Sharing Ownership in the Workplace

SUNY Series in the Sociology of Work
Judith Blau, Editor

Sharing Ownership in the Workplace

Raymond Russell

State University of New York Press
ALBANY

Published by
State University of New York Press, Albany

For information, address State University of New York
Press, State University Plaza, Albany, N.Y., 12246

Library of Congress Cataloging in Publication Data

Russell, Raymond, 1946–
    Sharing ownership in the workplace.

    (SUNY series in the sociology of work)
    Bibliography: p. 221
    1. Employee ownership. 2. Profit-sharing.
3. Employee motivation. 4. Employee ownership—United
States—Case studies. 5. Profit-sharing—United States—
Case studies. 6. Employee motivation—United States:
Case studies. I. Title. II. Series.
HD5650.R744 1985   338.6   84-8908
ISBN 0-87395-998-1
ISBN 0-87395-999-X (pbk.)

To Stewart E. Perry

Contents

Introduction

As this book goes to press, hardly a week goes by without news about some form of employee ownership appearing in some prominent portion of the American press. There are frequent articles about workers buying out closing plants, unions granting wage concessions in exchange for their employer's stock, and corporations using employee stock ownership as a new form of takeover defense. Employee ownership is now so popular that several airlines have recently begun to advertise the fact that they are at least partially employee-owned, and one of them has gone so far as to boast that it is now the most employee-owned.

These recently spreading forms of employee ownership will be discussed in this work, but not until its final chapter. The earlier chapters will instead be devoted to making a series of points that should help make the significance of these recent developments much easier to understand. Perhaps the most important of these points is that encouraging employees to share in the ownership of their workplaces is not a new idea. Economic reorganizations of this sort have been advocated repeatedly since the nineteenth century, and have already taken a bewildering diversity of forms. Thus much of this book will be devoted to sorting out the results of these various past experiments, in order to assess their relevance for the events that are taking place now. The point of these analyses will be to ask whether we are now merely repeating mistakes of the past, or are instead really embarked upon something new.

This effort to gain a historical perspective on the phenomenon of employee ownership will quickly lead into one of this book's major themes. In the past, labor-owned institutions of many varieties have shown repeated tendencies to revert back into conventional organizational forms. Among the advocates of these institutions, this phenomenon is often referred to as the problem of the "degeneration" of democratic firms. This book devotes a great deal of attention to this topic, because an understanding of it is crucial for assessing the prospects of the new generation of employee-owned firms that is in the process of emerging today. If employee-owned workplaces are inevitably destined to transform themselves back into conventional organizational forms, then it seems futile to try to create these firms at all. If these degenerative processes can be avoided, on the other hand, then it is also important to know how this can best be done.

This phenomenon of degeneration and the search for ways to prevent it lend special significance to the case studies that are presented in the three central chapters of this book. These chapters describe three populations of organizations located in the United States that are at least to some extent employee-owned, and in which at least some organizations have retained their employee-owned structures for more than fifty years. The fact that these organizations have such long histories allows them to serve two purposes at once. First, they provide opportunities to identify the most prominent causes that promote degeneration in firms of this sort. Second, the fact that these organizations have preserved their structures for so long makes them very promising sources of ideas about how these degenerative tendencies can best be held in check.

These common themes serve as the major rationale for the case studies presented in the central portion of this book, and will hopefully help to defend them against two criticisms that I can anticipate all too well. One likely objection is that the organizations described in Chapters 3, 4, and 5 are too different from each other to be referred to by the common label "employee-owned." Some of these organizations are cooperatives, some are partnerships, others are corporations whose stock is worker-owned. Describing all of these organizations as "employee-owned" or "worker-owned" thus contradicts the usage of a number of scholars who have attempted to maintain a firm demarcation between producers' cooperatives and corporations whose stock is worker-owned. The effort to preserve this distinction had already broken down, however, long before this book went to press. In this book, for example, the reader will encounter cooperatives in which memberships are bought and sold as readily as any corporate shares, and worker-owned corporations that faithfully adhere to the cooperative principle of one member, one vote. Thus this book will join Woodworth (1981), Rothschild-Whitt (1983), and Toscano (1983) in treating employee-owned corporations and producers' cooperatives as two alternate variants of worker- or employee-owned firms, rather than as totally incomparable organizational forms.

A second major criticism that is likely to be made of these analyses is that these organizations are not sufficiently employee-owned to suit some readers' tastes. All of these organizations make use of nonowner labor, and in some of them less than a majority of the labor force participates in the ownership of the firm. Readers are particularly likely to balk at my labelling of accounting firms and law partnerships as employee-owned firms. I would nevertheless defend this usage on both definitional and heuristic grounds. Definitionally, all of the organizations described in these chapters are employee-owned in the sense that only people who work in them are normally permitted to participate in their ownership, and also in the sense that a relatively large portion of the labor force shares in the ownership of these firms. More important than this purely definitional matter, however, is the issue of what there is to be learned from these firms. The fact that these firms employ nonowner labor should not come as a surprise; as will be discussed at length later on, the employment of nonowner labor is relatively easy to explain. But we know far less about the reasons that cause some organizations to decide that all or even a part of their labor force should be included in the ownership of the firm. So when any organizations determine that a significant portion of their labor force ought also to be owners, that fact is quite relevant to the subject matter of this work, and may also provide some important insights into both the degeneration and stability of more thoroughly employee-owned firms.

Since I have defined the subject matter of this work quite broadly, I have been forced to deal with an equally broad range of theory as well. Theorists as diverse as Karl Marx, Max Weber, Sidney and Beatrice Webb, Louis Kelso, and Peter Drucker have all had relevant things to say about the future of ownership, and their views are therefore discussed at appropriate places in the text. I would like to acknowledge at the start, however, that this is a theoretically eclectic work, and the selection of theorists to be discussed here was not intended to imply allegiance to any particular school. I take issue with the thought of each of the theorists named above, for example, in at least some portion of this work.

One of the most fascinating things about the current spread of employee ownership, in fact, is the large body of social theory that it appears to contradict. Max Weber, for example, left no room for employee ownership in the bureaucracies that he predicted would continue to dominate the world. For Weber, the rational allocation of both labor and capital required a strict separation of each. In one of his most thorough definitions of bureaucratic organization, Weber even explicitly stipulated that work within such structures is "entirely separated from ownership" (Weber, 1946:334). Efforts to allow workers to share in the ownership of their workplaces may appear superficially to provide more support for the prophecies of Karl Marx; but as should become clearer below, most of the forms of employee ownership discussed in this work are definitely not what Marx had in mind.

Before completing this introduction, I would like to express my gratitude to a number of people who made various important contributions to the completion of this work. My heaviest debt is to Stewart E. Perry. Stewart first sparked my interest in employee ownership when he hired me to work with him on his study of worker-owned scavenger companies in 1973. Much of both the theoretical and empirical content of this book was first roughed out while I was working with Stewart on that project. In later years, Stewart also helped to support my research on taxi cooperatives, and has become a close colleague and friend.

When I first went to work for Stewart in 1973, another member of the project team was Barry A. Stein. Some papers by and discussions with Barry did more than any other single source to clarify the meaning of ownership for me. It is largely ideas that I took from Barry that provide the major organizing principle behind Chapters 2 through 5 of this book.

Shortly after I began working with Stewart, Arthur Hochner joined the project. Thereafter, Art and I worked side by side on the study, interviewing scavengers together, reading and commenting on each other's papers, and co-authoring several reports. Charles Vidich, Jerry Sanders, Joseph Dewhirst, Ned French, John Havens, Dennis Redfield, and Stanley Reichgott also participated in this research for shorter periods of time. It was Charles Vidich who first pointed out to me that the taxi industry has given rise to numerous cooperatives, and who first suggested that I should study them.

Much of the content of this book is the result of large numbers of conversations with scavengers, taxi drivers, professionals, and scholars. Since most of these interviews were conducted under a pledge of anonymity, I cannot name the individuals here, but my debt to them will be apparent from the many quotations in the text. To scholars with whom I discussed this research I made no such pledge, so for their suggestions and encouragement I would like to thank George Homans, Daniel Bell, Arnold Tannenbaum, Joyce Rothschild-Whitt, Jane Mansbridge, George Strauss, David Ellerman, Katrina Berman, Derek Jones, Paul Blumberg, Avner Ben-Ner, Veljko Rus, Menachem Rosner, Paul Derrick, Bernhard Wilpert, Michael Shalev, Corey Rosen, and Katherine Klein.

Much of the research reported here was supported by grants from the Center for Studies of Work and Mental Health of the National Institute of Mental Health. Since coming to the University of California campus in Riverside in 1979, I have also had the benefit of several research grants from the Academic Senate and the administration of the campus. My department chairman, Edgar Butler, has also done much to make sure that I would have both the time and the resources needed to complete this book. Mark Wanamaker, Mokerrom Hossain, and John Prince also contributed invaluable research assistance during the later stages of the preparation of this book.

I first developed the idea of turning all of this research into a book in consultation with Magali Sarfatti Larson and Fred Block. I very much doubt that I could have completed the book without their warm encouragement. Magali and Fred also read and commented on long sections of the manuscript, and called attention to weaknesses in my arguments that I have subsequently done my best to correct. In September of 1983, Judith

Blau assumed the formal responsibility for editing the manuscript, and has contributed the advice and encouragement that were needed to bring this study to an end.

Unlike many recent authors, I have no personal computer to thank for helping me to draft this manuscript. Every word of this work was written out by hand, and was then laboriously typed in the old-fashioned way. In the early phases of this research most of this typing was performed by Kate Bramer, Susan Tritto, Laura Bachman, and Clara Dean. In the later phases I did have the use of a Lexitron word processor, which was expertly operated by Nancy Rettig, Marilyn Dick, and Susan Rivera. None of this typing under the constant pressure of deadlines could possibly have gone as smoothly as it did without the supporting efforts of Wanda Clark, Marge Souder, and Paul Otjen.

Riverside, California
May 1984

CHAPTER 1

Ownership, Work, and Public Policy

As the introduction has already indicated, employee ownership of work-places is an old idea; but it has also long been viewed as an impractical one. For centuries, the major trend in capitalist economic evolution has been not to unite ownership and work, but to separate them. That is, more and more workers have come to spend their lives in workplaces that they do not own.

Despite this fact, there is hardly a country in the world today that does not encourage workers to become owners of their workplaces through one mechanism or another. The governments of the Soviet Union and socialist Eastern Europe, for example, pledged themselves long ago to abolish capitalism and to establish a worker-owned economy in its place. In various parts of Western Europe, governments foster their cooperative movements (Thornley, 1981), help workers to buy out closing plants (Jones, 1980) and explore more far-reaching forms of worker participation in capital growth (Meidner, 1981). In the third world, governments often make support for producers' cooperatives a major part of their policies for economic development (Nash, Dandler, and Hopkins, 1976; Abell and Mahoney, 1980).

The United States is by no means an exception to this general trend. In 1974, for example, the U.S. government began offering tax incentives for firms to adopt Employee Stock Ownership Plans (ESOPs). In 1976, the Joint Economic Committee of the U.S. Congress resolved that "it should be made national policy to pursue the goal of broadened capital ownership" (U.S. Congress, Joint Economic Committee, 1976:100).

The present chapter is an attempt to identify some of the sources of this widespread interest in employee ownership, both in the United States and abroad. While such specific forms of employee ownership as ESOPs are relatively new, this chapter will argue that the idea of employee ownership itself has quite deep intellectual roots, and addresses problems that have been long-standing features of the economic and political life of the United States and other countries.

1

What is Ownership?

Few ideas in social thought are more difficult to pin down than the concept of ownership. Although we often think of ownership as unitary, it is actually a complex set of relationships between one or more human subjects, whom we call "owners," and a variety of material and social objects, which we refer to as "property." These relationships vary tremendously from one situation to another. Moreover, ownership is never an unmediated relationship between a human subject and an object of value. It always involves the judgment of other people. In the absence of other people, one never *owns* a valued object; one merely *possesses* it, or *uses* it. What transforms these relationships into ownership is the presence of other people who view them as *legitimate*, as *rights* which they must respect and perhaps defend.

Since Roman times, rights of ownership have been acknowledged to include such diverse elements as *usus*, or rights of use; *fructus*, or rights to enjoy and appropriate the fruits of use; and *abusus*, or rights of abuse, which include the rights to liquidate, sell, give away, or otherwise "alienate" the property. Although we are accustomed to seeing these rights lodged in the same individual, they can be and often are parceled out to different people. Thus, an owner may rent out a piece of property to someone else; or the owner may retain the property, but sell to another an option to buy it. Some ownership rights may go entirely unexercised, in which case they run the risk of being usurped by "squatters." Moreover, the prerogatives of owners are always subject in one way or another to their interpretation by the state. Summarizing all of these complexities, R.H. Tawney observed that "Ownership is not a right, but a bundle of rights, and it is possible to strip them off piecemeal as well as to strike them off simultaneously" (Tawney, 1920:104).

Despite the many complex forms which ownership may take, we normally think of ownership as simple. This is because most of our ideas about ownership have been shaped by one clear and striking instance of it — the exercising of all rights to a particular piece of property by the same individual. Much of this less complicated property extricated itself only recently from the encumbrances of its feudal past; but when it did, it hailed its victory so loudly, and argued its reasonableness so forcefully, that it now often strikes us as the only really "natural" form of ownership.

The private property of individuals is able to dominate our thinking about ownership as much as it does, moreover, by virtue of the rich set of meanings that we associate with it. An institution that so directly links a single human subject with a clearly identified object is capable of bearing a great deal of social and psychological freight. It forges one of the strongest possible bonds between an individual and his environment. This form of property is often so closely identified with its owner that we come to perceive and treat it as a part or expression of the owner himself. In the words of William James:

> It is clear that between what a man calls *me* and what he simply calls mine, the line is difficult to draw. We feel and act about certain things that are ours very much as we feel and act about ourselves. Our fame, our children, the work of our hands, may be as dear to us as our bodies are, and arouse the same feelings and the same acts of reprisal if attacked. . . . In its widest possible sense, . . . a man's self is the sum-total of all that he can call his, not only his body, and his psychic powers, but his clothes and his house, his wife and children, his ancestors and friends, his reputation and works, his land and horses and yacht and bank account (Beaglehole, 1931:298–299).

A somewhat more philosophical statement of the psychological significance of ownership was offered by Erazin Kohak:

> Ownership . . . is . . . the experience of a lived interaction between a subject and his world in the course of which meaning becomes actual and matter meaningful . . . . It is perhaps the basic fact of being human, as basic as "having-a-body," "belonging-to-a-context" (Kohak, 1972:458).

Other writers have focussed their attention not on the significance of ownership for the owner, but on the impact of ownership on the owner's relations with other people. For as Wilbert E. Moore and others have observed, property not only "defines the relations of persons to scarce values," it also necessarily "defines relations between persons" (Moore, 1943:35). Quite often, for example, property serves as a criterion of social rank. As Max Weber noted, "Property as such is not always recognized as a status qualification, but in the long run it is, and with extraordinary regularity" (Weber, 1946:187). More frequently still, private property creates a domain in which the individual owner is the acknowledged master, and which others may enter only on terms that the owner takes the lead in defining. Thus, property constitutes an institutional guarantee of the immunity of the owner from the interference of others.

In seventeenth century England, these two aspects of private property, as an extension of the personality of the owner and as a safeguard of the owner's autonomy, were combined in a struggle fought to secure simultaneously both the property and the liberty of the English gentry. One argument that did double duty for this cause was the idea that "each man has a property in his own person." The Levellers were the first to advance this principle, using it to win for civil rights the respect that Cromwell's men reserved for property rights (MacPherson, 1962:137–142). Later, after the victory of 1688, Locke used the same slogan to reverse the argument, claiming that a man's rights to property should be as unlimited as his liberty (Locke, 1924:130).

Property and Labor

When seventeenth century Englishmen defended their rights on the grounds that "each man has a property in his own person," they raised more issues than they resolved; for few arguments better illustrate the difficulties and ambiguities inherent in the concept of ownership. If one really owns one's own person, for example, does that ownership include rights of abuse? If yes, then how is it that suicide is prohibited? To what extent may other aspects of one's personhood and will be transferred or abdicated? Do people have the right to sell themselves into slavery? They do not, at least in the United States, where "life, liberty and the pursuit of happiness" are identified in the Declaration of Independence as "unalienable" rights.

In asserting a right of property in one's own person, however, the English revolutionaries had something more specific in mind than these vague rights. They were expressing the idea that each man is the proprietor of his own *labor*. In the hands of Locke, this principle of labor as property was transformed into one of the most popular arguments in defense of property rights (see Becker, 1977). For if a man owns his labor, Locke reasoned, then he is also entitled to appropriate the fruits of that labor. As Locke put it,

> . . . every man has a "property" in his own "person." This nobody has any right to but himself. The "labour" of his body and the "work" of his hands, we may say, are properly his. Whatsoever, then, he removes out of the state that nature hath provided and left it in, he hath mixed his labour with it, and joined it to something that is his own, and thereby makes it his property (Locke, 1924:130).

When a man's property is the result of his own labor, this may not only make his ownership seem more meaningful and legitimate; it can also do the same for his labor. Property that is a fruit of labor both motivates and rewards the labor that produces it. Thus, despite his preference for bureaucratic organization, Weber acknowledged that

> The appropriation of the means of production and personal control, however formal, over the process constitute among the strongest incentives to unlimited willingness to work (Weber, 1947:263).

A number of surveys of self-employment in the American labor force have documented various ways in which individuals who own their own businesses do indeed show greater involvement in their work than those who do not. For example, numerous studies have reported that the self-employed work longer hours than other workers, putting in an average of eight to ten additional hours per week (Fine, 1970:24–26, 72). The self-employed have also been found to be significantly less likely to be absent from work than individuals employed by someone else. In one national survey, for example, 55% of wage-and-salary earners reported that they had been absent from their jobs for at least one day during the previous year, whereas only 31% of the self-employed had been away from work this often (Fine, 1970:22–23, 41–42).

Despite its motivational advantages over other forms of employment, self-employment in the American labor force is now largely a thing of the past. The transformation from an agricultural to an industrial economy has been accompanied by an equally profound reorganization in the nature of employment. In 1780, an estimated 80% of the American labor force was self-employed. By 1970, the self-employed had been reduced to less than 10% of the labor force (see Table I).

Interestingly, the possibility that proprietary farming would someday be replaced by a system of labor for hire is inherent in the concept that each man has a property in his own person; for if a man's labor is truly his property, then he has as much right to sell it for wages as he has to use it himself. And when a worker sells his labor, he normally also sells his claim on the fruits of that labor. Locke took it for granted that when labor is performed in another man's service, the master, not the servant, is the proper recipient of the property rights created. "Thus," he wrote,

the grass my horse has bit, the turfs my servant has cut, and the ore I have digged . . . become my property without the assignation or consent of anybody. The labour that was mine [that is, performed by me or hired by me] . . . hath fixed my property in them (Locke, 1924:130).

Hence the irony that a chain of thought which starts from the unity of

Table I. Percent Self-Employed in the U.S. Labor Force, 1780–1979

1980	80.0
1880	36.9
1930	20.3
1950	17.9
1960	14.2
1970	9.1
1979	8.6

(Figures for 1780 to 1950 are from Reich, 1972:175, as modified in Zimbalist, 1975:52; figures for 1960, 1970, and 1979 are calculated from Fain, 1980:4.)

labor and property ends in justifying the separation of the laborer from the fruits of his work. As Marx expressed this point in *The Grundrisse*,

> It . . . seemed originally that proprietary rights were founded on the worker's own labour. But now property appears as the right to appropriate alien labour, and the impossibility of labour appropriating its own product for itself. The complete divorce between property (still more, wealth) and labour thus appears as the consequence of the law that originally identified them (Marx, 1971:105).

The increasing separation of work and ownership in modern economies has important consequences for each of them, as well as for the relationship between the two. Whereas work and ownership had formerly reinforced one another, there now exists a conflict of interest between them. Owners seek to maximize their profits while paying the lowest possible wage, and workers seek to maximize their wages with little concern for profit. Since there is no theoretical limit to the demands of either side, disputes between them often can only be resolved through strikes, appeals to governments, or other political tests of strength. Other conflicts between owners and workers arise not over the terms of employment, but over the labor process itself. This is because a worker who has forfeited any claim on the product of his labor has little material interest in the completion of his tasks, and must therefore be coerced or cajoled by the owner into performing his work.

Reinhard Bendix has demonstrated that property rights continue to be relevant to the modern labor process, but in a new way. Whereas formerly, property had motivated labor and rewarded it, property rights now help to legitimate the worker's subordination to the authority hierarchy of his workplace (Bendix, 1956). The remoteness of ownership from production, however, makes it increasingly less capable of playing even this purely ideological role.

As property has become more and more divorced from labor, it has also derived less and less support from the arguments made by Locke on its behalf. Claims for the legitimacy of private property are perhaps at their weakest in the modern large corporation. In the corporation, ownership gives up all pretense of being a lived interaction between a Lockean owner and the fruits of his labor, and is transformed instead into an abstract system of paper certificates. Walter Lippman observed in 1914 that ". . . the modern shareholder is a very feeble representative of the institution of private property" (Ransom, 1925:182). Joseph Schumpeter was equally critical of what the corporation is doing to the nature of ownership. "The capitalist process," he complained,

> by substituting a mere parcel of shares for the walls of and the machinery in a factory, takes the life out of the idea of property. It loosens the grip that once

was so strong—the grip in the sense of the legal right and the actual ability to do as one pleases with one's own; the grip also in the sense that the holder of the title loses the will to fight, economically, physically, politically, for "his" factory and his control over it, to die if necessary, on its steps. And this evaporation of what we may term the material substance of property—its visible and touchable reality—affects not only the attitude of holders but also that of the workmen and of the public in general. Dematerialized, defunctionalized and absentee ownership does not impress and call forth moral allegiance as the vital form of property did (Schumpeter, 1950:142).

In this way, argued Schumpeter, corporate ownership gradually undermines the legitimacy of the system of private ownership upon which it is based, and produces an incipient crisis of workplace authority and motivation. The shareholder's ownership grows increasingly less capable of commanding the authority upon which the capitalist factory depends. "Gone," lamented Schumpeter, "are most of the means of maintaining discipline . . . . Gone is the moral support of the community that used to be extended to the employer struggling with infractions of discipline" (Schumpeter, 1950:214).

For generations, criticisms of this sort have been leading many observers to regard the ownership of modern workplaces as no more than a "legal fiction" (Bell, 1973:294) or a "myth" (Dahl, 1970:127, 131–132; Ellerman, 1975a), and to urge that capitalist ownership be replaced by some alternative system in which work and ownership can more meaningfully be tied. For Marx, the only way to accomplish this would be by altogether abolishing private ownership of the means of production, and replacing it with a system in which workers collectively own industry on a nationwide scale. Even Schumpeter was inclined to grant that a day might soon arrive on which ". . . socialism might be the only means of restoring social discipline" (Schumpeter, 1950:215). R. H. Tawney argued, however, that

. . . it is not private ownership, but private ownership divorced from work, which is corrupting to the principle of industry; and the idea of some socialists that private property in land or capital is necessarily mischievous is a piece of scholastic pendantry. . . (Tawney, 1920:86)

Whether critics of capitalist property relations have sought to implement Marx's program or have advocated other alternatives, they have presented a tremendous challenge not only to current owners, but also to all modern states. States are forced to address this issue, first of all, because the state is the ultimate arbiter of all property rights; property rights could not assume the significance they have if they were not enforced by the coercive powers of the state. States also become involved in relations between workers and owners, moreover, because they play an ever growing role in regulating class conflict and maintaining industrial peace, and are being held increasingly responsible for the health of their national economies as a whole. Under these circumstances, it has become harder and harder for any government not to have a policy toward work and ownership. Thus, whether they do so out of fidelity to Marx, or in fear of him, or for reasons of their own, numerous modern governments have now formally committed themselves to the search for new ways in which work and ownership can more effectively be combined.

Toward an "Industrial Homestead Act" for the United States

In the United States, large scale government support for employee ownership is a recent phenomenon; but governmental concern for the distribution of property within the American population has quite old roots. In the first years after independence, for example, leaders were particularly attentive to the distribution of ownership in the American electorate, because the new nation had been organized as a democracy, and it had been widely believed since ancient times that democracy and a widely skewed distribution of property were incompatible. As early as 1787, for example, James Madison predicted that

> In future times, a great majority of the people will not only be without landed, but without any other sort of property. These will either combine under the influence of their common situation; in which case the rights of property and the public liberty will not be secure in their hands, or, which is more probable, they will become the tools of opulence and ambition; in which case there will be equal danger on another side (McClaughry, 1972:91).

In 1820, Daniel Webster expressed a similar concern. He wrote:

> The freest government, if it could exist, would not be long acceptable, if the tendency of the laws were to create a rapid accumulation of property in a few hands, and to render the great mass of the population dependent and pennyless. In such a case, the popular power must break in upon the rights of property, or else the influence of property must limit and control the exercise of popular power . . . (Coker, 1949:508).

America's Founding Fathers were alike not only in their perceptions of this danger, but also in having a common solution to propose. They urged that the American government should encourage as broad as possible a distribution of property ownership, so that most Americans would align themselves for rather than against the interests of the existing property owners. Thus Thomas Jefferson wrote that "legislators cannot invent too many devices for subdividing property" (Coker, 1949:460). Webster suggested similarly that:

> It would seem, then, to be the part of political wisdom to found government on property; and to establish such distribution of property, by the laws which regulate its transmission and alienation, as to interest the great majority of society in the protection of the government. This is, I imagine, the true theory and the actual practice of our republican institutions (Coker, 1949:508).

Not long after Webster made these remarks, the French visitor Alexis de Tocqueville reported that the strategy Webster advocated was so far apparently working in the United States of that day. In a nation of property owners, all had respect for the institution of property. Reported de Tocqueville,

> In America, the most democratic of nations, those complaints against property in general, which are so frequent in Europe, are never heard, because in America there are no paupers. As everyone has property of his own to defend, everyone recognizes the principle upon which he holds it (de Tocqueville, 1945, I:254).

The most ambitious application of Webster's strategy did not come, however, until the Homestead Act of 1862, which made available 160 acre farms in the West to whomever was willing to work the land. In a speech in favor of this act in 1850, Andrew Johnson predicted that it "would create the strongest tie between the citizen and the Government," and would provide "a great incentive . . . to obey every call of duty. . ." (McClaughry, 1972:91).

This strategy of increasing popular support for private property by broadening the distribution of property ownership has also won grudging tributes from the left. In a work on housing policy published in 1872, for example, Engels approvingly quoted the observation that "the cleverest leaders of the ruling class have always directed their efforts toward increasing the number of small property owners in order to build an army for themselves against the proletariat" (McClaughry, 1972:89). In 1920, Lenin also acknowledged the efficacy of this policy when he remarked, "It is a thousand times easier to vanquish the centralized big bourgeoisie than to 'vanquish' millions upon millions of small proprietors" (Lenin, 1940:35).

While appreciating the political significance of governmental efforts to expand the number of small property owners, most Marxists have also argued that in the long run, such policies cannot possibly succeed. This is because the dynamics of capitalism are seen as leading inevitably to a situation in which most small businesses will be gobbled up by larger ones. In

1846, for example, when Kriege and other German communists in the United States expressed too much enthusiasm for the Homestead Act, Marx used the following words to deride the foolishness of their hopes:

> Kriege fancies that he can prohibit by law the necessary consequences of this parcelization: concentration, industrial progress, etc. . . . It will soon be seen that one farmer, even without capital, by his mere labor and the greater original productivity of his 160 acres, would again reduce another one to his vassal (Marx, 1972:4).

On this prediction, of course, subsequent history has proved Marx largely to be right. Neither the Homestead Act, nor other policies like it, have prevented the transformation of the American people from a nation of independent farmers and shopkeepers into one of wage and salary earners. As large organizations with an employed labor force have become prominent and permanent features of modern economic life, the options available for the redistribution of property ownership have appeared much more restricted in scope. In most economic sectors, opportunities for individuals to own their own business are now largely a thing of the past.

In the United States and many other countries, governments have often abandoned all hope that more than a small number of workers might own their own businesses, and have instead concentrated their efforts on helping workers to acquire ownership of their homes. In the United States, in particular, government efforts to encourage home ownership have enjoyed an unusually notable success. According to the most recently available figures, 64.6% of American families owned their own homes in 1983 (*Los Angeles Times*, May 2, 1984, p. I-2). Thus the Founding Fathers' hope of interesting the great majority of Americans in the existing distribution of property is now principally being realized through Americans' ownership of their own homes.

As a mechanism of social control, however, home ownership has one major defect. While it does make the homeowning worker more sympathetic to the institution of private property, taken as a whole, it does little to overcome the conflicting interests of labor and capital within individual firms. In fact, it may even encourage workers to maximize their wages and purchasing power at the factory owners' expense.

Thus certain far-sighted government officials realized quite early in the game that new forms of ownership that could do a better job of reconciling the interests of labor and capital within industrial firms would eventually be needed. The earliest known call for employee ownership in the United States came from William Meredith in 1849, when he was serving as Secretary of the Treasury (Patard, 1982b). Another wave of interest in employee ownership occurred in the 1870s, in the wake of a series of major strikes. Congressman Abram S. Hewitt, for example, became an advocate of "joint ownership" between labor and capital while serving as chair of a Congressional committee that had been formed to investigate these strikes. Hewitt's service on this committee led him to conclude that "until labor becomes an owner it never will understand the capacity of business to pay" (Derber, 1970:62).

Interest in employee stock ownership reached a peak in the United States in the 1920s, but was dealt a severe setback by the stock market crash of 1929 (Patard, 1982a, 1982b). In the 1930s, the federal government's response to this failure was to lend its support to an alternative solution to the labor problem, namely the union movement. For many years thereafter collective bargaining reigned supreme as the nation's primary mechanism for reconciling the conflicting interests of labor and capital (Derber, 1970).

The idea of employee ownership did not completely die, however, and in 1958 a new assault on the separation between work and ownership was launched by Louis Kelso, with the assistance of Mortimer Adler. Kelso and Adler argued that as long as American workers do not own capital, they will constantly press for wage increases that exceed what either their firms or the economy as a whole can actually afford to pay. If workers could acquire enough capital to provide a significant portion of their incomes, however, Kelso and Adler believed that this would also lead workers to moderate their wage demands. The authors went on to suggest a number of proposals for bringing about a wider distribution of capital ownership, including the encouragement of employee stock ownership plans, and a variety of changes in the federal gift, inheritance, and income tax laws (Kelso and Adler, 1958).

Kelso's proposals languished in obscurity for a number of years, in part because he had a tendency to base them on a set of economic notions that most professional economists regarded as amateurish and often wrong (Jochim, 1982:12–16). Kelso finally found an opportunity to influence national policy, however, when he was introduced to Senator Russell Long in 1973. Long is a son of the Louisiana populist Huey Long, who became famous in the 1930s for his announced intention of making "every man a king." After meeting Kelso in 1973, Russell Long set out to use his position as chair of the Senate Finance Committee to make every worker at least a capital owner, if not a king (Speiser, 1977; Sloan, 1981).

Long's first practical step in this direction was to write a strong inducement for the formation of Employee Stock Ownership Plans, or "ESOPs," into a pension reform act in 1974. The bill authorized firms borrowing money for the purchase of new capital to deduct the principal as well as interest from their corporate income taxes as they repaid the loan, provided that they allocated an equivalent amount of stock to their ESOP. Since 1974, Long has promoted a number of other pieces of legislation designed to make the use of ESOPs more attractive to American businesses, and has supported bills to encourage a variety of other forms of employee ownership as well (U.S. Congress, 1981b).

By the late 1970s, employee ownership had attracted a number of additional supporters, and a variety of new uses and forms of employee ownership had begun to be advocated in the Congress. In 1978, for example, a bill was introduced that would have provided federal aid to workers who sought to prevent plant closures by purchasing their plants (Whyte and Blasi, 1980). This measure enjoyed widespread support in both the Senate and the House, but never became law as a result of disputes over some unrelated provisions of the bill to which it had become attached. A bill authorizing the Small Business Administration to assist a wide variety of employee-owned businesses did become effective, however, in July 1980 (Blasi and Whyte, 1981). These federal efforts to promote employee ownership have also increasingly been matched by numerous pieces of legislation at the state level as well (Rosen, 1981; *Employee Ownership*, December, 1982, pp. 9–10).

A noteworthy aspect of these legislative efforts on behalf of employee ownership is that they appear to have come not in response to pressures from constituents, but at the initiative of the lawmakers themselves. Writing of the period between 1977 and 1980, for example, Blasi and Whyte observed:

> Congress was never strongly lobbied for any form of worker ownership legislation. A variety of worker-owned firms, unions, and community groups expressed some interest, but . . . it was the members from the House and Senate themselves . . . who were excited by the idea (Blasi and Whyte, 1981:325).

Blasi and Whyte attributed much of the legislators' enthusiasm for employee ownership to its unique ability to appeal simultaneously to both Republican and Democratic values.

While employee ownership has continued to attract increasing support, Russell Long has remained its most effective spokesman in the Congress. His speeches on its behalf have often been quite reminiscent of sentiments that had been expressed by the nation's founders nearly two centuries before. On May 12, 1981, for example, Long argued in the Senate that employee ownership will "help create a stronger political base for our endangered private property system" (U.S. Congress, 1981b). In March of that same year, Long had elaborated that "Capitalism really needs a broader constituency. It needs more people who regard themselves as capitalists if this system is going to survive. . ." (U.S. Congress, 1981a).

In that same speech, Long made an additional argument in favor of employee ownership that has no counterpart in the concerns of the nation's early leaders, but instead reflects the country's more contemporary role as the major bastion of international capitalism. In Long's words,

> We are trying to prevent socialism and communism from taking over Latin America, from taking over Asia, from taking over Africa. We need a working model of what we would advocate for others throughout this world, and we ought to have it right here . . . (U.S. Congress, 1981a).

While he is clearly the most important advocate of employee ownership in the U.S. Congress today, Long frequently points out the extent to which his proposals enjoy widespread support among leaders of both major parties. The goal of "expanded ownership" has been a part of Republican Party policy for more than a decade, largely as a result of the persistent efforts of Vermont Republican John McClaughry (McClaughry, 1972; Rosen, 1983:10). In 1980, the Republican Party platform included a provision that states,

> The widespread distribution of private property ownership is the cornerstone of American liberty. Without it neither our free enterprise system nor our Republican form of Government could long endure (U.S. Congress, 1981b).

One of the most important Republican advocates of employee ownership is President Ronald Reagan. In 1975, candidate Reagan argued,

> Capitalism hasn't used the best tool of all in its struggle against socialism— and that's capitalism itself . . . . Could there be a better answer to the stupidity of Karl Marx than millions of workers individually sharing in the ownership of the means of production? (U.S. Congress, 1981b).

A year earlier, in July 1974, Reagan had told the Young Americans for Freedom,

> Over one hundred years ago, Abraham Lincoln signed the Homestead Act . . . . It set the pattern for the American capitalist system. We need an Industrial Homestead Act . . . .
> . . . it is time to formulate a plan to accelerate economic growth and production and at the same time broaden the ownership of productive capital. The American dream has always been to have a piece of the action (U.S. Congress, 1981b).

Worker Ownership and the American Dream

Clearly, there is a good deal of interest in employee ownership in American government today. As Blasi and Whyte pointed out, however, recent legislation to promote employee ownership has come not in response to the lobbying efforts of powerful interest groups, but at the initiative of legislators themselves. A legitimate question that remains to be asked, therefore, is to what extent the lawmakers' enthusiasm for employee ownership is shared by American workers themselves.

Although Ronald Reagan has asserted that to have "a piece of the action" is "the American Dream," there is an important sense in which this statement is not true. The traditional American Dream has not been to own a piece of someone else's business, but to own a business of one's own. Surveys of American workers have often documented how widely and intensely that particular aspiration is held (Mayer, 1953; Chinoy, 1955; Mayer and Goldstein, 1964). Other evidence also suggests that workers are far less interested in acquiring a piece of someone else's business than they are in owning a business of their own.

One sign of workers' lack of interest in acquiring a mere "piece" of someone else's "action" is the fact that workers rarely choose to purchase stock in corporations that employ them, unless the shares are offered to them at substantial discounts (Naylor, 1968). Unions, moreover, rarely seek employee ownership in collective bargaining situations, and they tend to accept it when it is offered only as a means to prevent a plant shutdown or to minimize the effects of paycuts (Moberg, 1981).

In all of these instances, it could be argued that both individual workers and their unions see employee ownership as desirable in itself, but as a luxury they cannot afford. Thus, whenever they are faced with a choice between short-term income and ownership, they choose income.

In the case of unions, however, it is clear that their reservations about employee ownership go far beyond this. In 1976, for example, the AFL-CIO issued a response to the new ESOP legislation that expressed a number of reservations about the plans. The statement particularly emphasized the possibility that employee stock ownership is an unwise investment strategy for workers, because if a firm were to fail, its employee stockholders would lose their savings along with their jobs (Jochim, 1982:154). Union leaders must always be concerned, moreover, that employers will once again use employee ownership, as they did in the 1920s, as a means to prevent unionization or to undermine support for unions where they already exist (Derber, 1970; Edwards, 1979; Patard, 1982a).

Despite these misgivings, there is one last piece of evidence to indicate that American workers would strongly welcome employee ownership in at least some of its forms. This evidence sheds no light on how workers would feel about owning a small piece of an otherwise conventionally-owned firm, but it does suggest that American workers would rather work for a business that they co-owned with their fellow employees than to work for one whose owners were outside the firm. In 1975, a poll conducted by the People's Bicentennial Commission asked 1209 Americans whether they would prefer to work for a company that was owned and controlled by "outside investors," by "the employees," or by "the government." Fully 66% of the respondents chose the employee-owned firm (Rifkin, 1977:176).

CHAPTER 2

Strategies For Sharing Ownership

The United States has thus recently joined the large number of countries that seek in one way or another to make their economies at least partially worker-owned. By the late twentieth century, the worldwide search for viable forms of worker ownership had already produced a long and diverse history. Numerous countries, for example, had already seen more than a century of experimentation with producers' cooperatives, utopian communities, and a variety of other mechanisms for promoting workers' ownership of individual enterprises. In Russia, the Bolshevik revolution of 1917 produced the world's first attempt to bring about worker ownership of an economy as a whole. In other lands, Israel has produced its well-publicized kibbutz, plus a unique national economy in which nearly a quarter of the labor force works in enterprises that are trade union-owned; Yugoslavia has contributed its system of "social ownership" and "workers' self-management;" and other important innovations have occurred in many other parts of the world.

The present chapter will attempt to survey these diverse experiences in worker ownership, with special attention to some common difficulties that they have all had to cope with. In the modern world, any plan by which workers are to become the owners of their workplaces has two major problems to solve. One is the need to forge a more meaningful and effective relationship between work and ownership. What is required is a link through which ownership and work mutually express and enhance one another—that is, ownership motivates and rewards the worker's use of the property, and work both reflects and enhances that ownership. Secondly, any new institution that seeks to restore the tie between ownership and work must also be a shared form of ownership, since modern workplaces bring together the labor of tens, hundreds, or even thousands of workers.

These are two objectives that cannot easily be pursued at one and the same time. A very old view holds that ownership and sharing do not readily mix, especially where work is involved. One of the first to express this opinion in writing was Aristotle.

It was in *The Politics* that Aristotle raised the question of whether property should be held in common or not, and answered firmly in the negative. One of his principal arguments was that common ownership would lead to a chaotic clash of individual wills. "In fact," he charged, "we find more disputes arising between those who share the use and possession of property than we do among separate owners. . ." (Aristotle, 1962:65). Years later, Hobbes was similarly to see in common ownership an anarchic "state of nature," in which "every man has a right to every thing," but each actually receives what "he can get; and for so long, as he can keep it" (Hobbes, 1929: 98, 99, quoted in Schlatter, 1951:139).

In addition to viewing common ownership as a social Pandora's box, Aristotle also considered it a psychologically weak link between an individual and an object of ownership. In this he disagreed with Socrates who had seen a great unifying force in the opportunity for everyone in a group to perceive a good as simultaneously "mine" and "not mine." "Is not our ordinary use of the word 'my,'" Aristotle asked, "better than this use of it by two thousand or ten thousand people all with reference to the same thing?" (Aristotle, 1962:58–59).

One source of this alleged psychological weakness of shared ownership may have been identified by Georg Simmel. The feeling of possession, Simmel observed, depends largely on "the strongly emphasized exclusion of all outsiders. For many individuals," he noted, "property does not fully gain its significance with mere ownership, but only with the consciousness that others must do without it" (Simmel, 1950:332).

The net result of all these difficulties, Aristotle believed, is that shared ownership is not a very fruitful way to build a closer tie between ownership and work. A form of ownership that is but weakly felt is not a very effective motivator. "People are much more careful of their own possessions," observed Aristotle, "than those communally owned." He generalized that "the greater the number of owners, the less the respect for the property" (Aristotle, 1962:58).

One problem with all of these criticisms, however, is that they are all based on an implicit contrast between shared forms of ownership and the individual ownership of the sole proprietor. But this is not the type of ownership that these shared forms are designed to replace. Their special target is the wage labor performed for the absentee and/or corporate owner. It was John Stuart Mill who argued that

If Communistic labour might be less vigorous than that of a peasant proprietor, or a workman labouring on his own account, it would probably be more energetic than that of a labourer for hire who has no personal interest in the matter at all (Mill, 1871:205).

While the criticisms of Aristotle and others who share his views look back to an older form of ownership, Marx often took an opposite point of view. He looked forward, and peppered his writings with allusions to the bright possibilities that a future of shared ownership would have in store. Unfortunately, these references are accompanied by only the briefest of indications as to how we are to get from here to there.

Consider, for example, Marx's famous idea that the future of property will unfold in two stages, which we now refer to as "socialist"and "communist" phases. This idea appears in only two of Marx's works, neither of which he chose to publish. The first of these was the *1844 Manuscripts*, in which Marx referred to the ultimate form of communism as "the positive transcendence of private property" (Tucker, 1972:70). In the set of notes called *The Critique of the Gotha Program*, Marx labelled it merely "a higher phase of communism" (Tucker, 1972:388).

In the published works written between these two, Marx made no effort to differentiate two types of communism, and applied a bewildering diversity of terms to the future of ownership. In *The German Ideology*, he demanded that the instruments of production "must be made subject to each individual, and property to all" (Tucker, 1972:155). In *Capital*, he referred to the future of ownership by a variety of names, including "individual property," "socialized property," "possession in common," "the property of associated producers," and "outright social property" (Tucker, 1972:318; Marx, 1967:437, 440). In *The Civil War in France*, he praised the Paris commune for seeking "to make individual property a truth," and for bringing us closer to the day when "united cooperative societies are to regulate the national production under a common plan, thus taking it under their own control" (Tucker, 1972:557). And in *The Critique of the Gotha Program*, we find the two phases of communism being jointly referred to as "common property," "common ownership," and "the cooperative property of the workers themselves" (Tucker, 1972:385–389).

What are we to make of all these cryptic and occasionally contradictory remarks? Eugen Duehring said of Marx's writings on ownership that "Herr Marx remains cheerfully in the nebulous world of his property which is at the same time both individual and social and leaves it to his adepts to solve for themselves this profound dialectical enigma" (Engels, 1939: 142–143). Engels responded to Duehring by denying that there was anything subtle in what Marx had to say about the future of ownership. "To anyone who understands English," he retorted, "this means that social ownership extends to the land and to the other means of production, and private ownership to the products, that is, the articles of consumption" (Engels, 1939:144). But what is this "social ownership," and what must happen to it for it to become "the positive transcendence of private property?"

Neither Marx nor Engels ever gave a fully developed answer to this question. Here and there throughout their published and unpublished works, however, they did leave a number of fragmentary clues. We know, for example, that social ownership cannot be identical with state ownership, because it will remain after the state itself has "been transcended," or in Engel's phrase, has "withered away." From *The Critique of the Gotha Program*, we know that Marx expected the new form of ownership to come into full flower only after "the springs of co-operative wealth flow more abundantly," and other preconditions are met. In such a time, when scarcity has been conquered, and work no longer serves as a means to life, but has emerged as "life's prime want," people will no longer have reason to be possessive or exclusive about the fruits of their labor. Thus, work and distribution in this society will follow the principle, "from each according to his ability, to each according to his needs" (Tucker, 1972:388).

Only in the *1844 Manuscripts* did Marx elaborate at all on the form that ownership would take in this future era. There, he conveyed the content of this new form of ownership by giving a new meaning to the term "appropriation." Whereas in Locke, appropriation had merely signified the act by which a material substance had been turned into property, Marx used it to summarize the complete range of processes by which man continually relates to the material world. Every sensation, every thought, and every other means by which an individual orients himself to an object constitute acts of appropriation of that object.

The great merit of the positive transcendence of private property, for Marx, is that it removes all the fetters from this process of appropriation, and brings about "the complete *emancipation* of all human senses and qualities" (Tucker, 1972:73). Under these circumstances, Marx believed, people would no longer find it particularly important to possess or consume nature; normally, they would be content to enjoy it in a non-egotistical fashion. In such a society, the rich man is not one who has many possessions; on the contrary, he is a man who is rich in need—"profoundly endowed with all the senses," he is rich in need of "a totality of human manifestations of life" (Tucker, 1972:75, 77).

This communist form of property, then, is one that can readily be shared with others. The involvement of other people, writes Marx, merely augments the individual's capacity to appropriate the material world:

> In the same way, the senses and minds of other men have become my *own* appropriation. Besides these direct organs, therefore, *social* organs develop in the *forms* of society; thus, for instance, activity in direct association with others, etc., has become an organ for *expressing* my own *life*, and a mode of appropriating *human* life (Tucker, 1972:74).

That is, certainly, an attractive ideal; but a fair test of shared workplace ownership lies neither in extolling the virtues of sole proprietorship, nor in the optimistic speculations of Marx. A more valuable approach will be to look closely at the history of some actual experiences in implementing worker ownership, and to evaluate the results. There has already been quite a number of these practical efforts. In the past century and a half, the present system of factory ownership has inspired such disparate alternatives as consumer cooperatives, worker-owned firms, utopian communities, nationalized industry, trade union ownership, and socialist revolutions. The experiments have been so numerous, in fact, that we might easily become lost in them without some systematic criteria to guide us through.

One useful set of distinctions for looking at these experiments in shared ownership can be derived from the form of property that all of them are reacting against — the corporation. For the corporation is the first and most successful form of shared ownership to be applied to industrial production, and most ostensible alternatives owe it a far greater debt than is customarily acknowledged.

The corporation is an extremely effective device for bringing together the capital of many separate owners into a single economic entity. One of its great attractions is that while uniting the capital of so many individual owners, it reserves for each of them a class of property rights that can be exercised independently of all other owners. These rights are, chiefly, the right to vote on certain major decisions; the right to receive a variable dividend; and the right to sell or otherwise transfer one's share in the ownership of the corporation.

All other ownership rights in the corporation are exercised not individually, but by the corporation acting as a unit. A shareholder in a corporation may still exercise some of those other prerogatives as well; but that he or she does so no longer follows automatically from the mere fact of being a shareholder or owner. Rather, it results from the added political fact that this shareholder is able to influence the organization's decision-making process. It is in such cases that we speak of a shareholder as having a "controlling" position in the corporation.

Two things are of interest here. One is the division of ownership rights into two differentiable classes. This distinction has been the cause of much confusion. It has given many people the habit of labelling the administrative side of corporate ownership as "control," and the residual rights of inactive stockholders as "ownership." But the right to control a corporation is not an alternative to, but a major part of, the ownership of it; and no one exercises very much control over a corporation who does not also own a quite respectable block of stock in it (see Zeitlin, 1974, and Useem, 1980:43–53).

It is much safer to apply to this dichotomy a terminology that makes it clear that *both* sides of it are aspects of ownership. This is what Berle and Means did, when they first brought the distinction to the attention of the

American public in 1932. In *The Modern Corporation and Private Property*, they referred to the rights of individual shareholders as "passive ownership" or "beneficial ownership," while treating actual control over the corporation as an instance of "active ownership" (Berle and Means, 1968). In this book, the value-laden connotations of the words "passive" and "beneficial" will be avoided by referring to the former rights as "equity ownership;" and, in deference to the modern convention, active ownership will usually be referred to as "control."

The corporation also invites us to draw one other distinction, for it demonstrates two alternative strategies for sharing these ownership rights. Jointly held rights can be distributed to the individuals who share in them, or they can be exercised collectively. In the corporation, equity ownership is shared distributively, and the rights of control are shared collectively. Barry A. Stein, from whose work I took these points, argues that this arrangement contributes to the legitimacy crisis that besets the corporation. For although the corporation attempts to share control rights collectively, its owners do not constitute a collectivity. That is, most owners have no relationship to one another, and do not even participate in the infrequent meetings of shareholders, where their own shares would be a feeble counter to the large number of proxies which fall, often by default, into the hands of management. And so, it sometimes appears that corporate control rights are "unowned," and are left to be usurped by whatever minority can successfully seize hold of them (Stein, 1976).

The corporate strategy for allocating these rights, however, is not the only way that ownership can be shared. It is also possible, for example, to share equity collectively, as occurs in the various forms of community ownership. And at least some control rights can be exercised distributively.

This last point is a controversial one. Stein, for example, suggests that rights of control are *not* capable of being shared distributively. He writes, "the necessity for rights conveyed by distributive ownership to be capable of independent and non-conflicting exercise prevents rights of use or control from being shared in that fashion" (1976:305–306). But while the organization of most modern workplaces does create formidable barriers to the distributive sharing of rights of control, the possibility of decentralizing at least some of these rights to autonomous work groups or individual workers cannot be entirely dismissed. One historical case of shared ownership in which many control rights were exercised distributively is the *mir* or land commune of the Russian peasantry. In many cases, the members of a *mir* would meet periodically to allocate portions of their common land by lot to each individual family. Then each family would cultivate its own land allotment separately and for its own benefit. One authority defines the Russian land commune as "an institution in which . . . the right of disposition of property belongs to the community as a whole, but the right of use belongs to each individual member" (Walters, 1968: 134). Some examples of more contemporary organizations in which many control rights are shared distributively will be offered in later chapters of this book.

Thus the corporation offers two distinctions, which point to a total of four possible elements from which to construct a system of shared workplace ownership. These elements, along with some labels by which they can briefly be characterized, are presented schematically in Table II.

From the perspective of this table, many ostensibly disparate models of workplace ownership appear to be but different instances of the same strategy for sharing ownership. For example, profit sharing, employee stock ownership plans, and most worker-owned firms all focus almost exclusively on the distributive sharing of equity ownership. Most utopian communities and instances of national, community, or trade union ownership share equity collectively. Efforts at workplace democratization aim to help workers share control rights collectively; and many attempts to upgrade the content of jobs aim to share some of these same rights distributively.

Before leaving this table, several words of explanation are in order. First, it should be emphasized that the cells presented here are neither exhaustive, nor mutually exclusive. While the two dichotomies drawn here have yielded a total of four cells, any number of other subdivisions of ownership rights and of strategies for sharing them might have yielded more complicated tables. And of the four broad strategies presented here, institutions can and often do pursue more than one strategy at the same time.

Secondly, it is necessary to add a few comments about the labels inserted in each of the cells of Table II. The purpose of these labels is not so much to describe completely the empirical content of each cell, as it is to characterize the essence of a given approach. Thus, individual workers can potentially share in the economic rewards of equity ownership through a wide range of devices, including bonus plans, cash payments upon ter-

Table II. Strategies for Sharing the Ownership of Workplaces

Means of Sharing ＼ Class of Rights	Equity	Control
Collective	Owning by Belonging	Democracy in the Workplace
Distributive	Workers as Stockholders	Ownership Through the Nature of Work

mination, the issuing of bonds or annuities, and other forms of investment. But the most striking and thoroughgoing instance of this strategy occurs when a firm is constituted as a corporation, the principal stockholders in which are the individual employees of the firm.

When equity is shared collectively, on the other hand, the individual participates in ownership only insofar as he or she enjoys membership in and takes part in the activities of the group that owns the firm. Thus, in this case, the worker "owns" the enterprise only to the extent that he "belongs" to the owning group.

Turning from equity to control, workers can share collectively in the governance of their enterprises through a wide range of mechanisms that have evolved for expressing the worker's voice in the workplace, including collective bargaining, codetermination, and the operation of workers' councils. All of these democratic innovations, to the extent that they become matters of legal right, transfer to workers at least some of the control prerogatives of ownership. But only when workers become self-governing within their workplaces, rather than outside of them, do they clearly begin to play the role of active owners in their firms.

Similarly, piecemeal increases in the autonomy and complexity of individual jobs can occur under any system of ownership. They are less likely when someone other than the worker owns the capital. When the worker is himself/herself the owner, one expects to see this ownership reflected in the nature of his or her work. This expectation derives not only from our experience with the self-employed sole proprietor, but also from the writings of Marx on work in the communist future, when workers are to appropriate the tools and products of their labor through a continuous process of meaningful and self-expressive work.

From the perspective of this table, it no longer appears quite so "enigmatic" to suggest, as Marx did, that the future ownership of workplaces will be both "social" and "individual." It seems both reasonable and desirable to suggest that institutional arrangements for worker ownership should adopt both collective and individual elements, and that they should embrace both equity and control.

Practical efforts to implement worker ownership, however, have often failed to take this broad a view of the sharing of workplace ownership. Instead, they commonly seize on one or perhaps two devices for sharing ownership and expect these fragments alone to constitute a new and significant ownership experience. For example, employee-owned firms, while often accompanied by workplace democracy, repeatedly show a tendency to abandon their democratic structures when these conflict with the primary role of the firms as personal capital investments of the individual worker-stockholders. Ownership of equity by a nation or community, similarly, carries the implication that rights of control should also be shared equally by the members of that group. In practice, however, these institutions may or may not be accompanied by a democratic distribution of control. The members of an Israeli kibbutz, for example, share both equity and control; but in the Soviet Union, theory and practice alike have tended to emphasize the sharing of equity while little effort is made to bring about an effective sharing of control.

The remainder of this chapter will elaborate on these points by examining in detail some major historical instances of each of these four strategies for sharing workplace ownership.

Workers as Stockholders

Over the past hundred years or more, the most common innovations in the sharing of ownership have been those that the corporation has most directly inspired. The cooperative movement, many profit-sharing plans, and most types of worker-owned firms take the corporate strategy for sharing equity as their point of departure and merely extend it to a new population of owners.

Beyond this fundamental similarity, these innovations have differed widely in their structures and goals. Consumers' cooperative, for example, seek to effect a more democratic distribution of equity ownership without concern for the relationship between ownership and work. Of greater interest here are those innovations that link the sharing of equity to the place of work. These range all the way from modest forms of profit sharing or employee stock ownership in conventional firms to instances in which workers own all the stock in an entire firm.

Of these innovations, profit sharing appears to be the most widely used. The world leader in profit sharing is probably France, where it has old roots, and has been mandatory for companies with more than 100 employees since 1967 (Meidner, 1981:305). In the United States, it was estimated in 1980 that more than 300,000 American companies have formal arrangements for sharing profits with their employees, and that 15 million employees are covered by these plans (Metzger, 1981:97; see also Metzger, 1974). Since 1974, Employee Stock Ownership Plans (ESOPs) have also proliferated rapidly throughout the United States. By 1983, more than 6,000 American companies had set up these plans (*Wall Street Journal*, July 16, 1983).

Profit sharing and employee stock ownership have achieved this popularity despite many theorists' claims that they can do little good for their firms. Since the nineteenth century, experts have argued that these innovations will have little influence on the relationship between employees and their work, because workers' shares will inevitably be too small, remote, and diluted to create a meaningful link between effort and reward (Derber, 1970:66–70, and Drucker, 1949:246–253; see also Yunker, 1977). In a large organization, they argue, an individual employee is only one of hundreds or thousands whose efforts influence the profits of a firm and the value of its stock; and whatever minor increments in either result from one employee's efforts, they will in turn be divided among hundreds or thousands of employees and owners before the employee receives any benefit from them. According to Derber (1970:71), F. W. Taylor's dissatisfaction with the motivational potential of profit-sharing schemes helped lead him to initiate his famous experiments with piece rates and other more direct means of evoking higher productivity from the worker.

Current advocates of profit sharing and employee stock ownership often acknowledge that these reforms may not forge very effective links between individual efforts and individual rewards, but they also argue that they do have important consequences for relations between individual workers and their firms. That is, these innovations are seen as improving the climate of industrial relations in a firm, and as encouraging employees to become more personally committed to the long-term interests of the firm. Some recent evidence in support of this view comes from a 1980 survey of 229 companies that had three or more years of experience with ESOPs (Marsh and McAllister, 1981). Personnel managers in 59% of these companies believed the plans had exerted a "good" influence on "employee morale," and 79% thought they had caused "employee interest in company progress" to improve (p.613). Similar findings have emerged from studies by Goldstein (1978) and by Christiansen (1980). Their generally favorable impact on industrial relations and morale may also explain why studies of the relationship between profit sharing or employee stock ownership and profitability or other measures of performance typically report favorable effects for each (Metzger and Colletti, 1971; Conte and Tannenbaum, 1978; Frieden, 1980:79–81; Marsh and McAllister, 1981; Rosen and Klein, 1983; but see also Livingston and Henry, 1980).

Thus both profit sharing and employee stock ownership do appear to promote more harmonious relations between labor and capital, as their advocates have long promised for them. In most cases, however, they appear to bring about only a cosmetic change in the relationship between labor and capital, rather than a structural one. One sign of the largely symbolic nature of these programs is the heavy stress that is often placed on the way these plans are communicated to workers (for example, see Metzger, 1981). Apparently, if workers are not frequently reminded by management of the existence of these plans, the danger is that they might easily forget about them, and the plans will then have no effect. It seems quite likely that one of the most important things being communicated by the existence of these plans is management's benevolence, and its appreciation of the contribution of the labor force to the success of the firm. Thus, these plans may best be interpreted as gestures of good "human relations" or "welfare capitalism" (Edwards, 1979), rather than as significant new material ties between workers and their work.

One important exception to this generalization is the use of stock ownership to motivate upper management. High ranking managers are few enough in number and important enough to the success of an organization that corporations have been able to motivate their executives with significant amounts of stock. For generations, numerous social scientists have been predicting a widening conflict of interest between stockholders, whose goal is profits, and managers, whose goal is assumed to be higher fixed salaries (Berle and Means, 1968; Dahrendorf, 1959; Williamson, 1964; and Galbraith, 1967). Actually, however, most corporations have quite successfully minimized this divergence of interests by compensating their top executives not only with salaries, but also with stock.

A pioneering study of this "ownership income of management" was reported by Lewellen in 1971. Lewellen found that already in the early 1960s, chief executives in 50 large American manufacturing firms were earning almost as much in stock options and other stock-based compensation as they were from their annual salaries. Moreover, the cumulative result of these stock options was that the typical chief executive by that time already owned between one and two million dollars worth of his company's stock, which in turn was subject to as much as three quarters of a million dollars in unrealized capital gains or losses per year (Lewellen, 1971:82, 85). A study of 218 of the 284 largest U.S. industrial corporations in 1975 and 1976 found the use of stock options in that sample to be somewhat more limited, but also reported that the chief executives in these companies already owned enough stock to earn an average of $186,400 in dividends alone in those years (Allen, 1981:1119; see also Herman, 1981:91–98).

As a result of this executive stock ownership, other stockholders have had far less to fear from these managers' control over their firms; upper managers have as strong an interest in maximizing profits as they do. Masson (1971) found that the more closely executive rewards are linked to the profitability of a firm, the better the firm performs on the stock market. Larner concluded from similar data that ". . . the system of financial incentives and rewards in large corporations makes executive compensation and income profit-dependent, and thus effectively links the pecuniary interest of managers to the pecuniary interest of stockholders" (Larner, 1970:63).

There is one other important instance in which equity ownership has an important opportunity to influence the motivation not only of managers, but of rank-and-file workers as well. That is the small firm in which *all* capital is worker-owned, and is shared equally by the entire labor force.

These are strict criteria, but they have been met from time to time by a wide variety of work organizations in the history of virtually every major economy. In fact, many of the numerous social experiments labelled variously as "workingmen's associations," "producers' cooperatives," or "worker-owned firms" have had structures of this sort.

To a diverse group of nineteenth century social theorists, these cases of worker ownership provided the most promising model of how the conflict between labor and capital could ultimately be overcome. Even Karl Marx had many words of admiration for these cooperative enterprises. In *Capital*, for example, he had this to say about their superiority to conventional corporations:

> The capitalist stock companies, as much as the co-operative factories, should be considered as transitional forms from the capitalist mode of production to the associated one, with the only distinction that the antagonism is resolved negatively in the one and positively in the other (Marx, 1967:431).

In his *Inaugural Address* to the First International, Marx was even more flattering of the cooperative factories. "The value of these great social experiments," he declared,

> cannot be over-rated. By deed, instead of by argument, they have shown that production on a large scale, and in accord with the behest of modern science, may be carried on without the existence of a class of masters employing a class of hands; that to bear fruit, the means of labour need not be monopolized as a means of dominion over, and of extortion against, the labouring man himself; and that, like slave labour, like serf labour, hired labour is but a transitory and inferior form, destined to disappear before associated labour plying its toil with a willing hand, a ready mind, and a joyous heart (Tucker, 1972:380).

Not very long after Marx had uttered these words, a number of doubts began to be raised in many quarters as to whether these firms really did justify the optimistic lessons that were then being drawn from them. As time wore on, many producers' cooperatives showed a tendency to fail or stagnate as businesses. Some observers concluded that worker-owners, in the end, make poor entrepreneurs—that they were hampered inevitably by a lack of capital and business experience, and suffered from a reluctance to innovate or take risks.

By the end of the nineteenth century, the worker-owned firm was widely judged to be an economically unviable institution. The Fabian socialists Sidney and Beatrice Webb were particularly vociferous proponents of this belief. In 1920 they flatly asserted, "All such associations of producers that start as alternatives to the capitalist system either fail or cease to be democracies of producers" (Webb and Webb, 1920:29, quoted in Jones, 1976:45).

Subsequent experience has shown that this negative evaluation greatly overstated the economic weaknesses of worker-owned enterprise. Jones (1975, 1976, 1980) has suggested that the Webbs' conclusions were unjustified even on the basis of data available in their day, and may have come more from the Webbs' preconceived notions than from the data alone. Jones' own surveys of the performance of producer cooperatives in a variety of countries have unearthed a mixed record, but one that generally fails to support the pessimistic conclusions of the Webbs (Jones, 1976, 1978, 1979, 1980). In particular, certain economic niches have been identified in which producer cooperatives manage not only to survive, but even to outperform conventional firms. One such example is the American plywood industry, in which a small group of producer cooperatives in the Pacific Northwest annually accounts for approximately 10% of the nation's softwood plywood production (Gunn, 1980a:394; see also Berman, 1967, 1982; Bellas, 1972; Bernstein, 1974, 1981).

A more serious criticism of producer cooperatives and other worker-owned enterprises has been the charge that even when they do succeed economically, they have a tendency to "degenerate" over time. As the Webbs expressed this complaint,

> In the relatively few instances in which such enterprises have not succumbed as business concerns, they have ceased to be democracies of producers managing their own work, and have become, in effect, associations of capitalists. . . making profit for themselves by the employment at wages of workers outside their association (Webb and Webb, 1920).

More recent investigations have tended to confirm the Webbs' impression that degeneration is indeed a common occurrence in many producer cooperatives and other worker-owned enterprises. In one discussion of the phenomenon, Paul Blumberg has noted that degeneration typically takes some or all of the following forms:

> Transforming the co-operative into a simple profit-making, profit-seeking business, indistinguishable from private enterprise; exploiting a monopoly situation, often to public disadvantage . . .; closing off of co-operative membership; raising the cost of membership to a prohibitively high level; and resorting to the anti-co-operative device of taking on hired labor (Blumberg, 1968:3–4).

The degeneration of producer cooperatives had become a common problem already in the nineteenth century, and writers of that era had already begun to offer explanations for it. For Marx, degeneration was an inevitable consequence of operating in a capitalist economic environment. In *Capital,* while praising these organizations for representing "within the old form the first sprouts of the new," he added that they "naturally reproduce, and must reproduce, everywhere in their actual organization all the shortcomings of the prevailing system" (Marx, 1967:431).

To the nineteenth century English cooperator George Holyoake, the degeneration of producer cooperatives was not inevitable, but was due to the fact that their organizers have "no clear conception of the place of capital" in them, and therefore allow it "to steal like the serpent of Eden from the outer world into the garden of partnership" (Holyoake, 1906, vol. II: 338). In these firms, as in the conventional corporation, ownership is derived from capital rather than from work. As Holyoake put it,

> The joint-stock system uses the labourer, but does not recognize him. At best it invites him to join the capitalist class as a shareholder . . . . Under the joint-stock plan labour is still a hired instrument — labour is still dependent, without dignity, because without rights (Holyoake, 1906, vol. II:339).

The impulse to make use of hired, nonmember labour is thus inherent in the structure of most worker-owned firms. These organizations acknowledge individual workers to be owners solely by virtue of the capital they have invested in the firm. As an enterprise prospers and hires additional laborers, these new recruits can become equal partners only by purchasing shares from the existing group of worker-owners. But unless they really need the money, most worker-owners would rather not sell to these new employees. For as Simmel would argue, to add to the number of co-owners would further dilute their own sense of ownership; the presence of nonowners within the firm, on the other hand, enhances it. Moreover, as the time approaches for worker-owners to retire, they often realize that they can obtain a higher price for their shares by selling them to outside capitalists rather than to nonshareholding workers in the firm.

In recent years, the processes leading to the degeneration of many worker-owned organizations have been increasingly better understood; and later in this chapter, a number of structures designed to minimize these tendencies will be discussed. In the late nineteenth century, however, these defects were more commonly seen as dooming these organizations to inevitable irrelevance. In the words of the nineteenth century socialist Laurence Gronlund,

> But admit that such associations here and there have succeeded and that others therefore likewise might succeed, it yet leaves the kernel of the Labor question untouched. These successful associations are brilliant examples of

workingmen raising *themselves out of* their class, not raising *their class.* They are not truly cooperative but virtually joint-stock companies . . . . They . . . hire and fleece laborers after the approved fashion of the age, and experience teaches that they are indeed the hardest taskmasters (Gronlund, 1965:57).

Marx, while offering many words of praise for these organizations, typically mixed his praise with qualifications of the following sort:

At the same time, the experience of the period from 1848 to 1864 has proved beyond doubt that, however excellent in principle, and however useful in practice, cooperative labor, if kept within the narrow circle of the casual efforts of private workmen, will never be able to arrest the growth in geometric progression of monopoly, to free the masses, nor even to perceptibly lighten the burden of their miseries. It is perhaps for this very reason that plausible noblemen, philanthropic middle-class spouters, and even keen political economists, have all at once turned nauseously complimentary to the very cooperative labour system they had vainly tried to nip in the bud by deriding it as the Utopia of the dreamer, or stigmatising it as the sacrilege of the Socialist (Tucker, 1972:380).

It was the bad luck of the cooperative workshops to be making known their faults at the very time that the socialist parties of Western Europe were first coalescing and beginning to debate what their political programs ought to be. At first, many socialists proposed to use the state to promote workers' cooperatives on a heretofor unprecedented scale. France's Louis Blanc, for example, had demanded, "What the proletariat lacks in order to free itself is tools, and it is the government's job to deliver them" (Buber, 1949:68). In 1875, largely under the influence of Ferdinand Lasalle, the German socialists included a call for "the establishment of producers' cooperative societies *with state aid*" in the program which they drew up at Gotha (Tucker, 1972:393).

In the end, however, the socialists had too many misgivings about the character of cooperative enterprise for this plank to long remain in their platform. In his *Critique of the Gotha Program*, Marx attacked the proposal without mercy, and concluded, "as far as the present cooperative societies are concerned, they are of value *only* in so far as they are the independent creations of the workers and not proteges either of the government or of the bourgeois" (Tucker, 1972:393–394). In 1891, when the German socialists adopted a new program at Erfurt, the proposal for state aid to cooperatives was dropped. Thereafter, most members of the International devoted themselves to using the state to promote collective rather than distributive strategies for sharing the ownership of industry.

Owning by Belonging

Insofar as a shared resource is distributively owned, relations among the owners need have no special consequences for their ownership. As the corporation demonstrates, it is not even necessary for owners to know one another to exercise and feel their ownership. When property is owned collectively, however, the opposite is true. In that situation, the extent to which individuals behave and feel like owners will be a function of their role in the group that owns.

This point was made by Marx in a discussion of the common ownership of land by primitive tribes. In this system, wrote Marx, *"Property . . . means belonging to a tribe* (community) . . . and by means of the relationship of this community to the land . . . there occurs the relationship of the individual to the land . . ."* (Marx, 1965:90). Shlomo Avineri has observed that in this discussion, Marx uses the same term (*Gemeinwesen*) to denote both the common property of the tribe and the fact of membership in the tribe (Avineri, 1968:112).

Ownership that is exercised collectively brings a number of potential advantages to workplaces that are employee-owned. It has been pointed out, for example, that amounts of profit that can seem paltry and insignificant when they are divided up and distributed to individual workers (Yunker, 1977) may acquire a far greater impact when aggregated into a collective fund (Drucker, 1949:248–250). When workers labor together for their common good, this may also give freer rein to the operation of moral incentives and peer group controls. The point here is not that collective beneficial ownership should depend on altruism. Rather, it appeals to collective self-interest (Wiles, 1977), to ties between individuals and groups that promote a "coalescence of material and ideal interests" (Rothschild-Whitt, 1979b:515; see also Rothschild-Whitt, 1979a).

Such ties between individuals and groups can contribute significantly to both the initial formation and later stability of worker-owned firms. Aldrich and Stern (1983) have argued that individualistic motives have rarely led to the creation of worker-owned firms, because individual founders prefer structures that allow them to monopolize the rewards of ownership. Worker-owned organizations are much more likely to be established by church groups, trade unions, and other collective bodies that seek to spread the benefits of ownership throughout their membership. It is also possible that collectively owned enterprises are slower to introduce hired nonowner labor than other worker-owned firms, because the common group membership between present and future employees may help to minimize the inherent conflict of interest between these two groups (see Chapters 3 and 4).

All of these potential advantages hinge, however, on the strength of the ties that link individuals to an owning group. Insofar as these ties are insufficiently strong, worker-owners are likely to revert quickly to the individualistic rationality that has led so frequently to the degeneration of many worker-owned firms.

Some valuable insights into the ties between individuals and groups in collectively owned organizations emerge from Rosabeth Kanter's survey of nineteenth century utopian communities in the United States. In the course of studying thirty of these institutions, Kanter identified a wide range of devices through which they sought to bind individual members more closely to the group. Kanter also found that it was precisely the institutions that had an abundance of these "commitment mechanisms" that showed the greatest ability to survive (Kanter, 1972).

Commitment in these organizations usually began, as in a case of distributive ownership, with an act of investment. But here, investment is not so much a purchase of an interest or share, as it is a symbolic act by which the member consecrates himself to the collective enterprise. The investment does not have to amount to some specific sum, but it has to mean something to the person who makes it. New members were usually required to turn over all their assets to the collectivity. Moreover, these investments were often irreversible, so that the recruits' economic fortunes would thereafter depend permanently on the success of the group.

Many other commitment mechanisms that Kanter identified were aimed at fostering an ongoing sense of membership in the group. These include isolation of the group, frequent interaction within the group, and the elaboration of group ritual. Kanter also found that in successful communities, these mechanisms were usually facilitated by an underlying homogeneity in ethnic background, economic status, and religion that preceded entry into the community. This common origin provided a foundation upon which to build a shared sense of mission, or "transcendence," that Kanter also found in most of the successful communities.

A related approach to group identification in these communities was an ascetic suppression of individuality. Kanter's report on the practices of the nineteenth century utopians is filled with such terms as "sacrifice," "renunciation," "mortification," and "deindividuation." The only personalities permitted to stand out in these communities were those of the leaders, who were often figures of charismatic authority.

These elements that Kanter observed in nineteenth century communities also go far toward explaining the success of the most celebrated of all twentieth century utopias, the Israeli kibbutz. Living in isolation, and sharing work, recreation, and living quarters, the kibbutz pioneers provided a textbook example of how to foster a new group identity. Moreover, the founders of this movement were able to fuse socialism and Zionism into an extraordinarily powerful sense of purpose. And what was a holy mission for the first generation of immigrant Jews who entered the kibbutz presented itself as a matter of group survival for the next. The urgency of its errand has enabled the kibbutz to set exacting standards for the behavior of its members. Kibbutzniks turn over all their assets upon entry into the collective, and work strenuously thereafter for the most minimal material rewards.

These features have enabled the Israeli kibbutzim to achieve an impressive record of both social and economic success. Since the first kibbutz was founded in 1909, the number of kibbutzim had grown by 1971 to 234, with a total population of 99,700. This represented 36% of Israel's rural population, and accounted for 38% of its agricultural output (Don, 1977:52, 59). The kibbutzim have maintained an impressive rate of capital investment, thanks to which their productivity nearly doubled from 1957 to 1973 (Barkai, 1977; Don, 1977:59). By 1973, the kibbutzim had also established 246 industrial plants, which together produced 5.5% of the nation's industrial output (Don, 1977:60–61). In a 1974 study that compared workers in ten kibbutz plants to workers in similar plants in the United States, Yugoslavia, Italy, and Austria, the kibbutz workers stood out as showing the least alienation and the best mental health (Tannenbaum *et al.*, 1974:155–166).

Even in this noteworthy instance of success, however, this group-based strategy for sharing ownership has revealed some characteristic limitations. For example, the shared values and identity that have linked kibbutz members to one another have been largely confined to immigrants from Europe, and have not successfully been extended to other sources of recruits. As a result, when Palestinian Arabs or even Sephardic Jews have worked in these organizations, they have done so as hired wage laborers, rather than as members of the kibbutz (Rayman, 1981; Leviatan, 1980). In addition, later generations born into a kibbutz have not shown the same intensity of commitment to kibbutz ideals as have individuals who entered the kibbutz by choice (Rosner, n.d.; Blasi, 1978). Perhaps partly for this reason, it has recently been shown that consumption patterns in all three major kibbutz federations have tended to become increasingly individualistic over time (Ben-Ner, 1982). There have also been tendencies for the use of hired labor to increase in the kibbutzim, with the result that by 1971 nonmember laborers constituted more than half the labor force in many kibbutzim (Ben-Ner and Neuberger, 1982:206).

Collective ownership has also proved to be less meaningful in situations that are less conducive to its success. A case in point is Israel's Histadrut, which has long served simultaneously as a trade union, a social service organ, and an agency of economic development. Through its subsidiary

Hevrat Ovdim, Histadrut owns many of the enterprises in which its members are employed. In 1970, the Histadrut empire employed 24% of the Israeli labor force, and was responsible for 23% of its net national product (Rosenstein, 1970:171; see also Kurland, 1947; Blumberg, 1966, Chapter 5; Tabb and Goldfarb, 1966; Yudin 1975). Histadrut industry is thus much more diffuse and also less morally elite than the kibbutz. Unlike the kibbutzniks, Histadrut employees do not live together, and tend to view their jobs as a source of income rather than an act of nation building. The union's leaders are frequently searching for new ways to infuse "a bit of the kibbutz spirit" (Jenkins 1973:86) into these enterprises; but so far, they have not found the way to translate the commitment mechanisms of the kibbutz into the vernacular of large scale, urban industrial organization.

A similar but much more challenging problem confronted the Russian Bolsheviks when they sought to reorder their entire society along collectivist lines (Wiles, 1977:23–24). How does one convey a sense of ownership to a group of collective owners, when the group is over a hundred million strong? From the beginning, the Soviet Communists' principal means of generating group commitment was broadly to instill a sense of common socialist purpose. In this effort, they were aided initially by a charismatic leadership, and later, by the proliferation of rituals and images that kept alive its memory. During the years of World War II, the socialist mission became also a national one, and Russians were called to fight fascism in the name of their Motherland as well as socialism.

A major problem with exhortations such as these, however, is that they tend to lose their force in periods that are relatively free from crisis. And for the person who is unmoved by these appeals, what is left of collective ownership? In 1840, the French anarchist Proudhon had warned that when ownership is shared collectively, the community and not the worker would be the true proprietor. In *What Is Property?*, he wrote that in this system,

> The members of a community, it is true, have no private property; but the community is proprietor, and proprietor not only of the goods, but of the persons and wills. In consequence of this principle of absolute property, labor . . . becomes odious. Passive obedience . . . is strictly enforced. Fidelity to regulations, which are always defective, however wise they may be thought, allows of no complaint. Life, talent, and all the human faculties are the property of the State . . . (Proudhon, p. 260, 1966).

This apparent paradox in which collective owners can themselves be perceived as the property of others is an accurate description of the role of the individual in an instance of all-embracing collective ownership such as the USSR. Individual workers do not own their own labor, because they are not free to sell or otherwise dispose of it according to their own wishes.

As individuals, they also do not own property, and cannot hope to reap personal gain by selling the fruits of their individual labor. The group, however, has need for their labor, and must induce or force it if it does not come spontaneously. It is only to the extent that they identify with the collectivity of owners that individuals in this system can be said to work freely, or as owners. Thus, while the group constitutes the *subject* of collective ownership, the individual is one of its *objects*.

In 1844, the young Marx appeared to take these concerns of Proudhon very much to heart; it was this thinking, in fact, that led him to posit a two-staged development of communism. He joined Proudhon in condemning the first stage as a "crude communism," that "generalizes" private property at the same time that it "annuls" it. In this system, he agreed, "The task of the *laborer* is not done away with, but extended to all men," and life is characterized by a "regression to the *unnatural* simplicity of the *poor* and *undemanding* man" (Tucker, 1972:68–69). Marx differed from Proudhon, really, only in suggesting that this "first positive annulment of private property" would be followed by a second one, which would not have these defects.

Both in the contemporary kibbutz movement and in the USSR, in the meantime, the role of the individual laborer as an object of collective ownership has received a number of explicit acknowledgements. Kibbutz regulations make it a matter of principle that "Every member of the kibbutz shall . . . place his full working capacity at the disposal of the kibbutz" and ". . . the kibbutz shall determine the member's work and everything connected therewith" (Yassour, 1977:315–316). In the USSR, the nation's right to the labor power of its citizens is even more absolute and has at times been ruthlessly enforced. In World War II, tardiness or absenteeism were punishable by the death penalty. After the war, a more benign set of "antiparasite laws" made unemployment a crime (Conquest, 1967). The Soviet Union also views education as an investment in its workers, and in 1972 imposed a "diploma tax" of up to 12,200 rubles on educated Jews who sought to emigrate to Israel (Sawyer, 1979:195). David Ellerman has remarked that in Soviet-type economies, workers "are essentially changed from being privately owned commodities rented on the labor market to being socially owned resources drafted into the industrial army" (Ellerman, 1975b:148).

To the extent that collective equity is unclear or ambiguous, it throws the other major component of ownership—control—into bold relief. Moreover, insofar as collective ownership fails to be an effective motivator of work activity, functions of administration and supervision grow all the more important. The work of Reinhard Bendix suggests that one of the most significant roles left to equity ownership in the Soviet Union has been to legitimate that country's hierarchial system of control.

In a collective economy as small as the kibbutz, where face-to-face relationships unite all the participants, and leaders are democratically elected, administration does not present an overwhelming problem. Elite formation does take place, and has caused some concern to kibbutz well-wishers (Etzioni, 1958; Ben-Raphael, 1976), but has so far done little to threaten the underlying unity of the community (Talmon, 1972).

Matters are different, however, in units as large as nations, where the centralized machinery of government is clearly differentiated from the mass of citizens. In these cases there is a strong tendency to ascribe ownership to whatever body or group actually exercises the rights of administration or control. Thus we often refer to collectively owned resources as being "state owned" or "government owned," even though in theory it is the people as a whole who own, and the state merely administers public resources on the people's behalf. Similarly, to critics of the Soviet system, it has often seemed that the Party or bureaucratic elites are the actual owners of Soviet industry. This idea, which was widely popularized by Milovan Djilas in the 1950s, had already become current in Marxist circles a number of years before. The Dutch Marxist Anton Pannekoek had written in 1942 that in the USSR, "The entirety of the ruling and leading bureaucracy of officials is the actual owner of the factories, the possessing class" (Pannekoek, 1975:475).

A more general theoretical conclusion that many Marxists have drawn from the Soviet experience is that although collective ownership can be meaningful, it will actually be so only to the extent that it includes mechanisms for the collective sharing of *control*. This is the theme of *Socialist Ownership and Political Systems*, a book by Polish economist Wlodzimierz Brus that appeared in English 1975. Some years earlier, Daniel Bell offered the following summary of the shift in priorities that this new conclusion has entailed:

> In recent years, there has arisen a sophistication which understands that the abolition of private property alone will not guarantee the end of exploitation . . . . In socialist thought the "new" answer is to raise again the theme of "workers' control" (Bell, 1962:387).

Democracy in the Workplace

Daniel Bell was correct in suggesting that "workers' control" is not a particularly new idea. As a demand and a reform, it has cropped up repeatedly since the early nineteenth century. What *is* new, however, is the system of "workers' self-management" that has emerged in Yugoslavia in the years since 1950.

The Yugoslav experiment is not only the first practical effort to organize the industry of an entire country along democratic lines, it is also the source of an important innovation in ownership theory: the Yugoslavs promote workplace democracy not as an end in itself, but as an integral part of the "social ownership" about which Marx wrote. They are thus the first theorists to treat workers' control as an integral part of the nature of ownership, not just something related to it.

Given the significance of this contribution, it is remarkable that the Yugoslav leaders thought it up in a hasty act of improvization. Following their quarrel with the Soviet Union in the late 1940s, the Yugoslavs were in urgent need of an ideological issue that could rationalize their defiance of Moscow. Milovan Djilas has published an illuminating account of how the idea of workers' self-management presented itself as the answer to this crisis. In *The Unperfect Society* he writes,

> The idea of self-management was conceived by Kardelj and me, with some help from our comrade Kidric. Soon after the outbreak of the quarrel with Stalin, in 1949, as far as I remember, I began to reread Marx's *Capital*, this time with much greater care, to see if I could find the answer to the riddle of why, to put it in simplistic terms, Stalinism was bad and Yugoslavia was good . . . . The country was in the stranglehold of the bureaucracy, and the party leaders were in the grip of rage and horror over the incorrigibly arbitrary nature of the party machine they had set up and that kept them in power. One day — it must have been the spring of 1950 — it occurred to me that we Yugoslav Communists were now in a position to start creating Marx's free association of producers . . . . Tito . . . knew nothing of the proposal . . . until he was informed by Kardelj and me in the government lobby room during a session of the National Assembly. His first reaction was: our workers are not ready for that yet! But Kardelj and I . . . pressed him hard, and he began to unbend as he paid more attention to our explanations. The most important part of our case was that this would be the beginning of democracy, something that socialism had not yet achieved; further, it could be plainly seen by the world and the international workers' movement as a radical departure from Stalinism. Tito paced up and down, as though completely wrapped in his own thoughts. Suddenly he stopped and exclaimed: "Factories belonging to the workers — something that has never yet been achieved!" . . . A few months later, Tito explained the Workers' Self-Management Bill to the National Assembly (Djilas, 1969:220–223).

Although the idea of introducing democracy into Yugoslav workplaces occurred to the Yugoslav leaders in a sudden burst of inspiration, the goal of workplace democracy itself has far older roots. For England's guild socialists it reflected a romantic nostalgia for pre-capitalist life (Houseman, 1979). Since the nineteenth century, labor unions have been described as a form of "industrial democracy," and it has often been argued that the unions are the most effective form of workplace democracy that workers will ever devise (Webb and Webb, 1897; Clegg, 1960; Derber, 1970).

Many others have often argued, however, that the labor union is an inherently limited form of workplace democracy. A labor union exists primarily to protect the interests of workers in their roles as wage earners. Through a process of collective bargaining, it seeks to influence the terms under which wage workers sell their labor to employers. When these negotiations break down, the unions resort to the use of the strike, which is in essence a declaration of "no sale" in response to management's latest offer. In the past, trade unions have exerted their greatest influence on such "bread and butter" issues as wage scales and job security, and have taken only an intermittent interest in companies' internal operations. Voices in the labor movement have occasionally called for unions to become more closely involved in decision making at the workplace. The role of the unionists may be limited, however, by the very nature of their principal weapon, the strike. A successful strike requires a high level of commitment and solidarity among the participants, and a good measure of hostility to management as well. To maintain the needed level of consensus, union demands usually stick close to fundamental issues that affect large numbers of wage earners. And to keep a proper combative spirit, union leaders can not allow themselves to be compromised by too great a complicity in the management of the enterprise. Such labor theoreticians as Hugh Clegg warn that if unions get too close to management, they will undermine the adversary relationship between labor and management on which their power rests (Clegg, 1960).

Considerations of this sort have often led to the conclusion that collective bargaining is inherently limited to what Lenin referred to as "economist" demands (Lenin, 1929). That is, unions are quite effective at influencing the price at which wage earners sell their labor, but are less appropriate for transforming the management of the workplace itself (see also Blumberg, 1968: Chapter 7, and Mason, 1982:161–162). Thus for other advocates of workplace democracy, a different institution has come to represent the embodiment of their hopes. That is the "factory council" or "workers' council" through which they seek to make the labor force of every economic organization a democratically self-governing unit.

The workers' council is a mongrel institution of obscure origin. It owes much of its occasional popularity to its ability to appeal to many diverse political perspectives at the same time. The councils were first advocated by liberal factory owners of the nineteenth and early twentieth centuries, who saw management-sponsored committees as an alternative to union militance. During World World I, most governments officially encouraged such labor-management bodies as an aid to their war efforts.

To the anarcho-syndicalist left of that era, self-governing councils also frequently suggested themselves as alternatives to the rule of the capitalist and the state. In 1905, and again in 1917, revolutionaries in Russia spontaneously organized *soviets*, or councils, in their factories and cities. After the October Revolution of 1917, the factory soviets in Russia were quickly subordinated to the discipline of Lenin's party machine (Avrich, 1963; Azrael, 1966; Brinton, 1970; Rachleff, 1974; Goodey, 1974; Bailes, 1978; Rucker, 1979; Sirianni, 1982). At the same time, however, workers' movements elsewhere in Europe were placing the creation of workers' councils at the top of their agendas (e.g., Callinicos, 1977; Sirianni, 1980; Silard, 1981). They differed principally in whether they sought to establish these councils by armed revolution, as in Bavaria and Hungary, or by plant seizures, as in Italy in 1920, or by law, as in Weimar Germany (Horvat, Markovic, and Supek, 1975, Vol. I:191–253).

It was in the years immediately after World War I that the idea of the workers' council received its first serious development in socialist thought. Two Marxist theorists, Antonio Gramsci and Anton Pannekoek, identified the councils as the key institution through which the proletariat was to make itself a self-governing class (on Gramsci's thought, see Gramsci, 1977, and the literature cited in Kaye, 1981; on Pannekoek, see Aronowitz, 1972; Pannekoek, 1975; Smart, 1978; and Bonacchi, 1967–77). In Pannekoek's words,

> We see now that council organization puts into practice what Marx theoretically anticipated but for what at the time the practical form could not yet be imagined . . . . Marx's conception of the dictatorship of the proletariat now appears to be identical with the labor democracy of council organization (Pannekoek, 1975:438).

When the Yugoslavs first announced their intention to transfer the control of their enterprises from the state to the factory councils, it was not clear to anyone how far-reaching or how permanent the change would prove to be. Since then, however, a series of new laws and constitutional amendments has gradually increased and solidified the authority of the councils. In 1958 the councils were granted parity with political authorities in the choice of the enterprise director. In 1969, they received the right to dismiss the director at any time. Similarly, the share of plant income at the disposal of the workers' councils grew from 20% in 1956–60 to approximately 60% in 1968 (Hunnius, 1973:294).

The organizational arrangements used to bring democracy to Yugoslav workplaces are in practice quite complex, and have tended to become increasingly so over time. Until the 1970s, the entire labor force of an enterprise constituted the work collective, which in turn elected the workers' council. Councils were initially composed of between ten and fifty members, and met once every one or two months. The executive arm of a workers' council was its managing board, which consisted of between five and fifteen elected members (Tannenbaum et al., 1974:30). At least three-quarters of the managing board were required to be production workers, and no members of any of these bodies could be elected for more than two consecutive two-year terms (Hunnius, 1973:278–279). Since 1974, a new Yugoslav constitution and other legal changes have further decentralized this system by basing it not on the enterprise, but on the basic organization of associated labor or "BOAL." A BOAL is equivalent to an internal division or profit center in a capitalist firm, and will apparently help prevent workplace democracy in Yugoslavia from being diluted by being stretched to cover too many workers or work sites (Sacks, 1983).

Since the 1960s, a number of Yugoslav and Western social scientists have attempted to measure the degree to which rank-and-file workers actually participate in the decisions of these bodies. One of the most ambitious of these efforts was the international comparative study reported by Arnold S. Tannenbaum and four associates in 1974. The study compared workers employed in ten matched industrial plants in each of five countries — in the United States, Austria, Italy, Yugoslavia, and Israel (kibbutz industry only). Plants were matched by type of industry and size. Participation in decision-making was measured by a number of questions developed by Rensis Likert and by Tannenbaum. These measures showed the sample of 350 Yugoslav workers to rank second only to the Israeli kibbutzniks in perceived participation by workers in decision making in their plants. Moreover, when the participation of different levels in the plant hierarchies was examined, the Yugoslav plants showed a more evenly distributed pattern of influence than those of any other country (Tannenbaum *et al.*, 1974:52, 58–60, 77). An even larger twelve-nation study of industrial democracy in Europe reported in 1981, similarly found the Yugoslav workers to rank first in influence over decision making in their plants (IDE, 1981).

The institutionalization of democracy in Yugoslav workplaces has occurred in defiance of a respectable body of thought that views such innovations as inherently unwise. One source of this skepticism is the emphasis placed by Weber and others on the technical virtues of top-down, bureaucratic decision making; from this perspective, democracy seems inherently inefficient and disruptive (Weber, 1947:247–248). The theoretical views of Weber are also supported by the empirical findings of the Webbs on the history of many past worker-owned firms. The Webbs claimed that the failure of many producer cooperatives was due to the inherent impracticality of democracy in the workplace. They wrote in 1920,

The relationship set up between a manager who has to give orders all day to his staff, and the members of that staff who, sitting as a committee of management, criticize his action in the evening, with the power of dismissing him if he fails to conform to their wishes, has been found by experience to be an impossible one (Webb and Webb, 1920; reprinted in Coates and Topham, 1970:72).

This pessimism about the practicality of workplace democracy has been challenged from a number of quarters. Theoretically, the most important response has come from the numerous social psychologists who argue that workers are more motivated to carry out decisions when they themselves have had a hand in making those decisions (e.g., Coch and French, 1948; Blumberg, 1968). Empirically, Yugoslavia has achieved a "respectable" record of economic growth since introducing workers' self-management, and some efforts have been made to show that the motivational consequences of workplace democracy have contributed to the economy's performance. But economic studies have generally found it impossible to disentangle the effects of workers' self-management from those of numerous other influences (Estrin and Bartlett, 1982). Perhaps the best indication that workplace democracy does enhance the productivity of Yugoslav workers comes from the research of Tannenbaum's group. In that study, Yugoslav workers along with the Israeli kibbutzniks stood out from the other three samples of workers in two striking respects: they were more likely to say that their co-workers would criticize them if they did their jobs poorly, and they were also more likely to say that criticism from co-workers bothers them when it occurs (Tannenbaum et al., 1974:70,73). Thus, in these democratic workplaces, the authority of the peer group appears to have been joined to that of management in encouraging diligent performance of one's job.

The more they succeed in democratizing their workplaces, the more firmly have the Yugoslavs insisted that their system of workers' self-management marks a new departure in the nature of ownership. This claim originates in the contrast they make between their own type of ownership and that of the Soviet Union. Since Soviet factories are administered not by their employees, but by and on behalf of the state, the Yugoslavs see the USSR as a case of state ownership. In Yugoslavia, on the other hand, where property is owned in common, but is administered directly by associations of producers, they claim to have established the "social property" which Marx had in mind in *Capital*.

In the Yugoslav formula, the worker participates in the ownership of industry in two distinguishable ways. First, he shares in the collective equity, or social property, that all members of his society own in common. And second, he exercises control over that property, and appropriates its fruits, by virtue of his work and his participation in the workers' council.

In 1919, Gramsci identified the workers' council as the best vehicle for expressing working-class democracy because it represented the proletariat directly in their role as workers rather than in some extraneous capacity. Its superiority to the trade union lay in the fact that it was "specific to the activity of producers, not wage-earners, the slaves of capital" (Gramsci, 1977:100). The Yugoslavs have given analogous reasons for conferring on the worker's councils the right to control and dispose of their collective capital. They thereby avoid the pitfalls of basing worker ownership on workers' ownership of stock, or their citizenship, or their membership in a class, and instead base it directly on workers' concrete participation in productive organizations. Yugoslav workers exercise their ownership *not* through their roles as owners, but through their roles as workers. In the words of their 1963 constitution,

> . . . nobody — not socio-political communities, nor organizations of associated labour, nor groups of citizens, nor individuals — may appropriate on any legal-property ground the product of social labour or manage and dispose of the social means of production and labour, or arbitrarily determine conditions for distribution.

> Man's labour shall be the only basis for the appropriation of the product of social labour and for the management of social resources (Vanek, 1975:71).

In this system, the nature of social property as equity follows logically from the principles of workers' self-management. Social ownership is that form of ownership that guarantees that appropriation will take place on the basis of labor rather than ownership. Social property constitutes the capital fund from which the worker derives his livelihood and economic freedom. Therefore, the workers' most important relation to this social property is the requirement that he protect it and make it grow. Yugoslav factory councils have the right to *use* social property, but not to *abuse* it. They are forbidden to reduce the capital fund of their enterprise or to realize unearned income on the sale of any part of it.

The Yugoslavs are uneasy with this concept of social ownership, for it lacks the clarity and vitality of workers' self-management. It is largely a negative concept, denying the possibility of ownership by any particular individual group, and limiting the rights of the social owners. It is also an incipiently statist concept, since in practice it is the state that protects society against any abuse of social property. The Yugoslav theorist Svetozar Stojanovic has written,

> Even a superficial glance at the real centers of social power in our country can show that a "self-governing, self-managing society" exists only in ideology, while a vivid dualism exists in practice — self-managing groups in the base and a rather strong statist structure above them (Stojanovic, 1975:469)

The Yugoslavs have now produced a vast literature in the effort to elaborate the positive meaning of social ownership (Carevic, 1974; Kardelj, 1979, 1981; Stanic, 1980). But even their most gifted theorists have failed to produce a concept one can really sink one's teeth into. Here, for example, are the eloquent but elusive words of Edvard Kardelj:

> The social means of production belong to all those who work. This is the most important objective condition for their labor and for their freedom as workers and creators.
>
> But no one can have private property title to these means of production. In this sense, social property is "everybody's" and "nobody's." At the same time, however, the social means of production are the workers' personal tools and thus the means with which they earn their personal incomes. Thus social property is both the common class property of all the workers and a form of individual property of those who work (Kardelj, 1975:40).

In 1975, the Yugoslav economist Branko Horvat published a review of the then-current debates over the nature of social ownership. His summary is perhaps the best available expression of the true state of this difficult art:

> If state ownership fails to promote socialism, what is a feasible alternative? The Yugoslav answer is: social ownership. But the answer to the next question — what precisely is social ownership — is not so easy and simple. The legal experts agree that social ownership implies self-government, that it is a new social category, that if it is a legal concept, it does not imply an unlimited right over things characteristic of the classical concept of property, and that it includes property elements of both public and private law . . . . In practically everything else, there is disagreement (Horvat, 1975:172).

The difficulties the Yugoslavs have had in clarifying social ownership, in contrast to their well-publicized successes in instituting workers' self-management, have permitted many people outside Yugoslavia to become enthusiastic about workplace democracy while showing no interest at all in social ownership. In Western Europe and the United States, there have recently been a number of efforts to introduce workers' participation in decision making into government and privately owned enterprises that pay little or no regard to the issue of ownership. These innovations range all the way from the sporadic experiments with "participatory management" in individual firms that have been common in the United States, to the legally mandated systems of workers' representation on company boards of directors and other forms of "codetermination" that have been established in many countries of Western Europe (Batstone and Davies, 1976; Garson, 1977; Windmuller, 1977; American Center for the Quality of Work Life,

1978; King and van de Vall, 1978; Pejovich, 1978; Jain, 1980; Thimm, 1980; Strauss, 1982).

Proponents of these various forms of workplace democracy have often advocated them with a range of arguments as diverse as those made for worker ownership as a whole. For some, these innovations are important victories for workers in their struggle for power (e.g., Gorz, 1967; Stephens and Stephens, 1982; Sirianni, 1983); for others, they are merely co-optative reforms (Ramsey, 1977; Clarke, 1978; Panitch, 1981). George Strauss attributes the popularity of these programs to the fact that they con-stitute "a happy melding of the ideologies of socialism and human relations" (Strauss, 1982:179; see also Greenberg, 1975). It has also been suggested that democracy in the workplace will strengthen democracy outside of it—not, as in arguments for worker ownership, because it will enhance the worker's stake in the legitimacy of the system, but because it will turn the workplace into a training ground for political participation (Pateman, 1970; Mason, 1982; Street, 1983).

Despite the great diversity of hopes and claims that have been expressed on their behalf, surprisingly little is known about the extent to which these various modest forms of workers' participation in management have actually lived up to their promise. Reviewing the American literature on par-ticipative management and autonomous workgroups in the 1960s, Paul Blumberg concluded that

> There is hardly a study in the entire literature which fails to demonstrate that satisfaction in work is enhanced or that other generally acknowledged beneficial consequences accrue from a genuine increase in workers' decision-making power (Blumberg, 1968:123).

Subsequent and more skeptical reviews of this literature have reported that the relationship between participation and work satisfaction remains robust, but indicate that only under narrowly circumscribed conditions does participation lead to higher productivity as well (Locke and Schweiger, 1979). With regard to worker representation on boards of direc-tors in Europe, some observers have argued that the worker directors' role has been too trivial to have any significant impact at all (Batstone, 1979). At least some evidence suggests, however, that access to board meetings has provided workers with an important new source of both information and influence, and that industrial relations have been altered significantly as a result (Thimm, 1980; Strauss, 1982:219–221).

Perhaps the most important issue raised by these various forms of workers' participation is their relationship to the ownership of a firm. In-sofar as these reforms are introduced at the discretion of management, and are given no permanent legal or constitutional base, it is probably just as well that they ignore the issue of ownership, since they introduce no real changes in it. The powers and prerogatives of the existing owners, whether they be private owners or governmental officials, remain essentially what they were before.

It is a different matter, however, when broad decision-making prerogatives are transferred to workers' bodies as a matter of right. In the Western European countries that have adopted systems of "codetermination," the representation of employees on company boards of directors is now provided for by law. Insofar as these reforms make meaningful inroads into the legal rights of management, they are changes in ownership, whether that fact is openly acknowledged or not. They diminish the rights of the titular owners by requiring them to share them with labor. In the succinct words of Svetozar Pejovich, "codetermination attenuates the right of ownership" (Pejovich, 1978:19).

These remarks apply not only to recent laws on codetermination, but to workers' more longstanding rights of collective bargaining as well. As Wilbert E. Moore observed in 1943,

> The legal recognition of collective bargaining as a "right," with workers maintaining their employee status during strikes or other labor disputes, and with enforceable claims on employment if illegally discharged, with back pay for the period of illegal withholding of employment—all this amounts to property, however unwilling the courts may be to offend traditional sentiment by use of the term (Moore, 1943:55).

only w/D thru & MOP

In a more general discussion of the implications of workplace democracy for the ownership of industry, Paul Bernstein summarized that "Democratization begins to transfer specific powers of ownership to the employees even before the formal, legal title of ownership may be transferred. Of course," Bernstein adds, "*complete* worker autonomy and self-management . . . is unlikely to occur without a transfer of the *majority* of rights belonging to the formal owner" (Bernstein, 1976:512).

Other theorists see ownership as important for workplace democracy, but only in the negative sense that no one should be permitted to have ownership rights that interfere with the operation of workers' self-management. This view is related to the tendency of many theorists to equate social ownership with an absence of ownership. For example, Elizabeth Mann Borgese of the Center for the Study of Democratic Institutions has written,

> . . . what is important is not that the worker should own resources or the means of production but that nobody else should own them and thereby be placed in a position of hiring and firing and otherwise directing and

manipulating the workers. If self-management need not be based on workers' ownership, it certainly excludes the possibility of ownership by others (Adizes and Borgese, 1975:xxiii).

This sort of thinking led the English authors R. H. Tawney (1920) and Paul Derrick (1947) to recommend an attractively simple device for establishing workers' self-management in their country. They proposed that legislation should be passed that would leave the existing distribution of capital essentially unchanged, but would strip capital ownership of all rights save the right to earn interest. All rights to make decisions and to appropriate variable economic returns would be vested in democratic bodies analogous to the Yugoslav workers' council.

According to the theories of some leading economists of worker's self-management, to cause ownership to "wither away" in this fashion would be not merely convenient, but ideal. Jaroslav Vanek and David Ellerman, in particular, have argued that ownership is harmful not only when it interferes from outside a self-managed firm, but when it is located within the firm as well (Vanek, 1970, 1971, 1975, 1977; Ellerman, 1977, 1982b). When workers own their own firm there is a constant danger that their desire to maximize the return on their capital investments will lead them to exploit hired labor or to sell off the firm. Vanek has also argued that worker ownership is undesirable on purely economic grounds, because when labor and capital are obtained from the identical source, a number of allocational inefficiencies can be predicted to result (Vanek, 1977:186–198).

To minimize the harmful effects of capital ownership on self-managed firms, Vanek and Ellerman make two major recommendations to the founders of these firms. First, democratic workplaces should follow the Yugoslav example in adopting structures that base the right to participate in decision making on contributing labor to the firm, rather than contributing capital to it. What is important, says Ellerman, is not that workers should have rights of "ownership" in their firms, but that they should have rights of "membership" in them (Ellerman, 1975a). For Ellerman, membership rights differ from ownership rights chiefly in the fact that they cannot readily be put up for sale. In the United States, this thinking has led Ellerman to recommend that self-managed workplaces should be legally constituted as cooperatives, rather than as corporations whose stock is worker-owned (Ellerman, 1977, 1982b).

In addition, Vanek and Ellerman have also recommended that self-managed workplaces should borrow their capital rather than owning it themselves. Vanek has argued that if capital is borrowed at interest, this will encourage sound accounting practices and a more rational allocation of resources. Moreover, if the firm does not own capital, workers will not be tempted to increase the return on their investments by using hired labor or selling the firm. The goal for Vanek and Ellerman, in short, is not to end the separation between labor and capital, but to reverse the power relationship between them; they propose to replace a system in which "capital hires labor" with one in which "labor hires capital" (Ellerman, 1975a).

While Vanek's system of "debt financing" appears to have some important allocational advantages, there are several grounds for questioning whether it is necessary or sufficient to prevent the degeneration of democratic firms. One frequent objection to debt financing is that if workers do not own capital, they will surrender *de facto* if not *de jure* control of their workplaces to whomever they obtain their capital from. Vanek recommends that self-managed workplaces should obtain their capital from the state, or from nonprofit support corporations established expressly for this purpose (Vanek, 1975: 34–35; Cornell Self-Management Working Group, 1975). A particularly successful example of such a support organization is the Caja Laboral Popular of Mondragon, Spain. Having been formed in 1959 to assist a mere handful of newly-formed cooperatives, the CLP's empire had grown by the early 1980s to include more than 85 industrial cooperatives with nearly 20,000 worker-members (Thomas and Logan, 1982; Ellerman, 1982a; Clamp, 1983). There have already been many complaints, however, that the CLP thoroughly dominates the management of its member cooperatives, and leaves them little practical scope to govern themselves (Eaton, 1979).

Partly for this reason, a number of capital structures have been recommended that can discourage degeneration while also allowing workers to own as well as control their workplaces. Vanek and Ellerman have themselves been increasingly inclined to grant that sources of capital need not be external to the firm, just as long as they are clearly differentiated from membership rights and do not threaten the long-term stability of the firm. Vanek, for example, has expressed approval of England's Scott Bader Commonwealth, a chemical firm that is owned by its workers through the legal form of a trust. The trust is a perpetual one, and employees become full and equal members in it without having to contribute any capital of their own (Vanek, 1975:24, 227–23). Ellerman has also become increasingly involved in promoting cooperatives in which individual members do supply and own the capital, subject to the constraints that: (1) their capital contributions are clearly labelled and accounted for as loans to the enterprise; (2) these loans earn interest; and (3) the loans along with accumulated interest and a member's share of any retained earnings are automatically paid back to members as they retire, without making it necessary for them to alter the cooperatives' structure in order to recoup these investments (Ellerman, 1977; 1982b; see also Vanek, 1977:171, 186).

There remain some important causes of degeneration, however, that none of the capital arrangements discussed so far does anything at all to eliminate. Avner Ben-Ner (1981; 1984) has recently demonstrated that self-managed workplaces are tempted to use hired labor not only by the dynamics of capital accumulation and recoupment, but also by the dynamics of the labor market itself. Ben-Ner argues that whenever there are laborers outside a cooperative who are willing to work for less than the earnings of co-op members, the cooperative is likely to make use of this cheaper labor, even if the hired labor is less motivated and productive than the labor of co-op members. This is because when the cooperative admits new workers as members, its profits can be expected to increase, but the number of people who share in those profits will also correspondingly grow. Thus the income per member will remain unchanged. If the cooperative hires nonmember laborers, on the other hand, profits will not grow as fast, but this disadvantage is outweighed by the fact that hired laborers have no claim at all on the profits of the enterprise. As a result, all profits from the use of hired labor become additions to the income of the existing co-op members.

Insofar as debt financing or alternative capital arrangements do not provide immunity from the temptation to degenerate, self-managed workplaces must rely that much more heavily on the constitutional provisions recommended by Vanek and Ellerman to prevent their demise. A chronic limitation of constitutional safeguards, however, is that they can usually be amended or circumvented by other means. Members of a cooperative can often progressively lengthen the probationary period required before a new employee can become a member, or can make increasing use of temporary help.

Workplace democracy is on somewhat surer footing when democratic arrangements within individual firms also enjoy the protection of the state. It has already been noted that workers' rights of collective bargaining and codetermination are often guaranteed by law. Many governments also discourage the degeneration of producers' cooperatives and other worker-owned enterprises through a variety of means. In the United States important tax advantages accrue to cooperatives, and attorneys for the plywood cooperatives have advised them that they could easily lose these advantages if they made too much use of hired labor in their plants.

Only in Yugoslavia, however, is the right of virtually all workers to manage their own workplaces guaranteed by law. In Yugoslavia, these rights of self-management are inherent in the concept of "social ownership," and are also embedded in a far older debate among Marxists over whether a socialist economy can best be coordinated through reliance on markets or a central plan (Brus, 1972; Bettelheim, 1975). In Yugoslavia, workers' self-management in individual factories is often seen as presupposing a decentralized economy in which autonomous firms respond to market opportunities, rather than the dictates of a central plan. Voices within Yugoslavia, however, have often complained that the tyranny of market forces can limit a firm's range of choices as effectively as any plan (Milenkovitch, 1971, 1977; Wachtel, 1973; Baumgartner, Burns, and Sekulic, 1979; Comisso, 1979; 1980). Insofar as the preservation of workplace democracy depends on legal safeguards, this may represent a particularly important instance in which market forces appear to be inherently inimical to the goal of workers' control, and in which the pursuit of this goal requires at least some assistance from the state.

Ben-Ner (1981) has recently argued, however, that even the Yugoslav system provides inadequate safeguards against the use of hired labor. He has pointed out that the creation of BOALs within Yugoslav enterprises may have consequences quite similar to the introduction of hired labor within a firm. In his words, contractual relations among BOALs "can be viewed as analogous to hiring wage laborers in groups, rather than individually" (Ben-Ner, 1981).

The Yugoslav system of workers' self-management has also drawn criticism on other grounds. Western economists have complained that the Yugoslav system of social ownership provides deficient incentives in a number of respects. Ichak Adizes faults social ownership for inhibiting the mobility of labor and capital (Adizes and Borgese, 1975:28). For Jaroslav Vanek, the most serious shortcoming is the failure to pay a scarcity rent on the use of a firm's accumulated capital.

The Yugoslav system of social ownership has its critics within Yugoslavia as well. The Zagreb sociologist Josip Zupanov has argued that Yugoslav workers do not share enough in the equity ownership of their firms. Zupanov reports that most Yugoslav workers "are not willing to take any responsibility beyond the limits of their own job," and suggests that the remoteness of their tie to social property may be at fault. The problem, writes Zupanov, is that the Yugoslav "institutional pattern . . . gives the employees enterpreneurial prerogatives but no property claim on the fruits of their entrepreneurial activity beyond their personal earnings [that is, their wages, plus their share of whatever earnings are distributed to the workers as bonuses]" (Zupanov, 1975:81).

Zupanov is also one of many social scientists who have called attention to another troublesome aspect of Yugoslav workers' self-management. Despite the formal equality among workers that prevails in workers' council debates, numerous studies have demonstrated the existence of systematic inequalities in the actual distribution of participation in these bodies. In particular, it has repeatedly been found that rank-and-file production workers participate in the workers' councils far less actively than do the managerial and technical personnel. Several observational studies have found that participation by rank-and-file employees is usually confined to personnel matters. Major technical and financial decisions, on the other hand, are often left to "the experts" (Zupanov, 1975:82; see also Obradovic,

1975; Obradovic and Dunn, 1978; and Verba and Shabad, 1978). Moreover, when surveys ask Yugoslav workers to rate the overall influence of various groups in their plants, their responses consistently disclose a hierarchical pattern. Zupanov summarizes, ". . . one may conclude that the hierarchical organization has survived within the new institutional shell of democratic organization" (Zupanov, 1975:82–83).

Such disclosures of inegalitarian patterns of decision making in the midst of democratic organizational forms are of course a long familiar theme in social science research. In 1911, Robert Michels argued that the degeneration of democracy into hierarchy was the result of an inevitable process, which he called the "iron law of oligarchy" (Michels, 1962; see also Scaff, 1981, and Meister, 1984). Among the various forms of workplace democracy, such tendencies toward oligarchical degeneration have been observed in labor unions (Lipset, Trow, and Coleman, 1956; Edelstein and Warner, 1976); In Israeli kibbutzim (Etzioni, 1958; Ben-Raphael, 1976; Rosner and Cohen, 1983); in German work councils (Hartmann, 1979); and in American producer cooperatives (Shirom, 1972). In his study of the history of producer cooperatives in the United States, Arie Shirom reported in 1972 that

> Although the norm of democratized management—periodical election by the members—was duly acknowledged, it very seldom materialized. This lapse occurred chiefly because of an unalterable fact of life: managerial talents are unequally distributed in any given human population. Consequently, a relativity permament managerial stratum emerged in almost every cooperative shop which endured long enough for this inevitable process to take place (Shirom, 1972:545).

Within Yugoslavia, a number of social scientists have so far resisted the thought that inequalities in decision making in Yugoslav plants are in any way "inevitable." Many of them have been inclined instead to ascribe these inequalities to the industrial division of labor that Yugoslavia has in common with the Soviet Union and the capitalist West. Figures reported by Veljko Rus show that participation in one sample of plants corresponds closely to workers' positions in the division of labor in their plants (see Table III). Zupanov concludes from such data that "participation by itself cannot alter the exisiting, asymmetrical distribution of power between managers and employees." He also suggests that "successful participation is likely to be the result rather than the cause" of a change in the fundamental division of labor and power within the Yugoslav enterprise (Zupanov, 1975:84).

Some similar inferences have been drawn from experiments in workplace democratization that have taken place outside of Yugoslavia. A study of the

Table III. Perceived Influence of Various Groups on
the Work of Workers' Councils

Group	Index of Influence*
Top Management	3.09
Staff	2.85
Middle Management	2.58
Supervisors	2.36
Highly skilled and skilled workers	2.36
Semi-skilled and unskilled workers	2.14

*Meaning of influence scores:
  1 = "very small"
  2 = "small"
  3 = "high"
  4 = "very high"

Source: Rus, 1970:151

participation of workers' representatives on company boards in Norway has pointed toward conclusions analogous to those reached by Zupanov. Authors Fred Emery and Einar Thorsrud reported,

> . . . the crux of the problem lies in the fact that in the day-to-day ongoing work of the enterprise, there is too low a level of individual employee participation. Without some higher degree of participation at this direct level, it seems unlikely that enough interest or knowledge could be generated to sustain the sort of difficult and extended effort required to work out policies with regard to major long-term changes. Briefly, what we are suggesting is that . . . the individual should have more elbow-room within his job, and . . . greater responsibility for decisions affecting his job (Emery and Thorsrud, 1969:30).

In Reinhard Bendix's summary of the work of Weber, he offers a principle that is relevant here. Hierarchical domination within a group, he writes, will be at a minimum only when "the members are by and large equal and possess a minimum of skill for the administrative tasks to which each might be called in turn" (Bendix, 1962:293; see also Weber, 1968, I:289–290, and II:948–949). Increasingly, workplace democrats around the world are beginning to realize that their factories do not meet this criterion. Repeatedly, inequality in jobs undermines their efforts to introduce equality in participation. And so, their interest in industrial democracy leads them to show more and more concern for the nature of industrial work.

Ownership and the Nature of Work

Previous sections of this chapter have associated the concept of worker ownership with such specific institutional arrangements as employee stock ownership, the nationalization of industry, and democracy in the workplace. Another line of thought links worker ownership with the content of individual jobs.

The idea that the ownership of workplaces has implications for the nature of the work within them has a number of sources. The idea owes much to the work of Marx. A relationship between work and ownership is implicit in the contrast Marx drew between the alienating character of labor performed in capitalist workplaces and the richness and freedom that he associated with life in a future communist era.

A link between work and ownership is also strongly implied by our everyday experiences with the sole proprietorship. In the popular imagination, the prospect of owning one's own business is virtually synonymous with "being your own boss." Research on the self-employed has also confirmed the impression that individuals who own their own businesses do indeed experience greater variety and autonomy in their work than do individuals employed by someone else (Eden, 1975; Kohn, 1976; Kalleberg and Griffin, 1980; Griffin and Kalleberg, 1981).

The preceding sections of this chapter have contributed some more practical reasons why advocates of worker ownership in one form or another must devote careful attention to the nature of work. The voluntary use of employee stock ownership in capitalist corporations, for example, has often failed to spread beyond a select circle of managers and other employees whose work makes them particularly important to the success of the organization as a whole; workers whose jobs do not have this significance, on the other hand, are frequently excluded from these plans. In the Soviet Union, the fact that most workers have jobs no different from those of workers in the capitalist West, and have no more influence on decision making in their plants, has often led observers outside the USSR to dismiss pretensions to worker ownership in that country as little more than a sham.

The Yugoslav response to the Soviet experience was essentially to blame the Soviet failure on the bureaucratic subordination of the firm to the state, and to assume that if firms were made autonomous and given a democratic organization, the problem would be solved. It now appears, however, that the Yugoslavs' effort to democratize their workplaces is being systematically undermined by a division of labor that continues to encourage some workers to have much more say than others over conditions affecting their work.

The experiences that both the Soviets and the Yugoslavs have encountered with inequalities in their workplaces have not been entirely unexpected developments, but instead have long been anticipated in social thought. Since the nineteenth century, numerous authors have argued that eliminating the inequality between workers and capitalists would not bring an end to inequality in the workplace, but would rather cause other bases of inequality to stand out in sharper relief. The inequalities most prominently discussed by these various theorists include those based on talent, as in the elite theories of Vilfredo Pareto; on education and other forms of "cultural capital," as in the work of Pierre Bourdieu; on organization, as in the work of Weber and Michels; and on the division of labor itself, as in the work of several writers to be discussed in detail below.

As a result of such factors, numerous socialists have often viewed it as desirable and/or inevitable that the workplaces of the future would be dominated by their best trained and most experienced workers. Alvin Gouldner has noted that in Saint-Simon's early model of socialism, authority "would no longer rest upon inherited office or on force and violence — *or even property* — but on skill and science" (Gouldner, 1979:35).

The anarchist Bakunin thought a socialist revolution would have a similar result, but he was far less enthusiastic about the outcome. He predicted that such a revolution would result in the "reign of scientific intelligence," which would prove to be "the most aristocratic, despotic, arrogant, and contemptuous of all regimes." Bakunin added that the intellectual workers under socialism would come to constitute

> a new class, a new hierarchy of real and pretended scientists and scholars, and the world will be divided into a minority ruling in the name of knowledge and an immense ignorant majority. And then, woe betide the mass of ignorant ones! (quoted in Karabel, 1976:124; see also Nomad, 1959:119–120).

Marx was well aware that such predictions were being made about the future of socialism, but he had a response: the division between intellectual and manual labor and the subordination of the latter to the former was not inevitable, but was a historically specific consequence of capitalism. This division of labor was therefore destined to disappear, once capitalism had been overthrown. Marx wrote that in communist society, it would become possible for each person to "become accomplished in any branch he wishes . . . to do one thing today and another tomorrow, to hunt in the morning, fish in the afternoon, rear cattle in the evening, criticize after dinner . . . without ever becoming hunter, fisherman, shepherd or critic" (Tucker, 1972:124).

Since the Russian revolution of 1917, many observers have looked upon the USSR as the first great test of Marx's ideas about the future of work. Much has therefore been made of the fact that Soviet society has made so little apparent progress toward a more egalitarian division of labor since 1917. Many authors have sought to blame this lack of progress on various circumstances that may have diverted the Bolsheviks' energies after the revolution, such as the defense needs created by capitalist encirclement, or Lenin's postrevolutionary infatuation with Taylorism (Braverman, 1974:12–24; Lieberstein, 1975; Bailes, 1977). Actually, both Marx and Lenin had always been inclined to associate a new division of labor only with the second, "higher" phase of communism; and both had always anticipated that the first phase of postrevolutionary society would accept the capitalist division of labor as it found it. Thus Marx wrote in *Capital* that the new society would begin by taking the existing capitalist machinery as it is and putting it to public use. And of the scientists and engineers, Lenin wrote on the eve of the revolution that "these gentlemen work today owing allegiance to the capitalists: they will work even better tomorrow, owing it to the armed workers" (Lenin, 1961:237).

That the Russian revolution did not produce a new division of labor should thus not be interpreted either as a failure or as a surprise (see also Bellis, 1979). Nevertheless, it has contributed strongly in the West to a tendency to treat differences in ownership as irrelevant to the nature of work, and to see the division of labor as determined by other factors instead.

In the United States, a particularly influential statement of this point of view appeared in the work of Robert Blauner. In a study of work alienation published in 1964, Blauner wrote that the most important determinant of alienation in modern workplaces is not ownership, but technology. Blauner argued that whereas "ownership powerlessness" is "a constant in modern industry" (Blauner, 1964:17), technology varies a great deal, and with important consequences (see also Kohn, 1976).

This tendency to see the nature of work as a result of technology rather than ownership encouraged Blauner and others to draw some optimistic conclusions about the future of work. Like England's Joan Woodward (1965), Blauner saw technology as undergoing a three-stage sequence of development, moving from the craft technologies that preceded the industrial· revolution, through the machine-tending and assembly-line technologies of the early industrial revolution, to a new generation of "automatic" or "continuous process" technologies. This sequence had op-

timistic implications because it suggested that a sharp differentiation between mental and manual labor was only a temporary consequence of an
early phase of the industrial revolution, and that the current phase of
technological evolution is favoring the reappearance of complex and
autonomous work.

The technological determinism of Blauner and Woodward has subsequently been challenged on a number of grounds. One set of theorists has
insisted that the division of labor and other structural features of modern
organizations are influenced less by technology than they are by size (Pugh
et al., 1969; Hickson, Pugh, and Pheysey, 1969; Blau, 1970). Another
school has argued that the features of modern organizations are not rigidly
"determined" by any of these factors, but are instead a result of "managerial
strategies" or "organizational choice" (Trist *et al.*, 1963). A leading
American representative of the "organizational choice" school is Louis E.
Davis of UCLA. Davis wrote in 1973 that

> The Marxist faith that ownership of the means of production will reduce, if
> not eliminate alienation is at best simply utopian and at worst an ideological
> argument disregarding reality.
>
> . . . alienation of the worker is related not to ownership of the means of pro-
> duction or even its management, but to what the technocratic staff believes is
> necessary for the success of the organization (Davis, 1973:89–90).

While the "organizational choice" school might conceivably imply that
the division of labor is inherently highly variable, its adherents have in fact
tended to join the technological determinists in suggesting quite optimistic
implications about the future of work. The most important source of these
implications has been the humanistic motivational theories of such
psychologists as Abraham Maslow, Frederick Herzberg, and Edward
Lawler. A common element in all of these theories is the thought that
workers will be most motivated by jobs that are complex, interesting, and
challenging. This in turn has suggested that managers will be well advised
to choose technologies that minimize the division between mental and
manual labor in their firms, since workers will be motivated to work
hardest only by jobs that include a significant component of intellectual
work. Thus the most practical consequence of this line of research has been
to encourage managers to seek productivity gains through the upgrading of
work — that is, by encouraging job enlargement, job enrichment,
workgroup autonomy, and similar reforms (see Davis and Cherns, 1975;
Davis and Taylor, 1979).

The widespread optimism about the future of work that had been fed
both by the technological determinists and by the humanistic psychologists

was abruptly shattered in 1974 by the publication of Harry Braverman's work, *Labor and Monopoly Capital,* subtitled *The Degradation of Work in the Twentieth Century.* In the early chapters of his book, Braverman offered a vigorous restatement of Marx's argument that capitalist firms inevitably seek technologies that degrade workers' skills and that deprive most workers of control over their work. In particular, Braverman uncovered an impressive amount of evidence indicating preferences for technologies that subject work to machine pacing, that separate mental from manual labor, and that permit the employment of labor at the lowest possible levels of wages and therefore of skill. In later chapters, Braverman used American census data and detailed analyses of recent trends in American factories and offices to paint a gloomy picture of what capitalism is doing to the nature of work (Braverman, 1974; see also Noble, 1978; Zimbalist, 1979; Wallace and Kalleberg, 1982).

Despite the persuasive force of his arguments, Braverman's work has in turn come in for its own share of criticism. Theoretically, the difficulties that have drawn the attention of the greatest number of critics have stemmed from Braverman's decision to ignore the consciousness of the worker. Throughout his analysis, Braverman appears to have assumed implicitly that workers under capitalism are uncooperative on the one hand, but on the other hand are too passive and politically impotent for their resentment to be of any practical consequence. Richard Edwards has argued, however, that workers' hostility to the "technical control" described by Braverman leads in fact to unionization, strikes, and hence to rising labor costs. As a result, Edwards suggests that capitalist employers often turn instead to "bureaucratic control," a strategy that uses job security and advancement opportunities to evoke the active cooperation of the labor force (Edwards, 1979). Michael Burawoy is one of several other Marxist writers who have faulted Braverman for neglecting the impact of capitalism on workers' consciousness, and therefore for underestimating the power of the capitalist to "manufacture consent" (Burawoy, 1978, 1979; Littler and Salaman, 1982).

These theoretical problems in Braverman's work may be linked in turn to an empirical one. Although Braverman saw capitalism as inherently destructive of skills, recent studies of the complexity and intellectual content of jobs in the American economy as a whole have repeatedly reported an upward rather than a downward trend (Berg, 1970: Chapter 3; Spenner, 1979; Rumberger, 1981; see also Spenner, 1983). A number of processes could potentially account for this trend, including those identified by Blauner and by the advocates of job redesign. Many of these processes can also be accommodated within the Marxist tradition, once it has been granted that the capitalist is capable of obtaining the active cooperation of the work force. For if such cooperation is forthcoming, then the capitalist may have no need to degrade workers' jobs in order to evoke high productivity from them. Moreover, if Edwards and the humanistic psychologists are right, workers will be even more cooperative if employers make efforts to upgrade rather than degrade their jobs.

At present, then, there is little basis for concluding either that capitalism is inevitably degrading to work, or that alternative ownership arrangements inevitably improve it. There are, however, some important relationships between worker ownership and the nature of work about which it is possible to generalize with much greater confidence.

One persistent link between worker ownership and the nature of work has to do with the incidence of producer cooperatives, partnerships, and other employee-owned firms. Insofar as the division of labor varies from industry to industry and from firm to firm, these various forms of employee ownership appear much more readily where work involves a substantial degree of skill and autonomy than where it does not. When work is autonomous, employee ownership often serves as a particularly valuable motivator that encourages employees to use their own autonomy in the interests of the firm. When work involves rare skills, these skills also often constitute a form of "human capital" or "firm-specific asset" (Williamson, 1981) that employee ownership also helps to tie more closely to the firm. There is also evidence that employee ownership is particularly consistent with the values of employees whose jobs are characterized by autonomy and skill. Kohn and Schooler have demonstrated that the more autonomy and complexity are involved in a worker's job, the more likely is the worker to value independence and self-expression in other spheres as well (Kohn and Schooler, 1969).

Such connections between the incidence of employee ownership and the nature of work will be pursued in detail in later chapters of this work. Those chapters will argue that employee participation in decision making is more meaningful and effective in workplaces in which skills are widely shared. Worker ownership that is thus linked to the nature of work may also be unusually resistant to tendencies toward "degeneration," because in these firms hired labor is less readily substitutable for self-employed labor than it is in other types of worker-owned firms. It will also be shown, however, that when worker ownership rests on such a technological base, it is also vulnerable to technological change. Thus Chapter 3 will describe an instance in which technological innovations that degraded workers' skills also contributed to the degeneration of one population of worker-owned firms.

While differences among firms in the nature of work thus have an important impact on the incidence and longevity of worker-owned firms, worker ownership is also strongly influenced by the division of labor within the firm as well. Insofar as a marked separation between mental and manual labor is present within worker-owned firms, it often appears that the intellectual workers are the major beneficiaries of these reforms. In capitalist firms that are only partially employee-owned it is typically the skilled and managerial employees whom owners are most eager to motivate with their stock ownership plans. In more far-reaching forms of shared ownership from which the capitalist has been completely eliminated, as in socialist enterprises or wholly worker-owned firms, the intellectual workers continue to occupy the highest posts, and also dominate decision making in democratic bodies as well.

The prominent role of the intellectuals in allegedly worker-owned institutions has often led to the conclusion that they are of no real benefit to the manual working class, and instead serve the interests of the intellectuals alone. In these organizations, it is argued, the manual workers remain subordinated to the managerial ones, just as before. For the managerial employees, however, these innovations constitute important gains, allowing them to displace the capitalists as their society's dominant class.

Once it is argued that the intellectuals have the most to gain from the elimination of capitalism, it requires just one more step to conclude that anti-capitalist ideologies are espoused by intellectuals in a cynical effort to dupe the working class into assisting them to power. The first complete statement of this position appeared in a work by Waclaw Machajski published in 1898 (Nomad, 1932, 1959; Avrich, 1965; Shatz, 1967). Most recently, Alvin Gouldner has attempted to update Machajski's thesis, suggesting that the "new class" of intellectuals has even closer affinities with the ideology of workers' self-management than it has with socialism as a whole (Gouldner, 1975–76, 1979). In support of this latter idea, it is pertinent to note that during agitation for workers' self-management that occurred in France and in Czechoslovakia in the spring of 1968, it was the intellectuals who made the earliest and the loudest demands for these reforms (Zukin, 1977–78).

Gouldner's account differs from that of Machajski in one other important respect. Gouldner asserts that the intellectuals' attraction to the ideology of self-management is not cynical or manipulative, but is rooted in the struggles, preoccupations and values inherent in their work. Like Kohn and Schooler, Gouldner argues that as a result of their needs for autonomy in the conduct of their work, "the deepest structure in the culture and ideology of intellectuals is their pride in their own *autonomy*" (Gouldner, 1979:33). This in turn leads Gouldner to draw the following contrast between the consciousness of the intellectual and manual workers:

> Like the working class, the New Class earns its living through its labor in a wage system; but unlike the old working class, it is basically committed to controlling the content of its work and its work environment, rather than surrendering these in favor of getting the best wage bargain it can negotiate. The New Class's consciousness is thus not "economic." . . . The New Class thus

embodies any further hope of working class self-management (Gouldner, 1979:20).

If intellectual workers are the leading advocates and beneficiaries of worker ownership in its various forms, it remains to consider whether these institutions have anything to offer the manual workers at all. Many authors have sought to warn workers to be wary of intellectuals who bear such gifts as workers' councils or worker representation on company boards. Mauk Mulder and Eric Batstone have argued that workers' participation in such bodies may often merely increase the power disparity between managers and the rank and file, by inducing workers to accept managers' decisions as their own (Mulder, 1971; Batstone, 1979). Such manipulative consequences of workplace democracy led Hugh Clegg to recommend that workers should resist these reforms, and should rely instead on their traditional sources of power, the union and the strike (Clegg, 1960). Similar recommendations have emerged from the recent experiences with self-management in Yugoslavia and with codetermination in Europe (Sirc, 1979: 179–180; Comisso, 1981; Zukin, 1981; Ogden, 1982).

Other authors, however, have challenged the notion that workers' councils are inherently manipulative, and have argued that workers have little to gain by refusing to participate in these bodies at all (Blumberg, 1968). Some important support for this view was contained in the results of Tannenbaum's five-nation survey. In that study, rank-and-file workers in Yugoslav and kibbutz plants clearly exercised less influence than managerial elites, but also appeared to exercise more influence than most of their counterparts in capitalist plants (Tannenbaum et al., 1974:59).

Findings of this sort have led many authors to conclude that at least modest increments in rank-and-file power do result from democracy in the workplace. In some cases this idea is linked to the "pluralist" models of democratic decision making that have emerged from the work of authors like Joseph Schumpeter and Robert Dahl. In these models, direct and egalitarian forms of democracy are acknowledged to be rare, but democratic choices between alternative elites are treated as an acceptable substitute. Lipset, Trow, and Coleman suggested in 1956 that even within exclusively blue collar organizations like labor unions, this may be as much democracy as can reasonably be achieved. Thus many advocates of workplace democracy now confine their hopes to the issue of how leaders are selected, and the extent to which power differentials between leaders and the rank-and-file can be narrowed if not erased. Reflecting this more limited view, Derek Jones wrote the following in response to Arie Shirom's complaints about oligarchical management:

> . . . the establishment of a stable management stratum is not necessarily inconsistent with other interpretations of the "norm of democratic

management." Most of these deny the need for mandatory rotation of management but instead require that the opportunity for management turnover exists and that power rests with the work-force — officers . . . should be periodically elected by all employees on the democratic basis of one-employee–one-vote (Jones, 1977:306).

Arrangements have also been developed that can help to close the power differentials between managers and rank-and-file workers by institutional means. That is, it is possible to tilt the distribution of power in favor of blue-collar workers by establishing a set of council seats and offices that only they are permitted to fill. This practice is observed in Yugoslavia and in many individual worker-owned firms as well. In many plywood cooperatives in America's Pacific Northwest only rank-and-file workers are eligible for membership, and managers serve the members as their hired employees.

Other strategies for reconciling an unequal division of labor with the goal of sharing ownership attempt to establish some minimal core for the concept of worker ownership that can apply to blue- and white-collar workers alike. In many individual experiments in worker ownership, this purpose has been served by policies calling for equality of pay among the worker-owners. Such policies are constantly threatened, however, by the operation of labor markets external to the firm. For if worker-owners perform different jobs, their labor typically also commands different prices outside the firm. This means that a worker-owned firm with a policy of equality of pay is probably offering its most skilled workers less than they can earn in another firm, and is therefore likely to have trouble recruiting and retaining qualified workers for these jobs.

This inherent tension between unequal work and the goal of equality of pay has led to a number of interesting contradictions, compromises, and improvisations in many types of firms. On the eve of the Bolshevik revolution Lenin announced as an "immediate aim" of his revolution the goal that "technical experts . . . should receive no higher wage than the working man" (Lenin, 1961:192); such egalitarian hopes would nevertheless soon be denounced in the Soviet Union as a utopian dream. In many contemporary experiments such as the cooperatives of Mondragon, equality of wages is seen as an unrealistic demand, but it nevertheless remains a point of policy that wage differentials within the cooperatives should be narrower than they are outside of them (Thomas and Logan, 1982). In the plywood cooperatives of the Pacific Northwest, the fact that managers are not members permits them to be paid high salaries while the worker-owners themselves adhere to a policy of equality of pay.

Another result of efforts to find an irreducible core of worker ownership that can apply with equal force throughout the labor force is the argument that if worker ownership means anything at all, it means that workers "own their own jobs," and therefore cannot be dismised (Meyers, 1964; Gramm, 1981). In practice, however, a firm's ability to guarantee job security to its worker-owners is also limited by markets. In many plywood cooperatives worker-owners have been traditionally seen as owning their jobs in this sense (Berman, 1967:202, 228; Greenberg, 1981), but worker-owners have occasionally had to be laid off during industry-wide recessions. The cooperatives are noticeably reluctant, however, to take this step, and have often accepted firmwide cuts in pay or hours worked as alternatives to putting individual worker-owners entirely out of a job. This resistance to the idea of laying off worker-owners has also often been turned into an argument in favor of the use of hired labor in these cooperatives. The hired laborers are seen as providing a buffer of marginal labor that can be laid off in slack periods while keeping the worker-owners' jobs intact (Gunn, 1980a: 405–406).

The most ambitious strategies for coping with inequalities within worker-owned firms seek neither to deny these inequalities nor to accept them as inevitable, but attempt instead to attack them at their root. One such strategy grants the desirability of a differentiation of roles, but calls for worker-owners to be rotated among those roles; thus, each worker-owner has an opportunity to take a turn at a leadership post, and a distinct class of leaders or managers has no opportunity emerge. A major defect of this strategy is that it requires leadership positions periodically to be taken away from individuals whose abilities, training, and experience make them well prepared to fill them, and reassigned to individuals who lack both experience and perhaps other qualifications as well. Among existing experiments, the most prominent instances of shared ownership in which leadership positions are rotated are the Israeli kibbutzim. Even there, however, there are in fact strong tendencies for elites to emerge, and for leadership positions merely to be reshuffled among an existing elite, rather than being filled by new recruits from the rank and file (Etzioni, 1958; Ben-Raphael, 1976).

Another approach to overcoming inequalities in the workplace concentrates on educating rank-and-file workers to make them better qualified to participate as equals in meetings attended by management, and perhaps also to take turns at leadership posts. An implicit assumption behind this approach is that workplace inequalities do not result solely from the organization of work, but also from the monopolization of esoteric knowledge, scarce credentials, and other educational and cultural advantages (Gouldner, 1979; Bourdieu and Passeron, 1977; Larson, 1977; Collins, 1979; Heller and Wilpert, 1981; DiMaggio, 1982). This strategy therefore seeks to bring about a demystification of managers' technocratic expertise, and to equip rank-and-file workers with the know-how, vocabulary, and self-confidence they need to participate with managers on equal terms. For some concrete examples and additional discussions of this strategy, the reader is referred to the special issues of *Economic and Industrial Democracy* that were devoted to this topic in May and August 1981.

Finally, one last set of strategies for overcoming inequalities within worker-owned firms addresses the division of labor itself, and asks to what extent it is possible to create a more egalitarian organization of work. In recent years, interest in this question has surfaced in such diverse environments as the Israeli kibbutzim, the Mondragon cooperatives, and the USSR. In each case, no one has been so radical as to suggest that a division of labor of some kind or another can entirely be dispensed with; but what has been proposed is that work should be restructured in such a way that every worker can experience some degree of complexity and autonomy on the job. It is widely argued that while such job characteristics may be merely dispensable luxuries in a capitalist firm, they are of greater importance in institutions that purport to be worker-owned.

While there is widespread agreement that work restructuring is a desirable end, it has been far less clear how this end is to be achieved. When the Mondragon cooperatives and Israeli kibbutzim became interested in this issue in the middle 1970s (Johnson and Whyte, 1977:26–27; Cherns, 1980; Leviatan and Rosner, 1980), their first step was to familiarize themselves with the job redesign techniques then in use in Europe and the United States. The Israelis consulted with such well-known figures as Norway's Einar Thorsrud and Phil Herbst, Albert Cherns from the United Kingdom, and Louis Davis of the USA. Both in Israel and in Mondragon, these fact finding efforts were soon followed by a number of pilot projects in work redesign. It was in this implementation phase, however, that a number of obstacles began to be encountered that seriously dampened the hopes of the work redesign enthusiasts. Plans to restructure work at Mondragon's largest plant were blocked by the high retooling costs they would involve (Johnson and Whyte, 1977:27). In kibbutz factories projects have been undertaken in a number of plants, but in even more instances proposed projects were nipped in the bud by many of the very same problems that they were designed to help resolve — that is, managers often perceived the projects as a threat to their power and therefore withdrew their support; or managers would cooperate, but researchers would find themselves unable to overcome the apathy of the rank-and-file; or one manager would initiate a project, and new managers who later rotated into that position would subsequently allow the project to die (Shelhav and Golomb, 1980:158–159).

Similarly disappointing results have emerged from the USSR. Since the early 1960s, social scientists in that country have been pointing out that Soviet workers cannot be expected to show a "communist attitude toward labor" until major improvements are made in the content of their jobs

(Zdravomyslov, Rozhin, and Iadov, 1970:288). Actual planned efforts to restructure work in the Soviet Union have been rare, however, and one unusually far-reaching experiment in workgroup autonomy in the early 1970s was quickly terminated because of the political threat it appeared to pose (Yanowitch, 1978:414–417). Since then, the Soviets have been largely content to document passively the favorable effects that technological changes are spontaneously exerting on the nature of work in their plants (Kozlova, 1969; Krevnevich, 1977; Ussenin *et al.*, 1979). In 1968, one of the leading Soviet sociologists of work issued the following discouraging pronouncement about the prospects for job redesign in the USSR, which may also stand as a fairly indicative summary of the current situation in many other parts of the world as well.

> The socialist revolution has abolished the greatest social injustice, namely, the division of society into ruling and exploited classes. But it has not eliminated in one magic stroke the existing division of labor into simple and complex, monotonous and varied, routine and creative, mechanical and organizational, attractive and unattractive. The social division of labor and narrow professionalization are the hallmarks of the world in which we live and in which each of us must find his place.
>
> Scientific socialism differs from magnanimous utopian socialism in that it takes into account the real objective laws and trends of social progress rather than basing itself on good intentions and notions about justice and humanism "in general." "In general" it would be just and humane to maintain an organization of labor in which workers would carry out complex, highly skilled work in alternation with simple work requiring a low level of skill, so that all would be equal in status as working people.
>
> It would also be "just" from the point of view of abstract humanism (and indeed, from the point of view of the narrow conception of equality that identifies it with the leveling out of wages) to limit the opportunities of administrative workers to maintain a large staff responsible for preparing information, seeing to it that decisions are acted upon, and other "bureaucratic red tape."
>
> However, modern production or scientific work is impossible without a clear-cut functional division of labor betwen different kinds of workers . . . .
> . . . the objective laws of social production and the development of the material and technical foundations of communism dictate certain definite requirements with regard to the occupational division of labor, which continues to grow steadily (Iadov, 1979:4–5).

Toward Richer Models of Shared Ownership in the Workplace

The preceding survey could easily cause one to grow discouraged with the concept of ownership. A common complaint about capitalist ownership was that it "takes the life out of the idea of property," and no longer creates a meaningful tie between individuals their surroundings. The net result of more than a century of experimentation with alternative forms of ownership, however, is that the concept now appears even more fragmented than before. The goal of enabling workers to own their own workplaces has been transformed into a bewildering diversity of institutions and meanings, including such phenomena as employee stock ownership, producers' cooperatives, utopian communities, socialist economies, workers' self-managment, and a variety of strategies for enabling workers to be their own bosses and own their own jobs.

Perhaps the most immediate issue raised by all this diversity is the question of whether these vastly different phenomena can legitimately be compared. Does employee stock ownership in a capitalist corporation in the United States have anything in common with socialism in the USSR? Granted that there are radical differences in purpose and context among these phenomena, some important bases of comparison do nevertheless exist. One such basis lies in the formal similarities among these organizational forms: decision makers in each of these contexts consider it desirable that their employees should also be owners; in both cases there is more emphasis on the sharing of equity or beneficial ownership than of active ownership or control. Of possibly greater importance than these purely formal bases of comparison, however, are some historical ones; for one should beware of making too much of the difference between advanced capitalist and early socialist institutions. All of the institutions considered here share a common historical era and a similar division of labor. Despite the important qualitative differences among them, each is characterized by varying degrees of reliance on markets, and of state support for workers' rights. In Marx's words, all of them may therefore also be considered to represent "within the old form the first sprouts of the new."

Having affirmed the right to compare all these things, it still remains to ask if it is really appropriate to designate them all by the same common term. There are several possible grounds for arguing that the terms "worker ownership" or "employee ownership" are unsuitable generic labels for the organizational phenomena examined here. One such ground is that the concept of ownership has lost its utility now that it has been so thoroughly decomposed. Writing with reference to Yugoslavia, Robert Dahl commented that

> In this kind of system the great myth of the nineteenth century stands exposed; ownership is dissolved into its various components. . . . The point is that "property" is a bundle of rights. Once the pieces in this bundle have been parceled out, nothing exactly corresponding to the conventional meaning of ownership or property remains. (Dahl, 1970: 131–132).

Another objection to referring to all the various institutions examined here as "worker-owned" is that many authors in this field use the label "worker ownership" in a narrow sense, and differentiate it from many of the phenomena discussed under that label here. In one common usage the term "worker-owned firm" refers solely to a capitalist corporation whose stock is worker-owned. In this narrower meaning, worker ownership is often contrasted to producers' cooperation, social ownership, or workers' self-management, and is therefore rejected on the grounds that it is less democratic and more likely to degenerate than these alternative forms.

In the work of Jaroslav Vanek and David Ellerman, this empirical distinction has also been linked to a theoretical point. These authors have argued that ownership rights differ from "membership rights" (Ellerman, 1975a) or "usufruct" rights (Vanek, 1977) chiefly by virtue of the fact that they include rights of abuse in addition to rights of use and to the fruits of use. Since rights of abuse have been a fatal flaw in many worker-owned firms, encouraging such practices as the sale of memberships and the use of hired labor, these authors hope to prevent these problems by dispensing entirely with the concept of ownership itself.

Although these arguments contain much truth, to use the concept of worker ownership only in this limited and pejorative sense seems inappropriate on several grounds. First, as the work of authors like Blumberg, Ben-Ner, and Shirom has shown, the processes leading to the degeneration of democratic firms can by no means be reduced to the question of ownership alone. Most of these processes apply to producers' cooperatives and socially owned institutions as well as to corporations whose stock is worker-owned. The use of hired labor seems due as much to labor markets as it is to capital structures, and the most effective way to discourage it may be through the policies of the state. And as was previously discussed, even Vanek and Ellerman have been increasingly inclined to give their blessing to organizational models in which most of the capital is in at least some sense worker-owned.

More broadly, it seems neither feasible nor desirable to reduce the concept of ownership to rights of abuse. It is not feasible because the public will continue to use the term in its traditional sense, regardless of what academics may say. It is also not desirable because it suggests that workers sould renounce forever the opportunity to say and feel that they own their own workplaces. This is one mistake that Karl Marx was too politically astute to make. Although Marx was quite critical of the capitalists' rights of abuse (Tucker, 1972:152), he never sought to turn these rights into a synonym for ownership itself. Instead he always maintained that the workplaces of the future would be both individually and collectively "owned".

If the concept of workers owning the means of production is indeed to be retained, will it ever be possible to reach agreement about what it means? If past experience is a reliable indication, this will present a formidable challenge indeed. Most previous experiments in worker ownership have typically seized upon only a single fragment of the concept of worker ownership, and have attempted to make it stand for the whole.

There are some signs that advocates of worker ownership in many countries are becoming increasingly aware of the dangers of relying too single-mindedly on any one strategy for sharing ownership. The various fragmentary forms of shared ownership are being rejected not simply because they are incomplete, but because they have shown themselves to be unstable as well. Thus, exclusively individualistic forms of the sharing of equity soon degenerate into institutions that are not worker-owned at all. Institutions in which equity is entirely collectively shared also degenerate, as the group ties and value consensus upon which collective ownership is based tend to weaken with the passage of time and with increases in size. When this occurs, the question of who really owns any collectively-owned resources becomes inseparable from the issue of who controls them. Efforts to share control collectively, however, are also subject to degenerative tendencies of their own, as typified by Michels' famous "iron law of oligarchy." These problems in turn highlight the desirability of finding individual as well as collective strategies for sharing control.

There is thus a growing recognition that it is both possible and desirable to create forms of worker ownership that in Marx's words are both "social" and "individual," and that involve the sharing of both equity and control. Of the many fragmentary forms of worker ownership, perhaps the most widely discredited has been the worker-owned corporation in which both equity and control rights are lodged in fully marketable individually-owned shares. More than a century of experience has made it clear that when a worker-owned firm is structured like a conventional corporation, it will not long resist the temptation to behave like one.

In institutions in which equity is shared collectively, on the other hand, there has also been a growing acknowledgement of the importance of giving individual members a greater personal state in the success of group investments. In Israel, Histadrut has shown an interest in sharing profits with its members (Yudin, 1975:85; Agassi, 1974:72–76). Within the kibbutz movement many kibbutzim have begun to recognize the right of members who leave the community to receive payments that reflect at least a part of the contribution they have made to the collective equity. One Israeli has commented on this change in the kibbutz,

. . . in agreeing to give monetary remuneration there is something of an admission that despite the fact that the kibbutz economy is a *social organism with indivisible capital* belonging to the *collective*, it is nevertheless obliged to consider the prerogatives of the individual. These prerogatives may not be violated because of adherence to the sacred principle of the integral nature of kibbutz capital. As a result of this principle of the indivisibility of kibbutz property, on occasion members have left empty-handed, after long years of work and effort and after having invested all their strength in the farm-home (Goldberg, 1969:179).

Similar developments have occurred within the Yugoslav system of social ownership. Between 1971 and 1974, the Yugoslavs revised their constitution to make it possible for workers to receive income not only from their current labor, but also from their "past labor"—that is, from earnings that were retained and reinvested during the period of their employment. So far, this provision has been used within Yugoslavia only to legitimate the payment of pensions to retired workers after they leave their plants. Some more far-reaching possibilities of this same principle were recently illustrated in Peru, when that country began to experiment with a "social ownership" sector in 1974. In the Peruvian model, a special class of bonds was created, to be issued to workers upon retirement in proportion to their contribution to the internal capital of the firm. The bonds were non-negotiable, and could be used only by the worker, his widow, and minor descendants. After the descendants reach majority, the bonds would revert to the National Social Property Fund (Covarrubias and Vanek, 1976; Knight, 1976; Stephens, 1980).

The growing demand for ways to share capital that are both individual and collective has stimulated much of the international interest that has been shown in the cooperatives of Mondragon. In these cooperatives, much of the capital is individually owned, but workers have neither the opportunity nor the need to recoup their investments by putting their memberships up for sale. Instead, each member's capital is carefully accounted for, and is returned to members when they retire (Saive, 1980). These individual accounts consist of contributions made by workers at the time they took their jobs, plus individual portions of the earnings retained by the cooperatives each year, plus accumulated interest (Gutierrez-Johnson, 1978; Thomas, 1980). Until they are distributed to individuals upon their retirement, however, all of these sums remain part of the collective funds. The collective aspects of equity sharing in the Mondragon cooperatives are further enhanced by the fact that a portion of members' initial contributions to their cooperatives is nonrefundable, and by the strong national, religious, and ideological ties that unite the Basque members (Johnson and Whyte, 1977; Thomas and Logan, 1982). Mondragon's success at creating a form of ownership that is both individual and collective has caused a good deal of discussion about the feasibility of exporting the Mondragon model to other countries, particularly the UK and the US (Campbell *et al.*, 1977; Oakeshott, 1978; Eaton, 1978, 1979; Labour Party, 180; Bradley and Gelb, 1981, 1982a, 1982b; Thornley, 1981:33-36; Ellerman, 1982a).

In addition to this interest in ways to share equity that are both individual and collective, there is also a growing acknowledgement that shared ownership will be more meaningful if it involves the sharing not only of beneficial ownership, but also of control. Thus Israel's Histadrut has experimented for years with ways for its ostensible worker-owners to become more involved in decision making in their workplaces (Tabb and Goldfarb, 1966; Rosenstein, 1970, 1977; Strauss, 1982:195-198). Some rather daring calls for workplace democracy have also emerged from within the USSR. One 1969 survey conducted by the Soviet Sociological Association reported that 89% of Soviet workers were in favor of granting workers the right to elect at least some of their managers (Kapeliush, 1979:69). That same survey and others also showed, however, that Soviet managers themselves were generally opposed to the idea, which is perhaps an important reason why the proposal has so far born little practical fruit (Yanowitch, 1978: 411-414). Some fourteen years later, in 1983, Soviet workers did receive a right to veto possible brigade leaders selected for them by management, but this of course still left them far behind their Yugoslav counterparts in decision-making rights (Teague, 1983).

There also appears to be a growing acknowledgement that the sharing of control, as of equity, can be both individual and collective. Thus in kibbutz factories and in the cooperatives of Mondragon, existing collective forms of workplace democracy have recently been supplemented by at least a sporadic interest in job redesign. In Scandinavia, on the other hand, there have also been reminders that the region's achievements in work restructuring should not be allowed to preempt entirely the goal of giving workers a voice in plantwide decision making as well (Abrahamsson, 1977: Chapter 11; Bolweg, 1976).

In *What is Property?*, Proudhon argued that what the world needs is neither absolute private property nor absolute communism, but a synthesis of the two. In constructing that synthesis, Proudhon warned, we should not "unite communism and property indiscriminately; such a process would be absurd eclecticism." Proudhon recommended that we should instead "search by analysis for those elements in each which are true, and in harmony with the laws of nature and society, disregarding the rest. . ." (Proudhon, 1966:281).

It would seem that the knowledge to effect such a synthesis is now slowly being accumulated. Chapter 3 will illustrate how the elements of shared ownership identified here have been brought together to produce a rich blend in one unique group of worker-owned firms in the US. That chapter will also demonstrate, however, that the processes that threaten the stability of worker-owned firms and cause their degeneration are as broad and diverse as the concept of worker ownership itself.

CHAPTER 3

The Worker-Owned Scavenger Companies of the San Francisco Bay Area

In the early part of this century, refuse collection in San Francisco and other nearby cities was handled by a large number of independent dealers. Most of these men were Italian immigrants, coming from such northern Italian cities as Genoa. In the absence of municipal regulations governing refuse collection, each of these operators made his own arrangements with customers. Competition among them was fierce. It is said that often, three or four men vied for customers on the same street.

Such competitive conditions imposed strict economies on the men who collected the refuse of these cities. The tools of their trade were simple—a horse, a wagon, and perhaps also a gun, since they did business mainly in cash. To make ends meet, the carters salvaged everything that might have resale value—rags, bottles, you name it. In the case of especially valuable refuse, such as the food wastes from restaurants or boarding houses, which could be sold as swill to pig farmers, the carters *paid* for the right to haul the wastes away. Because of their recycling function, refuse collectors in this region have long been known as "scavengers."

The coming of World War I produced a crisis among the scavengers. War-induced inflation brought about dramatic increases in the cost of labor, horseshoes, and feed grains. Some scavengers were in a position to pass these cost increases along to their customers, but others were not. The amounts paid by householders for the same services began to vary tremendously from one part of the city to another.

The situation obviously called for some form of regulation, and both scavengers and city governments began to take steps to bring it about. San Francisco's first worker-owned scavenger company, the Sunset Scavenger Company, was first formed in either 1912 or 1916 (company documents give both dates).In 1921, the San Francisco city government passed an ordinance setting uniform rates for collection services, and dividing the city into collection districts. The city council also announced that it was prepared to receive bids from competent private companies to collect refuse on contract for the city government. These developments no doubt encouraged the formation of the city's second worker-owned scavenger company, the Scavengers' Protective Association (SPA), which was incorporated in 1921. But to the city's consternation, neither Sunset, nor SPA, nor anyone else, bid on the proposed city contract. As a substitute, they city established a system of licenses and regulations that still exists today.

Under the new system, it did not take long for the two young companies to begin flexing their muscles in their dealings with the city and competitors. In 1932, when public pressure forced the city to shut down its polluting incinerator, SPA stepped in to pioneer a sanitary landfill operation outside the city. In 1935, the two companies formed a joint venture to handle the city's waste disposal problems. At the same time, they obtained permits to divide between them the residential collection services for the entire city. A politial scandal erupted in 1940, when an investigative agency charged that the success of these companies was due in part to secret contributions and other illegal favors extended by them to city politicians and their cohorts. But this political furor came too late and was not sufficient to deprive the two firms of the monopoly they had gained over residential refuse collection in the city.

In the years following World War I, scavenger companies were also being formed and rising to prominence in communities adjacent to San Francisco. In all, perhaps a dozen or more such companies were formed. The three largest of the group—Sunset, Golden Gate Disposal (formerly SPA), and the Oakland Scavenger Company—today each account for hundreds of employees. The others range from as few as two to three shareholding scavengers per company to as many as fifty.

In 1966, the sociologist Stewart E. Perry began a study of the Sunset Scavenger Company. Perry had first become interested in the refuse collectors of San Francisco because it seemed to him that they were somehow different from their counterparts in other cities. They seemed more confident, or perhaps just friendlier. When Perry investigated, he discovered the firm's unique structure and began his study.

Perry's major source of information about Sunset was a series of candid interviews with the company's outspoken president, Leonard Stefanelli. Stefanelli had been working "on the trucks" until he was elected president just ten months previous to Perry's first interview with him, and seemed eager to share the new perspective this change had given him. Most of Perry's interviews with Stefanelli were tape recorded.

Perry supplemented these interviews by spending a total of ten days accompanying Sunset crews as they worked their way through the streets of San Francisco. Many of these days were spent with the crew of Fred Fontana, the gregarious chairman of Sunset's customer relations committee. Conducted intermittently from 1966 to 1977, Perry's interviews and field observations were eventually reported in his book *San Francisco Scavengers: Dirty Work and the Pride of Ownership* (1978).

In the meantime, in 1973, Perry broadened his study and began collecting data on other worker-owned scavenger companies, and on refuse collection organizations that were municipally and privately owned. This additional data collection was facilitated by a grant from the Center for Studies of Metropolitan Problems of the National Institute of Mental Health. It was at this point that I joined the study. Between 1973 and 1977, I conducted interviews and field observations at Sunset and four other scavenger companies, and at four municipal or private organizations. I also found much useful information by reading through back issues of the *San Francisco Chronicle* and by examining court records pertaining to the scavengers. During this same period Jerry Sanders produced an intensive case study of one worker-owned scavenger company, and Arthur Hochner conducted interviews and field observations at a variety of worker-owned, municipal, and private organizations.

In 1977, the results of this qualitative research were supplemented by 708 standardized interviews with refuse collectors employed by a variety of organizations located in and around the San Francisco Bay Area. Of these interviews, 406 were with employees of six worker-owned scavenger companies, 165 of whom were shareholding partners in these companies, and 241 of whom were nonshareholders or "helpers." Of the remaining 302 respondents, 162 were employees of seven privately-owned firms, and 140 worked in four municipal departments. The procedures used to draw this sample and conduct these interviews are discussed in detail in Hochner (1978) and Russell (1979).

The present chapter is a synthesis of the materials gathered in both the qualitative and quantitative phases of this project. It explores how the elements of shared ownership identified in Chapter 2 are combined in these scavenger companies, and with what effect. To respect pledges of anonymity that were made in the later phases of this project, the names of individual scavengers and scavenger companies will in many places be withheld. Remarks attributed to Leonard Stefanelli and Fred Fontana are in all cases derived from Steward Perry's interviews with them.

Sharing Ownership in a Scavenger Firm

When the scavengers first created their worker-owned companies, they wee guided by no explicit concept of worker ownership. They were acting out of necessity, rather than choice, and were interested in whatever structure would bring about the least amount of change in their traditional ways of doing business.

An essential part of the scavengers' traditional ways, however, had been the fact that each man worked at his own direction, and for his own profit. As the scavengers joined together their formerly independent operations, they successfully transferred many elements of their former experience of owning their own business to the new organizations. The structures that resulted constitute an unusually rich form of worker ownership, blending together many of the devices for sharing ownership that were identified in the previous chapter. The use the scavengers have made of each of these devices will be discussed in detail below, in an order parallel to that in which these elements were presented in Chapter 2.

Owning Stock in a Scavenger Company

When Sunset's pioneer scavenger company was created, the first thought of its founders had been to organize themselves as a cooperative. Their attorney advised them that this would not be feasible, and recommended that they incorporate instead. The corporate structures that the Sunset and other scavengers adopted reveal that a great deal of egalitarian thinking lay behind the founding of the companies. All companies prohibited any shareholder from owning more shares than any of the others, thereby insuring the principle of one shareholder, one vote. Compensation for officers was set equal to that of all other shareholders. Shareholders who left the company for any reason, including retirement, were required to give up their shares, selling them either to a nonshareholding employee or back to the company.

One issue on which the company rules were ambiguous was the role of hired labor in these firms. There have always been hired laborers, or "helpers" or "extra men," as the scavengers call them, in these companies. However, as the Sunset 1934 By-Laws explicitly state, these helpers were treated by the company not as conventional employees, but as "apprentices or novices," who have entered the company "not for the salary, but for the opportunity of becoming a boss scavenger after they have become tried and experienced scavengers."

Opportunities for helpers to become shareholders were for many years enhanced by a tendency for the number of shareholders in each company to grow as the company expanded. The number of shareholders at Sunset grew from about 100 at the time the company was founded to 320 in the mid-1960s. By that same time, Golden Gate Disposal had grown to include 183 shareholders, while the Oakland Scavenger Company had a total of 178.

Over the years, the steps in becoming a shareholder have been essentially the same at each of the scavenger companies. The first step is usually to take a job as a helper at one of the companies. On a scavenger crew, a helper does essentially the same work as the "partners," as shareholders are often called, except that he rarely handles money. A prospective partner then waits anywhere from six months to a number of years for the shares of a retiring partner to become available. After he and an outgoing shareholder agree on a price for the shares, the helper expresses to the board of directors his desire to purchase them. If the board approves, and a majority of the members do also, he is in. After a probationary period of six months, he becomes a full partner in the company.

When a helper buys a share in his scavenger company, what does he gain economically? Partners derive income from their companies in three principal forms—annual dividends, capital gains on the sale of shares, and wages. Among the Sunset scavengers, dividends have normally been relatively small—that is, rarely more than 1–2% of the current value of a share. In many scavenger companies, it appears that dividends and corporate earnings have deliberately been kept low, both because company profits are regulated by the cities in which they operate, and because distributed earnings are "double taxed" by the Internal Revenue Service—first as corporate profits, and then as personal income. Thus partners prefer to take as much as possible of their income as wages, which are taxed only once, rather than as dividends.

Turning to the capital gains that partners make on the sale of their shares, Perry's data indicate that these can be more appreciable. A block of shares in Sunset that cost $12,000 in 1954 had risen to $21,000 by 1966, and would bring $50,000 in 1976. This averages out as a compound rate of appreciation of 5–6% per year. Thus dividends plus capital gains on shares add up to a return of 6–8% per year. This is not a very impressive performance for a capital investment, especially given the illiquidity of the asset. If one were to evaluate share ownership in a scavenger company on these criteria alone, one would have to conclude that partners would be better off making bank deposits or buying bonds.

The size of dividends and capital gains, however, have never been the most important considerations for a helper who is contemplating the purchase of a share. When you buy into a scavenger company, says Sunset's Fred Fontana, "You could say that you're buying a job." This statement is true in at least two senses. A scavenger owns his job, first of all, by virtue of the tenure his shareholding secures for him. It guarantees that he will not be fired, or even laid off, unless the company can prove gross dereliction on his part. Secondly, in purchasing his shares, the scavenger buys the right to earn a much higher income than he would earn as a helper. In 1976, partners in San Francisco's two scavenger companies were guaranteed an income of between $19,000 and $20,700 per year, depending on their jobs, and had the opportunity to earn as much as $4,000 or more per year in overtime pay. Helpers, in contrast, were paid between $13,000 and $14,000 per year, and would have had trouble making more than $2,000 per year in overtime.

The fact that scavenger shareholders derived income from their shares largely in the form of wages rather than dividends appears to have contributed significantly to the preservation of worker ownership in these firms. In a study of worker-owned plywood companies in the Pacific Northwest, Berman (1967) identified the practice of paying income to shareholders in the form of wages instead of dividends as a "crucial" source of stability in those firms. As she explained,

> Since in most companies no dividends are paid on shares, and in all the major source of income from a share is the wage paid for work actually performed in the plant, shareholders are encouraged to remain at work in the plant. The practice also discourages the accumulation of stock by individuals . . . as little or no additional income will result from ownership of extra shares (Berman, 1967: 217).

While this circumstance thus helps explain why partners did not seek to acquire additional shares, other aspects of the economics of these companies help explain why partners were not reluctant to share the benefits of shareholding with new generations of scavengers. Since each company's rates were regulated, partners had little opportunity to increase their incomes by minimizing labor costs. Both the dividends and the wages paid to scavenger partners were carefully scrutinized by public officials, and were not permitted to exceed what the regulators considered to be appropriate amounts. Thus any gains that might potentially accrue from the use of helpers in place of partners would eventually result in lower rates, rather than higher incomes for partners.

While the scavengers thus had little opportunity to profit from hired labor, they also had several positive reasons for extending opportunities to become shareholders to the helpers in their firms. In at least one known instance the sale of shares to helpers was used as a means of raising capital for a scavenger firm. In fact, the first major increase in the number of shareholders at Sunset resulted from considerations of this sort. In the 1930s, the Internal Revenue Service first informed the scavenger companies that it viewed them not as cooperatives, but as corporations for profit. As a result, Sunset suddenly owed $350,000 in back taxes. To raise the money to pay this fine, new shares were issued and sold to some of the company's helpers.

More regularly, Sunset and the other scavenger companies saw shareholding as a way to attract and motivate a high quality labor force. During World War II Sunset's wages were frozen, and the company felt a need to offer partnerships to prospective employees in order to compete with the wages being offered in war-related industries. Even earlier, Sunset's 1934 By-Laws had declared the motivational consequences of worker ownership to be essential to the operation of the firm. According to that document, the company's founders

> realized that the success of their common undertaking . . . was impossible unless: first, each associate or employee was a boss scavenger, for it was not to be expected that a hired scavenger would work as well and as willingly as one who is a shareholder . . . .

The preceding statement must be interpreted with some degree of caution, as it was written at a time when the Sunset scavengers were negotiating their tax status with the IRS. In that situation, the shareholding scavengers had a special interest in claiming that their higher wages were a fair reward for higher productivity, rather than a hidden form of company profit. It is possible, therefore, that this comment is a mere reflection of that intent.

If owning shares in a scavenger company does in fact have motivational value, it is worthwhile to ask what it motivates a scavenger to do. Since scavengers derive most of their income from shareholding in the form of higher fixed wages, rather than dividends, share ownership gives scavengers at most only a marginal interest in the annual profitability of their firms. Shareholding scavengers may have a stronger stake, however, in protecting the market value of their shares, and in ensuring their privileged access to the markets they serve.

What this suggests, therefore, is that shareholding might more readily motivate scavengers to maximize service than it would encourage them to minimize costs. As long the public is satisfied with the scavengers' service, legitimately rising costs can always be recovered through increases in rates; but should service quality noticeably deteriorate, a company's very right to stay in business could be lost. The scavengers appear to have understood this fact since their earliest days, and have provided an extraordinarily high level of service in each of the cities they serve. San Francisco is probably the only major city in the United States in which residents can have their refuse collected not only from alleys or curbs, but also from backyards, basements, and upper floors. The scavengers are also willing to carry keys for their customers, and to provide minor janitorial services as well.

One particularly vivid illustration of the care that many scavengers show toward their customers appears in the following observation from the qualitative phase of our research. The excerpt is taken from a report filled by Jerry Sanders after a day on a scavenger truck. According to Jerry, the leader of this crew

> . . . established himself as one of the most conscientious and fastidious workes I have ever seen anywhere. His first words to me were "sshh. . . we have to hold down the talking in these residential areas at this time of day" [shortly after 4:30 a.m.].

> . . . He has an obvious pride in the job and identifies fully with the company. At one point he said to me, "Look it's Jerry isn't it? Jerry, if you want to work along with us that's fine, but watch the spillage in the street when you dump your sack into the hopper." Now my "spillage" consisted of candy wrappers and peach seeds, not watermelon rinds and beer cans.

After thus admonishing Jerry to show more care, this scavenger softened the reprimand by explaining, "Public relations you know. It means everything for the company. That's what makes us."

Not every shareholding scavenger is as meticulous as this one man; but evidence that scavenger partners take unusually good care of their customers comes from a number of other sources as well. In the quantitative phase of this research project, shareholding scavengers reported significantly better relations with the public on a variety of measures than any other respondents (Russell, 1979: 198–212). There is also some independent support for the idea that the scavengers are unusually conscientious in taking care of their customers. According to a San Francisco city inspector who was interviewed in 1971,

> The companies make more than 300,00 pickups a week, and we receive about 30 complaints. Of those, maybe twelve are valid. Figure it out. The scavenger companies have a damn good record when you consider that they have more contact with the public than telephone, electricity, or any other public service. Garbage collection is a delicate personal relations job (Kazan, 1971: 43).

There is thus a good deal of evidence that the scavengers of San Francisco and the cities around it are unusually responsive to the needs of their customers. It would be a mistake, however, to attribute the high level of service they provide to the effects of share ownership alone. While scavenger partners have much to fear from a disaffected public, the possibility that they could lose their exclusive franchises is normally far too remote and long-term a danger to motivate them day to day. To maintain their responsiveness on a more short-term basis, therefore, the scavengers have relied not on share ownership, but on a variety of non-material work incentives and disciplinary procedures that will be the subject of later subsections of this chapter.

"E cosa nostra"

In Chapter 2, it was noted that ventures in shared ownership frequently derive important sustenance from a variety of ethnic, religious, and other cultural ties among their participants. This is certainly true of the scavengers as well.

Perhaps the most important cultural basis of solidarity among the scavengers has been the enduring Italian identity of these worker-owners. The vast majority of partners in all the companies are descendants of Italian immigrants, if not recent arrivals from Italy themselves. There are still many scavenger crews whose members communicate better in Italian than they do in English. When a scavenger wants to tell you how well a non-Italian has succeeded in integrating himself into the company, he may tell you that the man "speaks Italian as well as I do." Partners sum up the sense of shared ownership that unites the Italian scavengers with the words, *"E cosa nostra"* ("it's our thing").

Overlapping and reinforcing the ethnic link among scavengers are their family ties to their jobs. The names of the families that founded the companies continue to be well represented on their rosters today. Some families have already provided three generations of workers to the companies. Partners who can list fathers, uncles, brothers, cousins, sons, and/or nephews who have worked for the companies are commonplace. When one inquires of the few non-Italian partners how they came to buy into their companies, it often turns out that it was an Italian scavenger in-law who recruited them. Overall, 54% of the shareholding scavengers who participated in the 1977 survey reported that at least one other relative had also owned shares in the same firm.

These ethnic and family ties among the scavengers appear to have been another important source of stability in these firms. That is, partners have apparently been more willing to extend ownership opportunities to their sons and nephews and to fellow immigrants from Italy than to just anyone off the street. In this the scavengers have not been appreciably different from the sole proprietors of small businesses, or from members of Israel's well-known bus cooperatives. In the latter organizations, according to Viteles (1966–68: Book 5, p. 151),

> Sons and sons-in-law of members have preference when candidates are selected for membership. This has been a part of the rules of the (bus) co-operatives for many years. It represents a continuation of a long established owner's psychology . . . .

The ethnic and family ties among the scavengers appear also to have contributed to the strong sense of community and the rich occupational culture that have grown up around these companies. Many scavengers learned their trade by working alongside their fathers or uncles as unpaid family help, and have participated in the social lives of their companies since the time they were kids. For these scavengers, such early socialization into the culture of their companies has lent the sanctity of family and tradition to the companies' worker-owned institutions, and to their standards of good service and hard work.

One widespread manifestation of the scavengers' sentimental attachment to their companies' past is the large assortment of memorabilia that typically adorns scavenger offices and meeting rooms. Photos of company founders and their vehicles are a particularly common sight. The larger scavenger companies each maintain at least one old truck in like-new condition, which they bring out for parades and other special occasions. References to company founders are also a frequent theme in scavenger advertisements.

Ties among scavengers are not limited to individual companies. Quite commonly, a partner in one company will have relatives working in one or two others. Of the 165 partners who responded to our 1977 survey, for example, 27% reported that they had at least one relative who at one time or another had owned shares in another firm. Also, many activities and traditions of the scavengers bring together partners from several different companies. This has often been true of bowling and golf, and applies also to such scavenger traditions as "lunch at the dumps" and old timers' days.

The common culture of the scavenger companies finds formal expression in the numerous organizational ties among them. The partners in the Sunset Scavenger Company and in Golden Gate Disposal together form a society that provides a sick benefit and a funeral benefit and throws a couple of parties every year. A number of miscellaneous ancillary operations, such as container companies and disposal sites, are owned jointly by two or more scavenger companies.

It is difficult to draw a line between where the community of scavengers ends and where a city's Italian-American community begins. Many scavengers belong to their cities' Italian clubs. The companies also contribute regularly to community functions like Columbus Day parades. In return, their partners have always felt especially at home in their cities' Italian neighborhoods.

Leadership and Democracy in the Scavenger Firms

In Chapter 2, a diverse set of ideas about the consequences of workplace democracy was briefly reviewed. These views ranged all the way from the Webbs' contention that workplace democracy is inherently incompatible with managers' authority (Webb and Webb, 1920), to Mulder's suggestion that workplace democracy merely enhances the ability of managers to manipulate the rank and file (Mulder, 1971). Somewhere between these two positions was the view of Arnold Tannenbaum, who has argued that it is possible for workplace democracy to increase both workers' influence and managers' authority (Tannenbaum, 1968; Tannenbaum et al., 1974).

Before looking at the relationship between scavenger leaders and their rank and file, it is necessary to consider for a moment what the scavengers' collective decision-making apparatus is designed to do. As will be discussed in the following subsection, many important aspects of the scavengers' operations were traditionally decentralized to individual scavenger crews. The scavengers have required a centralized leadership, however, to allocate manpower and equipment among crews, and to protect the organization against scavengers who mishandle money, are rude to customers, or in any other way endanger the organization's image in the eyes of the public. Sunset's old By-Laws threaten various sanctions against any partner who fails to come to work on time, to take proper care of company property, or to obey the orders of the officers. Other provisions detail punishments for partners who use abusive language, fight, "create friction or discord," or "bring the corporation . . . into disrepute."

Within the scavenger companies, therefore, the fundamental adherence of partners to discipline and the authority of their leaders has never been in question. What has been at issue, however, is the exact balance of power between the companies' democratic bodies and the officers who wield authority in their name. In many companies, it appears that a chronic tension exists between the powers of the company leadership and the rights of the rank and file.

The formal structure of the scavenger companies provides the partners with two major means of influencing officers' decisions. First of all, they elect the officers. In each company, elections are held once a year to select all or part of the eleven-man board of directors. The board members, in turn, designate the president, vice-president, dispatcher, and any other officers, from among the directors. The second formal check on the actions of the officers is the requirement that all major issues be put before a meeting of the shareholders for final approval. "Major" decisions include purchases of equipment, the sale of assets, the admission or expulsion of a partner, and anything affecting the structure of the company.

Despite these formal limitations on their power, officers in fact have a formidable array of assets in their dealings with rank-and-file partners. Many of these have to do with company politics. To be elected in the first place, an officer must usually be a popular and respected member of the company. Typically, a politically successful scavenger also has the advantage of family and social ties to the company leadership extending all the

way back to the company's founders. As leaders remain in office and acquire expertise, their opinions are likely to carry more and more weight at
shareholders' meetings — many partners will tell you that members'
meetings merely rubber stamp the directors' decisions. We were also told
that board members can be quite adept politicians — one man charged that
he is kept off the board by the presence on 'the ballot each year of
superfluous candidates whose only function is to split the votes of
challengers.

Once a leader has been elected to office, the scavenger companies' institutions create and legitimate a wide range of powers for him: control over a
company's disciplinary apparatus provides numerous opportunities to
punish enemies and reward the faithful. Leonard Stefanelli related the
following story of how Fred Fontana was once railroaded out of the company by a former president:

> Fred is outspoken. He spoke out against . . . [the president], and they went
> through his books and found $86 or something over a 42-year period [exag-
> gerating for effect] that he couldn't account for, so they humiliated him by
> saying he was a crook, and they suspended him indefinitely . . . . They let
> some guys off, like a board of director's son with $1,600 shortage in his book
> in four months. All he got was a $500 fine.

On a day-to-day basis, the disciplinary powers of leaders may not be as
important as the many small penalties and favors they routinely mete out.
For example, the leadership has the power to reassign partners from one
neighborhood to another. One Sunset partner with seventeen years' experience on his route still felt this as a threat — "I don't know what I'd do, if
they took me off." Alternatively, they may give a man a new truck, or let
him have an extra man on his crew, or take something off his route. Said
Sunset President Leonard Stefanelli about these favors: "I have to take care
of everybody — I've become Big Daddy of the whole operation."

Once a scavenger gets elected to a position of leadership, he normally remains within the company's ruling circle until he retires — that is, for 20,
30, or even 40 years. At none of the companies is there a tradition that elite
positions should circulate. As soon as a scavenger is elected to the board of
directors, he is required to relinquish his union membership, and usually
never resumes it. If he becomes an officer, that means that his days of "car-
rying the can" are over for good. He begins to report for work wearing a tie
each day, has some business cards bearing his name printed up, and for all
practical purposes takes on the form as well as the function of a professional
manager.

As executive officers grow accustomed to their positions, the discrepan-
cies in power between them and the rank-and-file members can foster in

them quite highhanded attitudes toward the rest of the men. At Sunset, Leonard Stefanelli's predecessor developed a reputation for talking down to the men. According to Fred Fontana,

> He kept us down. It was his attitude toward us. He'd say that garbage men are dumb, and that people wouldn't accept our getting better pay.

All this is not to say, however, that leaders have things all their own way in these companies. Company presidents claim that partners are not at all bashful about speaking their minds when they happen to disagree with the leadership. According to Leonard Stefanelli, many men assert the attitude,

> Well, I'm a shareholder, I've got as much rights, voting power, earning the profits, as you, the president, and I've got as much to say as who's running the business down here.

Certain issues seem especially likely to provoke reactions from shareholders. In a couple of companies, we heard that there is resentment whenever any new white-collar job is created. No matter what you tell them, the guys "on the trucks" will be convinced that someone has just landed himself a "cushy" job. Another sensitive issue is the pay of officers. As has already been mentioned, officers have traditionally been forbidden to earn more than a rank-and-file partner. They do, however, control modest expense accounts. They may also have the use of a company car, and may earn additional income by holding offices in company subsidiaries. These perquisites are viewed with hostility and suspicion by many rank-and-file partners, and their disposition is jealously watched.

Finally, although turnover among leaders is rare, all three of the major companies provide examples of unpopular leaders having been turned out of office by the men: we heard of a hardnosed dispatcher in one company having lost his job just a few years before; and two top men of another were once deposed by the board of directors. We were told that the reason for this was that "they weren't doing their job"—that is, they weren't coming to meetings and were "hard on the men." Most dramatically, Leonard Stefanelli of Sunset swept into power in a fullfledged "revolution" [his word], in which the entire board of directors was voted out.

Leonard Stefanelli's revolution is a good illustration of the constantly shifting balance of power between a scavenger leader and the rank and file. The man Stefanelli replaced had for years defeated all comers in company elections. But in 1965, he committed a politically fatal mistake. Without consulting the members, he began paying company officers higher wages than the other partners. When this came to light, the partners were outraged. A group of 235 partners (out of about 320) demanded the immediate resignation of the present board of directors and elected a new one in its place.

The ouster of Stefanelli's predecessor was followed by a series of reform proposals aimed at reaffirming the equality of partners. Stefanelli recommended permitting nondirectors to be officers, in order to make of the board of directors a circulating body whose members return to the rank and file at the end of their terms. Possibly out of fear of Stefanelli's future power, the partners chose instead to retain a strong board that included all executive officers, and created the office of board chairman as an apparent foil to the presidency.

In this period, the company also considered a number of proposals having to do with the compensation of officers and other employees. Stefanelli felt the company should be making more use of financial incentives, and therefore advocated unequal pay. The wording that ultimately went into the 1967 By-Laws, however, read as follows:

> Ever since the creation of this corporation, it has been the invariable policy to pay to all stockholder members equal compensation for their respective work, labor or services, irrespective of the nature or type of employment or office held. It is hereby declared to be the intent of these By-Laws that such policy be continued in force and effect, and therefore all directors and all executive officers shall be entitled to receive equal compensation as the corporation is paying from time to time to all of its stockholder members.

This qualitative evidence about relations between leaders and rank-and-file shareholders in the scavenger firms thus provides at least some support for each of the views cited at the opening of this subsection. Clearly, workplace democracy in these firms has occasionally been disruptive. Clearly, too, workplace democracy has also at times contributed to quite substantial accumulations of managerial power. Overall, however, it is to Tannenbaum's position that this record lends the greatest support. That is, both strong management and an unusually high degree of rank-and-file influence appear to have routinely coexisted in most of these firms.

This impression that emerges from the qualitative phase of this study is also supported by some evidence collected during its quantitative phase (Russell, Hochner, and Perry, 1979). One set of questions included in the 1977 survey asked respondents how much "say or influence" each of several groups "actually have on what happens in your company [or department]." For each group, respondents were asked to indicate whether its members exercise "quite a lot" of say or influence (scored "3"); "some" say or influence (scored "2"); or "very little, if any" (scored "1").

Responses to several items in this series suggest that worker-owners in the six scavenger companies included in this survey are indeed perceived as exercising a greater amount of influence within the organizations than is characteristic of comparable groups of workers in other types of firms. Worker-owners rated the influence of "the men on the trucks who are shareholders" at 2.13, and hired helpers in the same firms gave them an even higher estimate of 2.45. At the seven private firms, in contrast, the influence of "the men on the trucks" was given an average rating of 1.75. For employees of the four municipal departments, the figure was 1.63.

The distributions of perceived influence across three hierarchical levels in the worker-owned, municipal, and privately owned organizations are presented in Figure I. Influence scores for the worker-owned firms are the average responses of shareholders and nonshareholders taken as a single group. Following Tannenbaum (1968), lines have been drawn between the scores from each set of organizations to form a "control graph," even though the data collected were discrete rather than continuous.

Three aspects of the data in Figure 1 are worthy of note: the differences in scores at each hierarchical level, the overall steepness or flatness of each hierarchical gradient, and the average height of each curve. Comparing the influence of managers and supervisors in the three types of firms shows their influence to be greatest under worker ownership. However, the much greater disparity between the influence of worker-owners and workers from other organizations causes the overall structure of the scavengers' influence hierarchy to be both flatter and higher. Thus, there appears to be a greater total amount of influence exerted in these organizations and a more equal distribution of that power.

The Work of a Worker-Owner

The scavengers have retained from their former days of independent operations an unusually intimate set of relations with their customers. Each customer is still billed individually for refuse collection service, and pays a sum proportional to the amount of service received. Many customers contract for such optional extra services as the use of keys, collection from upper floors or from basements, and janitorial services.

For most of the scavengers' history, this system has required each shareholder to function not only as a refuse collector, but as an entrepreneur as well. Traditionally a partner has been responsible for maintaining records about each household in his territory, and for seeing that each family pays for the services it receives. In practice, this has been a quite complex undertaking. The records for each household have had to include such information as the amount of service the family has contracted for (2 cans per week from a second floor apartment; 3 cans per week col-

FIGURE I

Distribution of Influence by Hierarchical Level in
Worker-Owned, Private, and Municipal Organizations

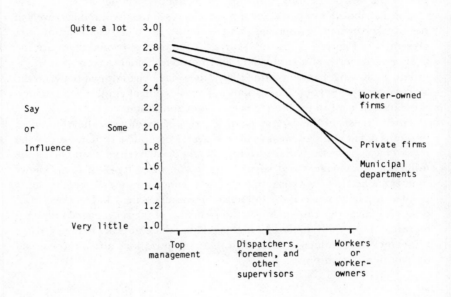

Source: Russell, Hochner, and Perry, 1979: 335

lected at street level, etc.), when they go away on vacation, when they receive extra services, and so on. During the day, the partner must remember how much service a household is entitled to, and has to assess and record extra fees for any refuse that exceeds that amount. In the past, partners were also required to go calling in the evenings to collect payments from each of their customers. Now, centralized mail billing has made most of this unnecessary, but partners still become involved when it becomes necessary to apply pressure to delinquent accounts.

For most partners, these business responsibilities have constituted a set of chores that they feel they could just as easily do without. When asked what he dislikes most about his work, one of Fred Fontana's crew members answered, "Collecting is a pain." On another occasion, Fontana himself confided,

> I don't like that part of it [the business] at all. I am sick and tired of dealing with the public. It makes you hate people. That's not my nature, but it's made me that way. They are all liars and what-have-you.

Despite their unpopularity, however, the scavengers' proprietary duties may have some extremely far-reaching implications for the nature of the scavengers' work. What these responsibilities essentially do is to inject a significant component of mental labor into an otherwise manual job. As Leonard Stefanelli observed,

> The scavenger business is . . . not just a strong-body weak-mind type of operation. A person has to have a certain amount of intelligence . . . has to have a certain amount of appreciation for values, especially money values— respect for his job and this type of thing.

An aging scavenger in another firm came close to expressing this same idea during a field observation conducted in 1973:

> "You know," he said thoughtfully, "they say anybody can collect garbage, but really, there's a lot to keep track of—books, banking. . . ."

The scavengers' proprietary duties not only require know-how and intelligence, but also involve a good deal of autonomous discretion as well. It has traditionally been the scavenger's prerogative to decide how much credit to extend to each of his customers. Sooner or later, the line has to be drawn—"We'll pick it up this time. I'll see her tonight and let her know this is it." What to do about extra refuse above and beyond what has been contracted for is the most common matter for the exercise of the scavenger's discretion. He must decide whether the additional refuse merits an extra charge, and if so, how much. Stewart Perry wrote after a 1972 observation at Sunset,

> I can't make out when and when not they will decide to pick up a little extra without charge for a customer—a carton or so in addition to the full cans. Mainly it seems to be the relation to the customer, the number of times the extra work occurs, perhaps how the scavenger feels at the moment.

Because of this unusual degree of discretionary power, at the scavenger companies and in no other ownership context did our researchers hear talk about whether or not refuse collectors are "fair" to the public. Says Fred Fontana,

> We try to be fair. Just a little bit extra we don't mind. Normally the scavenger is pretty fair. Oh, there's a couple guys that gouge customers, but the normal scavenger is pretty fair.

There appears to be an intimate connection between these unique features of the scavengers' work and the worker-owned structure of their firms. First, it seems that only in the context of worker ownership is such a large scale range of individualized services made available to the public at all. Certainly, the services that San Francisco residents receive from their scavenger firms appear unique among major cities in the United States [*Solid Wastes Management*, 13, No. 9 (1970), pp. 48, 91]. Within the San Francisco Bay Area, a number of smaller municipal and private firms provide many of the same services that the scavengers offer, but they clearly seem to be following the scavengers' lead (Russell, 1979:290–291).

While worker ownership appears to be an important source of the scavengers' unique proprietary duties, these duties have in turn provided an important rationale for preserving the worker-owned structures of these firms. That is, many scavengers have felt that worker ownership is necessary to attract and motivate the labor required by this work. Thus, they have wanted to maintain a large number of shareholders in their firms, so that a large number of workers would willingly share in these proprietary duties.

The incentive provided by ownership, however, has often proved to be an inadequate guarantee that these proprietary responsibilities will be faithfully discharged. Many stories are told of partners who have made unsophisticated deals with customers, who have neglected to keep their accounts up to date, or who have pocketed money they should have turned in to the company. And in their face-to-face interactions with the public, partners have not always proved to be good representatives of their companies. As the president of one scavenger company explains, it is unreasonable to expect men who don't specialize in dealing with the public not to be rude or short-tempered once in a while. These are, therefore, the most heavily scrutinized areas of the scavenger's activities, and an elaborate set of sanctions is used to encourage partners to be conscientious in their handling of money and customers.

Perhaps the most important of these incentives is the method used at many companies for determining the size of a route. Unlike other organizations in this industry, scavenger companies do not aim solely to equalize the amount of effort required to complete each route. A more important criterion is usually the dollar yield of each route. The more money a scavenger crew can collect from each account on their route, the fewer homes they have to collect from. Here is how Leonard Stefanelli explained the system in 1966:

> If a truck brings in — if the collector's good and brings in a lot of customers and he brings in an extra $300 a month [where normally that route in that area would be set at the average price, say $4,500 a month income], . . . they would change that and take $300 off that route and pass it on to a truck, say, bringing in $4,200. Even though customer per customer, the one with $4,200 worth of work probably has just as many customers [and work] as the $4,800 truck. Maybe the other driver can't raise more money; maybe they're all residential customers or something like that; and he can't get the money that this $4,800 truck is getting.

Stefanelli thus acknowledged that this system is often unfair. Fred Fontana feels particularly victimized by it, because of the special problems of his hilly route and residential customers with a high incidence of poverty and transience.

> "There's no justice to it," he said. "You see how we have to work here, and you know what it's like in Sunset [the district]. And yet with very little adjustment our route is set up to be large enough to make about the same money as a Sunset route, where there are no hills and no problems with customers. And it's dirtier work too. Sure, we could try to get a little adjustment in the route, but we are too tired to argue by the time we get home."

Despite its injustices, this system appears to be a highly effective means of motivating each partner to maximize the economic return from his route. It creates a permanent competition among partners to see who can bring in more money for the company. Years later partners still recall with pleasure the satisfaction of "slipping a block" to an adjacent route during annual readjustments.

Thus for many scavengers the experience of sharing in the ownership of their companies begins with the sense that "you own your own route." Their proprietary duties are a nuisance and a pain, but can also instill a sense of ownership and pride. They may also be an effective preparation for participation in shareholders' meetings, as well, as they involve initiative and judgment, and make each partner an expert on the economics of his own route.

Processes of Degeneration in the Scavenger Firms

Over the last ten or twenty years, a number of developments at the scavenger companies have had the effect of moving the companies away from their worker-owned institutions toward more conventional organizational structures and practices. Although the "degeneration" of other worker-owned firms has sometimes been attributed to a single cause, it appears here to be a broader and more multifaceted process. The demise of worker ownership in these firms, like its flowering, has been a complex phenomenon made up of a number of related elements. These changes will be reviewed in this section.

New Sources of Profit in the Solid Wastes Management Industry

For most of the years of their existence, the scavenger companies offered their partners an income whose chief merit was not its size, but its security. One Sunset partner recalled how he was once advised that if he became a scavenger, he would never get rich, but he would "always have two bits in his pocket." A major limitation on the scavengers' earnings was that they came in the form of wages, rather than returns on capital. Moreover, since scavengers' wages were scrutinized by regulatory bodies, they could never go far beyond the levels standardly paid to other laborers in their cities.

In the 1950s and 1960s, however, a number of developments called for new infusions of capital into the scavenger operations, and in turn provided new opportunities for partners to profit from these investments. A growing volume of commercial and industrial wastes, for example, created a role for a new breed of specialized collection vehicles. The new "debris-box trucks" and "front-end loaders" made use of containerized and mechanized loading processes that enabled crews of just one or two men to do the work of many. In this same period, San Francisco's two scavenger companies were forced to make expensive changes in the way they disposed of the city's refuse. As disposal sites close to the city were closed off to them, the scavengers had to build a large transfer station on the edge of the city, from which refuse would be off-loaded onto transfer trucks and hauled to new landfill sites, twenty miles or more away.

At the two San Francisco companies and in other firms as well, these new collection and disposal operations were handled not by the parent firms, but by new subsidiary companies created especially for those tasks. The proceeds from these new activities would thus be accounted separately from the earnings of their tightly-regulated parent companies. Although the finances of these subsidiaries were still closely watched by regulatory bodies, they nevertheless offered new forms of returns on capital that the formerly simple structures of these companies had never made possible.

While these developments were taking place, the scavengers were also coming to be influenced by other organizational innovations that were national in scope. In 1965, for example, a National Solid Waste Disposal Act was passed. In that same year, the National Solid Wastes Management Association was formed to promote the interests of the refuse collection industry. Representatives of the scavenger companies quickly took an active role in this new organization and have been frequent participants in its conferences, trade fairs, and other professional meetings.

The role of the scavengers in the burgeoning solid waste management industry, however, does not rival the part played by a more newly arrived set of organizations: the "agglomerates." Since they appeared in the late 1960s, these new giants have rapidly achieved positions of preeminence in the industry by acquiring the leading refuse contractors in many American cities. For several years in the early 1970s, shares in these firms were among the glamour stocks of Wall Street. When one reads this industry's trade journals, it is easy to get the impression that the future of waste collection in the United States lies in the hands of these agglomerates.

This impression receives further support from the goings-on at meetings of the solid waste management industry. One scavenger partner told about a convention he had attended in Monterey, California, in the early 1970s:

> [He] . . . said at that time there was a real fear (mixed with a certain attraction to being seduced by the easy riches promised by the big companies) that companies like . . . [the scavenger firms] were going to be swallowed up by these operations [the agglomerates]. He told me about how "smooth-talking attorneys from Harvard" continually bought drinks, and spread out portfolios, for the scavengers gathered there . . . . [His company president] would say to him in the bar, "Look out, here comes an SCA man." He said that he was there when "they" offered . . . [the president] an executive salary "that would knock you off your stool" (couldn't reveal how much though) and an unlimited expense account to boot if he would join forces with their national operation.

Researchers for this project observed a widespread interest among many scavengers in the possibility of allowing themselves to be acquired by an agglomerate. When he learned of our research at other firms, a partner in one company asked what it was like to work in a company that had been taken over by one of the giants. An officer at Sunset predicted in 1973 that the long range future facing the company will be a choice between going public and being acquired.

More generally, these firms have taught many scavengers the lesson that the refuse collection business does not have to be an unlucrative one. As the industry has become more capital-intensive, scavenger worker-owners have been less and less willing to see their incomes confined to the price they set on their own labor. Instead, they have become increasingly impatient to find ways for their profits to grow in keeping with the amounts of capital they have invested in their firms.

The Decline of Group Ties Among the Scavengers

As the scavengers have participated more and more in the national culture of the solid waste management industry, they have also shared less and less in the Italian-American identity that formerly helped to hold their firms together. Since World War II, there has been a marked decline in the ethnic and family-based patterns of recruitment on which the scavengers formerly depended.

One aspect of this change is that it has become more and more difficult to attract the sons and other descendants or partners into the scavenger companies. According to Leonard Stefanelli, the major source of this problem is that "most of the garbage men want their sons to be something better than they were." The response of an immigrant scavenger interviewed by Jerry Sanders appears typical in this regard. Sanders reported that this partner

> . . . told me quite frankly that he would not like to see his son continue in the garbage business. With much modesty he told me that it was all right for an immigrant like himself who didn't speak English well or write the language; in fact, he felt that he had done very well by the system, but that it wasn't good enough for a person born in the US. "If you're born in this country you don't want to carry garbage. Me, that's all I can do. But for him, it's different."

An alternative means of preserving their Italian identities which the companies have made some use of is the hiring of recent immigrants from Italy. But this leads to problems of a different sort. Fred Fontana remarked in 1966,

> We can't get good people. For instance, we have to depend on immigrants from the old country. Not that they are dumb, they just don't know the language; and they don't know how to figure things.

More recently, as the companies have sought to streamline their operations, this observation has become even more applicable. One partner complained in 1974 that the presence of Italian immigrants in his company makes it harder for the company to innovate. The key recent stumbling block has been the use of a computer for keeping account records. The only way an expensive piece of equipment like a computer can be effective, says this partner, is if the collector understands the process of feeding it information and is willing to use its services. In this man's judgment, the new system is being sabotaged by Italian-born old timers who do not make proper use of it.

There are also other processes at work which further dilute the companies' traditional Italian identities. With each succeeding generation, the sons and grandsons of partners feel less and less the sense of ethnic community that united the early scavengers. They are less and less likely to speak Italian or to live in Italian neighborhoods. And they may be inclined, like the partner just cited, to be critical of the Italian immigrants in their companies.

As they have grown, the companies have found it increasingly necessary to look beyond the families of partners and the Italian-American community for recruits. This they do with great reluctance. As Leonard Stefanelli put it,

> . . . the people we have the most trouble with are people who never had any historical connection with the company — the people who came off the street and who have never had another job and probably have no qualifications for another job, so they take the garbage job and they have the attitude that they're doing us a favor by being here.

The most important consequences of the recruitment of outsiders has been its impact on the ethnic composition of the companies. Two groups in particular have entered the companies in large numbers: Latins (Mexicans, Chicanos, Puerto Ricans, Portuguese) and blacks. As members of these minorities have come to occupy an increasingly prominent role in the companies, their relations with the Italian-American scavenger have become extremely sensitive.

Like all other employees of the scavenger companies, these ethnic minorities have entered the companies at the bottom, as helpers. The problem is that they have tended to remain in those positions. A mere handful of Latins and only two black workers had succeeded in becoming partners in the companies by the middle 1970s. Minority employees who have been with the companies for years can recall helping to break in Italian-Americans who later bought shares and were promoted over them.

Many Italian scavengers deny that the slow advancement of these minorities in the companies has been due to a policy of deliberate discrimination. They will say that most non-Italian employees in their companies never asked for the right to buy shares. Or they will tell you that this or that minority employee just didn't work out.

For their part, most minority employees of the scavenger companies seem convinced that the companies are discriminatory. An intelligent, ambitious Puerto Rican with 14 years' experience in one firm said of his company, "It's a good company, but you've got to be Italian to become a partner." In another firm Jerry Sanders asked a Mexican who had been with the company for nine years, why he is not a partner. "Because they don't like Mexicans," he was told.

There is some social interaction between Italians and non-Italians in the companies, up to and including an occasional after-work beer. More common than such mixing, however, is the tendency for non-Italians in some of the companies to create well-developed communities of their own. One man estimated that his home village in Mexico had supplied San Francisco and the cities around it with 150 refuse collectors. We were told that many of one company's black employees live close to one another and meet socially quite often. Another firm has a Portuguese enclave, some of whose members raise rabbits and regularly sell them back and forth to each other.

What the presence of these new groups in the companies has done, or in some cases still only threatens to do, to the once solidary communities of the scavenger companies is illustrated in the following scene. It was described by Jerry Sanders, and took place early one morning in the dispatcher's office, as he waited to begin his first day on a scavenger truck.

> The Spanish-speaking workers stood outside in mass, despite the chilling cold, coming in the office only for coffee, looking only slightly less uneasy and expectant than I imagined I must have looked. The Italians, on the other hand, moved into the room with the ease and assurance of those who are in familiar environs. . . . [Two black helpers] ambled from inside to outside and to the corners of the room, while the younger black man took a seat and remained silent. For the most part the men waited silently, the quiet occasionally broken up by isolated pockets of Spanish or Italian spoken among two or three people.

Management and Oligarchy

As indicated earlier, there has always been some degree of tension in the scavenger companies between the power of leaders and of the rank and file. Recent developments within the companies, however, are increasingly tilting this power balance in favor of the management group.

The most important source of the increasing power of managers is the growing complexity and expertise involved in the operation of these firms. When the scavenger firms were initially organized, their leadership jobs were merely part-time positions, and officers spent most of their time like everyone else, working their routes. Over time, however, company offices have been transformed into full-time jobs, and officers have been responsible for directing the work of ever larger and more specialized staffs.

The growing salience of technical expertise for the scavengers' operations has been expressed structurally in their companies in a number of ways. Within a year after he had assumed the presidency of Sunset, Leonard

Stefanelli had increased the number of managerial positions in his company from three to seven. At all three of the larger scavenger companies, rank-and-file scavengers had become dwindling minorities on their companies' boards by the early 1970s. Boards of directors were now dominated by officers and by specialists in such technical areas as computers, maintenance, debris boxes, and container operations.

The widening gulf in work and expertise between managerial and rank-and-file scavengers has been expressed in other ways as well. Scavenger leaders clearly dress, act, and think quite differently from the men on the trucks. They often seem to identify more closely with the other managers they read about in trade journals and associate with at professional meetings than they do with their partners in their firms. Scavenger leaders also seem increasingly inclined to speak about the rank and file not as a constituency they serve, but as a set of passive resources to be allocated according to the dictates of the managers' expertise. The words of one scavenger president about his fellow shareholders are illustrative in this regard:

> Of course they are part of the company, but they think they should run it. They want to tell you how to do this or that. They just don't know. We tell them what to do.

Some similar thoughts were also expressed by Sunset President Leonard Stefanelli as early as 1967:

> . . . Years ago, when the company was formed — you can look at the minutes, and a very simple set of By-Laws was drawn up — there weren't the problems we have now. The god-darn business is becoming more and more politically and technically complicated. . . .

> . . . The way our system is set up — well, I mean, that's all fine and good in the past, but I don't think it's going to be good enough to withstand the trials of the future . . . it's going to be a system of specialization. A man's going to have one job, and he's going to do that good. If he don't do it, we're going to replace him with somebody.

The Redesign of Jobs at the Scavenger Companies

It is not hard to understand why Leonard Stefanelli's predecessor as president had hesitated to introduce packer trucks on his company's residential routes. It was clear that this change meant far more than the mere substitution of one truck for another, but instead would entail a major transformation in the scavengers' traditional ways of dealing with their customers.

The problem originated in the fact that when the scavengers still used open trucks, there was a rough equivalence between the scavengers' output as refuse collectors and their productivity as bill collectors. A crew made up of three partners and one helper could typically stop at 400-500 households per day, for a total of 2000–2500 customers per week. (This is a respectable figure, considering that collection was carry-out, often from second or third stories, and that the restricted capacity of open trucks necessitated frequent trips to the disposal site.) This volume of business left 700–800 customers for each of the three partners to keep records for and collect bills from. That is about as many as a man could handle, using the scavenger's traditional face-to-face methods of doing business.

When packer trucks were introduced at Sunset, this correspondence between the company's refuse collection operations and the bill-collecting side of the business was threatened with disruption. For the packers to be economical, crew sizes had to be reduced. Otherwise, the new trucks' greater productivity would mean that crews would finish their work before nine o'clock every morning, and their trucks would sit idly in the lot for the rest of the day. For the trucks to pay for themselves, one man would have to be taken off each residential collection crew. And that man would have to be a partner, since to eliminate the cost of the helper on the crew would not save enough money to justify buying the packer. But how could two partners service as many accounts as three?

The solution adopted was centralized mail billing, with the aid of an office computer. With the office handling routine billing chores, all that the partners had to do was to record charges for any extra services they performed, and to apply pressure to delinquent accounts. Eventually, even this latter job was taken away from many scavengers, when the city government of San Francisco agreed to act as collection agent for the scavengers. With these changes, the scavengers' bill collection operations were made even more streamlined than their household refuse collection, and it became feasible for a single partner to handle a route book with a much larger number of accounts.

These innovations occasioned some layoffs, but not for partners. Partners displaced from residential routes found work in several growing spheres of their companies' activities. Many of them became drivers of debris-box trucks or front-end loaders. Others were assigned to their companies' new disposal operations, most of these as drivers of transfer trucks. Some partners, too, were assigned to new staff positions in their companies, such as overseeing their centralized office billing operations.

For the partners who have remained on residential routes, the introduction of packer trucks and office billing have had mixed effects on the nature of their work. On the one hand, they may now find their work cleaner and more efficient, and they are probably glad not to have to ring doorbells to collect their bills anymore. But on the other hand, these changes have also left the scavengers much less scope for exercising their traditional skills and responsibilities. The packer truck has eliminated most opportunities for salvaging recyclable materials, and office billing has greatly reduced the scavengers' contact with customers.

As a result, the work of a scavenger partner no longer differs as much as it once did from that of any hired refuse collection laborer. The changes that made it possible to remove one partner from each residential crew have thus undermined the rationale for having three, two, or even one partner per truck. Increasingly, officers and rank-and-file scavengers alike are wondering how much money could be saved by replacing more partners now engaged in residential collection with lower-paid hired help.

In addition, the shift of numerous partners into commercial operations, transfer truck driving, white-collar jobs, and so on, has greatly complicated the once simple division of labor among the scavengers, and has subjected it to increasingly rational calculation. The diverse mix of skills now required to run the scavenger companies has thrown into question many of their time-honored internal labor policies, such as the idea that every new employee should start out as a helper, or that every partner should be paid the same wage. At Sunset and at Golden Gate, the number of wage levels for partners was expanded in 1970 to three, and similar gradations in wages have emerged in other scavenger firms. At Sunset, a new set of By-Laws ratified in 1973 for the first time omitted the requirement that officers and specialists be paid no more than other partners.

The Retreat From Worker Ownership

Over the past decade, these various developments have contributed to several major alterations in the structure of the scavenger companies. One of these changes has been an increasing use of hired labor in all of these companies. At Sunset and at Golden Gate Disposal, this development has been accelerated by a policy that beginning in 1967 required the shares of retiring partners to be sold back to the company, rather than being sold to helpers. By August 1973, the number of partners in Sunset had fallen from a peak of 320 to 288. From June 1966 to February 1974, the number of share blocks in Golden Gate had dropped from 183 to 160, of which eight were in the hands of people outside the company.

To some it appeared that this policy of retiring shares was directed against the companies' non-Italian helpers, who might otherwise have been expected to enter the ranks of partners in increasing numbers. But as Leonard Stefanelli explained in 1966, the initial impetus for the share retirement policy came from the introduction of packer trucks. In order for the new trucks to pay for themselves, one partner had to be taken off each residential route which converted to packers. Thereafter, there was general agreement that the company now had more partners than it could put to good use. As Stefanelli outlined in 1966, this was an important factor behind both the share redemption program and subsequent innovations in the company's structure:

> We eventually hope to get down to a point where we'll have in the area of 150–200 shareholders down here, because as we get these [new] trucks, it consequently is going to eliminate jobs unless we expand our operations and branch out—which we are contemplating to do.

To many people in the scavenger companies, however, it has seemed possible that the policy of retiring shares will not stop at this relatively minor adjustment. For once office billing has been introduced, it becomes possible to remove not just one partner from each truck, but all of them. Partners who have learned to like the advantages of "fewer ways to cut up the pie," as one Sunset scavenger put it, may not want to give up the game when it is just getting interesting. One hears fantasies about the process continuing until the point is reached where either the management or some lucky individual owns a whole company.

All these developments have placed the nonshareholding helpers in these companies in a more and more difficult position. They are now faced with the prospect of becoming perpetual second-class citizens in a democracy of privileged workers. And they are learning that the scavenger's institutions can be most unkind to a permanent caste of helpers. The best jobs in the companies are reserved for partners. The top wages for helpers are less than 70% of the pay of most partners. Helpers also charge that partners monopolize the most lucrative overtime opportunities.

This situation has made the role of unions in the companies increasingly significant. All three of the largest companies were organized years ago by the Teamsters, but their locals have usually been dominated by partners, who are quite sympathetic to their fellow partners in management. When Sunset and Golden Gate were first brought into the Teamsters in the 1930s, the International was so concerned about the preponderance of owners in that local that it established a special trusteeship to govern it. In the 1940s, the local became self-governing, but has been slow to show much independence from management. Partners say that they would never approve a strike vote, because "we'd be striking against ourselves."

As the proportion of hired laborers to partners has risen, unions have become increasingly important potential power centers in these companies. In a number of firms, unions have begun to attack such traditional management prerogatives as control over job assignments and labor discipline. At one unionized company where there are already two or more helpers for every partner, jobs are allocated by seniority rather than at management's discretion. But one non-Italian helper in that company believes that the union is still too pro-management to suite his tastes. He claims that it lets the partners get away with occasional violations of the seniority system. He blames this weakness of the union on the fact that its tone is still set by shareholders and certain of the helpers—perhaps those who expect or hope to become partners—who are sympathetic to management.

A similar ambivalence saps the strength of the union that represents the shareholders and helpers of Sunset and Golden Gate. This lesson was forcefully driven home to the helpers when their contract was up for renegotiation in 1973. At the union meeting to ratify a new contract, attendance by shareholders was unexpectedly poor, giving the helpers enough voting strength to reject the terms offered by management. A new meeting was called, and this time, the companies took steps to make sure the partners would be there. At this meeting, the contract was approved.

This experience left many helpers with the feeling that they had no other recourse but to take legal action. In December 1973, a group of black and Spanish-surnamed employees of Golden Gate Disposal filed a class action suit against the two companies and the union. They charged discrimination in hiring, in promotions, and in the sale of shares. In June 1974, two Sunset employees added their names to the suit. In January 1975, a similar suit was filed against the Oakland Scavenger Company by five nonwhite helpers in that firm.

In filing suits against their companies, the minority employees of these companies were following an example that had been set even earlier by an Italian helper in one scavenger firm. On April 19, 1973, the nephew of a partner in Golden Gate Disposal filed a complaint against the company for failing to transfer the title to his uncle's shares to his name. The uncle had sold him the shares for $72,500, after refusing an offer of $59,500 from the company. Spokesmen for the company countered that the sale was invalid, because it did not have the approval of the shareholders. They had rejected the proposed sale at a meeting on January 18, 1973, by a vote of 96 to 53. The case was soon settled out of court, for terms which were not disclosed.

In the middle 1970s, there were also a number of signs that nonwhite helpers and disaffected young Italians in the two San Francisco companies were joining together to make their union more and more militant. In 1976, the union demanded a seniority system for job assignments, and more control over the adjudication of grievances. For the first time, contract negotiations reached the brink of a strike; and there were even rumors that the bad feeling between union leaders and management had been vented in sabotage. Management escaped from this confrontation with most of its powers intact; but if present trends continue, it is hard to see how it can do so for much longer.

In the meantime, another set of developments has produced some more irreversible changes in the structures of several scavenger companies. In the early 1970s, two smaller scavenger companies allowed themselves to be acquired by a large solid waste agglomerate. One of these had approximately 50 partners when it was sold to a major agglomerate in February 1973.

At the same time, some of the larger scavenger companies have shown an intention to beat the agglomerates at their own game, and have begun buying up smaller refuse collection companies in nearby communities before the agglomerates can grab them up. In 1973, partners at Sunset turned in their shares in their company in exchange for shares in a newly formed holding company with the impressive-sounding name of Envirocal. This new organization embraced both the Sunset Scavenger Company and its subsidiaries, *and* a few smaller refuse collection companies that the Sunset scavengers had recently acquired.

The Dynamics of Degeneration in the Scavenger Firms

Why have the scavengers abandoned their traditional structures so rapidly, after so many years of successful operation as worker-owned firms? Any answer should begin with a reminder that the scavengers had initially adopted their worker-owned structures by accident, rather than by design. That is, there has never been any explicit commitment to the ideal of worker ownership in any of these firms. The scavengers had quite practical reasons for adopting worker-owned structures in the early years of their firms; and when practical considerations later suggested the desirability of a different organizational model, the scavengers had little reason not to change.

Given this fact, perhaps the most remarkable thing about the scavenger firms is not that their structures have changed, but that they remained stable for so long. Some of the factors that for many years contributed to the retention of worker ownership in these firms have already been reviewed. The economic and regulatory structures affecting the scavengers sharply limited partners' opportunities to profit from the use of hired labor in their firms. Partners were also inclined to offer ownership opportunities to helpers, because they saw this as a way of assisting the family members and fellow immigrants from Italy who worked in their firms. The scavengers saw no need to abandon workplace democracy, because their workplace democracy seemed to work. Certain characteristics inherent in the tasks performed by the scavengers, moreover, seemed to require the motivational consequences of worker ownership in order for the job to be done right.

By the time the scavengers had begun to transform their structures, however, all of this had changed. The business of solid waste management had become more capital-intensive, and more profitable as well. The firms had come to rely increasingly on the labor of workers with whom the partners had less and less in common. Scavenger leaders were becoming increasingly differentiated from their rank and file, both in occupation and in expertise. And finally, the incentive and reward structures associated with worker ownership had come to seem increasingly less appropriate to the scavengers' work.

If one sought to identify one single force or process that was most responsible for the scavenger firms' demise, what would that one factor be? The accumulation of capital, or the existence of a market for hired labor? The destructive impact of time, size, and differentiation on the scavengers' formerly strong occupational culture and sense of community? The "iron law of oligarchy?" The importation of inappropriate technologies? Clearly, all of these forces were at work in these firms, and it is therefore extremely difficult to say which ones, if any, played the most important roles.

The multiplicity of the processes that contributed to the transformation of the scavenger firms is well illustrated by the case of the 50-partner firm that was acquired by an agglomerate in February 1973. I visited this firm several times between December 1973, and August 1975, in order to find out what had led these scavengers to accept the agglomerate's offer. It soon appeared that these scavengers would not have fallen under the spell of the agglomerate as rapidly as they did, if prior developments had not already left their worker-owned institutions in a severely weakened state.

In deciding to "merge" with this agglomerate, as they put it, the most prominent consideration for these partners was of course the financial aspects of the deal. The sale made it possible for partners to realize a large return on the capital invested in their shares. The agglomerate paid these scavengers an undisclosed sum in cash plus, reportedly, quite a sizeable chunk of the agglomerate's stock. This financial settlement had been especially welcome, given that quite a few partners were approaching retirement at the time of the sale. One partner said that if he had been ready to retire at that time, he would have wanted $100,000 for his share, and he was not sure he would have been able to find a younger worker who was willing to pay that.

But beyond the immediate dollars and cents aspects of the deal, many other factors had contributed to the decision to sell. Growth and modernization had already taken the company to a point where worker ownership no longer seemed integral to its operation. Out of a labor force of 240, fewer than 50 were actually working partners (some partners were in a state of semi-retirement, involving themselves only to the point of helping to keep the books on their old routes). Increasingly centralized accounting and the growth of the management team had greatly reduced the skill and responsibility involved in work on residential routes.

The sense of community, the feeling that "everybody pulled together," had also "already gone," according to a company officer. That feeling had been strongest when the company was still small. Thereafter, the company "got too big," the officer said. Factions developed. People began to turn their interests elsewhere. I asked this officer whether or not the influx of non-Italian workers into the company had had anything to do with that. He granted that maybe it had.

One symptom of this loss of solidarity had been a decline in the once-customary cooperation among crews during the workday. Instances of one crew voluntarily helping another had once been quite common at this company. This happens less often now than it used to, largely because the young workers are not so inclined. It's not that they're lazy, one former partner explained, it's just that they don't want to stay late. Many of them work other jobs.

The demise of worker ownership in this firm had also had a family aspect, according to another former partner. This scavenger acknowledged that he had been for the merger "all the way" when it came before the partners for a vote, but said he would not have been if he had had a son who could have taken his share. This partner was himself the son of a partner, and would have liked to keep his share in the family if he could have.

Decision making in this company had also been centralized well before the merger. Although meetings of partners continued to be held, they served merely to ratify company policies, not to make them. As one manager put it, "A guy couldn't come out of left field with an idea" and expect to see it adopted. He had to work through the leadership.

These scavengers' decision to sell their firm to a nationwide agglomerate was thus a culmination of all of the processes outlined above. Their once close-knit community was largely a thing of the past. The company's democratic institutions had deteriorated to the point where no one considered them worth preserving. Technological innovation had deprived worker ownership of much of its economic rationale. The agglomerate's stock, in the meantime, was booming, and looked like a better investment than stock in an aging worker-owned firm.

Not long after they had decided to divest their firm, however, these scavengers had occasion to express a few second thoughts. No doubt the greatest source of dissatisfaction was the fact that within a year or two of the sale, the price of the agglomerate's stock had fallen to barely a fifth of what it was selling for when the scavengers first received it. Although the price of this stock eventually recovered, the scavengers also regreted the passing of some things that had irrevocably been lost. When I asked a few former partners what kinds of changes had occurred since the company was sold, one man immediately responded, "It all boils down to the loss of one thing — *pride*." Another man joined in, "You had *a voice* in running the company [emphasis his]." A third, whom I asked on another occasion, began:

I miss the meetings . . . . It was a terrific feeling to own a company at 22 . . . . I used to walk out of here at night, look back at all the trucks, and say to myself, "This is mine. I own one of these trucks."

While for these scavengers there is no going back, it would be premature to proclaim the complete demise of worker ownership in the other scavenger firms. There remain some reasons for thinking that the scavengers may yet emerge from the present transitional period with at least some of their institutions intact. It is possible that the changes in crew structure touched off by the introduction of packers may not go as far at Sunset and Golden Gate as they did at some other scavenger companies. As of February 1972, Fred Fontana told Stewart Perry that he thought that Sunset should keep a minimum of two partners on each residential crew — he felt that business matters are still too complicated for one man to handle adequately alone.

Leonard Stefanelli and others are also quick to point out that the sword of technological innovation cuts both ways at the scavenger companies. While it eliminates or degrades some roles of the worker-owners, it can create others. The stress Stefanelli places on the need to diversify and expand his company's sphere of operations is designed in part to see that the modernization of the company will do just that. Stefanelli tried to convey what the introduction of more modern jobs and equipment can do to increase a scavenger's enthusiasm for the company and his work, and to make him more inclined to encourage his children to enter the company:

I know that down deep in their hearts, they would like their sons to carry on the tradition of the company. There's no question about that. But I don't think they really get out and *push* it, bcause they say, "Well, Jeez, I broke my back all my life." But now, since they see the company starting to progress, and they see these new trucks . . . . For example, we gave one to this new guy . . . the other day, and if you took his *wife* away, he wouldn't feel so bad [as] if you took that truck away!

A partner in another firm too, indicated indirectly that an upgrading of the jobs at his company would make him more eager to see his son go into the business. When asked about his aspirations for his son, the scavenger answered that he "would be pleased to have him work for [this company], but as a mechanic not as a garbageman." By the same token, this man would probably also look favorably upon a future for his son in the company as an automatic equipment operator or computer specialist — two types of careers that are becoming more and more prominent in the scavenger firms these days.

There is also reason to believe that the differences between the Italian shareholders and the minority employees of the scavenber firms are beginning to be resolved. In July 1979, it was announced that an out-of-court settlement of the discrimination suit against the Sunset and Golden Gate scavengers had been approved. Under the terms of this settlement, the two companies agreed immediately to sell a specified number of partnerships to minority buyers nominated by the plantiffs, and also accepted an "affirmative action" formula for the disposal of shares that become available in the future. According to this formula, the first bloc of shares to become available would have to be offered to a Hispanic buyer; the second to a black, the third to a Caucasian, and the fourth could either be retired or sold to any buyer of the company's choice. This formula was to remain in force until the representation of minorities among the partners equals their representation in the firms' labor force as a whole. A preliminary settlement of the suit against the Oakland Scavenger Company was also reached in April 1980, but the case had to be returned to the courts in June of that year when a new group of plaintiffs intervened in the suit.

Outside the scavenger companies, in the meantime, the nationwide wave of mergers created by the solid waste management agglomerates in the early 1970s has long since come to an end. And while the growth of the agglomerates has tapered off, the prestige of the scavenger companies within the Northern California region has remained quite high. While many aspects of the scavengers' work methods have recently become outmoded, others have been widely imitated, and are standard throughout this area. In recent years, the modernization of Sunset and other large scavenger companies has reaffirmed their position of local leadership within the industry.

Thus it has become increasingly clear to the scavengers that there are no better organizational models for them to follow than their own accumulated experience. Chances are good that for one reason or another, at least a few of these firms will see merit in retaining some semblance of a worker-owned structure for at least another generation or two. But ultimately, as Carl Bellas observed of the cooperative plywood companies in the Pacific Northwest, the scavenger companies are "a phenomenon, not a movement" (Bellas, 1972: 97). A unique set of circumstances called them into being, and ever since, they have been pulled by a variety of forces into more conventional directions.

CHAPTER 4

Taxi Cooperatives In The United States

The record of the scavenger companies discussed in the previous chapter contributes significantly to our understanding of employee-owned firms in a number of ways. They provide a rare example of a group of firms that have been successfully owned and operated by their manual employees for more than fifty years. In their institutions, they show how a variety of mechanisms for the sharing of ownership can be blended together to produce a uniquely rich and complex whole. The story of the gradual deterioration of these institutions also demonstrates that the so-called "degeneration" of democratic firms can be as complex a phenomenon as the phenomenon of employee ownership itself.

Valuable as these implications are, the lessons that can be drawn from the scavenger firms alone are also circumscribed in some equally important ways. Taken in and of themselves, the scavenger companies appear to be little more than a curiosity or historical accident. They are confined to a single industry and region, and were formed during a relatively brief period of time. Their success was due to a rare combination of economic, political, technological, and ethnic influences that might arguably never be repeated again. So how can one possibly generalize from such an idiosyncratic group of firms?

The present chapter and the following one result from efforts to break beyond these limitations of the scavenger experience by identifying parallels between the scavenger companies and more widespread populations of firms. In this chapter, the findings of several studies of taxi cooperatives will be reported. Cooperatives in the taxi industry will be shown here to have achieved many of the same successes and to be subject to many of the same processes of degeneration that were observed earlier in the scavenger companies. Unlike the scavenger companies, however, taxi cooperatives are not confined to any single region or period of time. Cooperatives are instead a widespread and standard feature of the American taxi industry.

This chapter is based on interviews with members of taxi cooperatives in such diverse cities as Boston, New York, Washington, Denver, San Francisco, and Los Angeles. Other published reports have described the operations of taxi cooperatives in Seattle, Portland, San Diego, and several other cities (Gelb, Donnelly, and Boccia, 1980; Gelb, Colman and Donnelly, 1980; Gelb, 1981; Bergman and Stein, 1983).

What is it about the taxi industry that makes it such an unusually fertile ground for forming cooperatives? The answer begins with some special features of a cab driver's work. Driving a cab is a labor-intensive activity that is not easy to supervise, because it is performed at widely scattered locations throughout a city. As a result of these circumstances, independent owner-operators have always competed well against the labor of hired cab drivers who work for fleets. These independent drivers, however, have in turn had many needs that have led generation after generation of them to organize themselves into cooperatives.

Many taxi cooperatives begin, like agricultural co-ops, as purchasing and marketing agents for their members. They arrange volume purchases of gas or insurance, and may also play a role in procuring relief drivers for their members. On the marketing side, most taxi cooperatives start by providing their members with a common name, insignia, and color scheme to paint on the sides of their cabs. Many also take the more ambitious step of operating a radio-dispatch service.

In addition to the help their radios give them in finding passengers for their cabs, co-op members often report some important non-economic reasons for putting radios in their cabs. Both in New York and in Boston, several co-op members reported that they like having radios in their cabs not primarily for the business it brings them, but for the security it provides. They see their radios as a way to summon help in an emergency, such as when they might become targets for crime. Radio users even work out codes with their dispatchers that enable them to signal that they are in trouble without arousing the suspicions of the passenger. The dispatcher will then notify the police or ask some other cabs to come to the rescue. Owner-operators may also see their radios as a source of companionship, and a way to keep in touch with home while they work. "It's like a family," explained a member of one New York cooperative.

This capacity of co-op members to look out for each other's interests has important political consequences in addition to its other effects. Every cab driver is aware that his work is shaped in countless ways by policies that emanate from the local city hall. But how many cab drivers have the time and energy to see to it that their perspective will be listened to when those policies are made? When they organize themselves into cooperatives, however, they also create organizations that can give them effective representation at their local city hall. Taxi co-ops participate regularly in negotiating fare increases with city governments, and also go to bat for individual members who feel they have been treated unjustly by local commissions or police. Thus a member of Boston's Independent Taxi Operators Association boasts of his cooperative that

> We are the ones that go to the commissioner, we are the ones who write letters, we are the ones who complain, we are the ones who go to the city hall, the [city] council. Who do they recognize? The ITOA.

With a few exceptions that will be noted below, members of most taxi cooperatives retain title to their own individual cabs, and operate their cabs with almost complete independence. Even when cabs are owned collectively, members typically rent their cabs out from the co-op, and then pocket all the fares they collect from passengers.

The fact that members continue to earn incomes individually, rather than collectively, is a source of conflict in many taxi cooperatives, and a potential economic liability as well. When a cooperative provides radio dispatching, members tend to become jealous of radio business that other members get, and elaborate rules are needed to satisfy members that the allocation of all radio business will be fair. If a regular customer asks to have the same cab driver sent to him when he calls every day, a cooperative may have to deny such a request, because its rules may require that each order be given to the cab nearest the job. Similarly, taxi cooperatives are said to be slow to go after newer and more specialized types of business, such as programs for the elderly and handicapped (see Fielding and Teal, 1978), because they have no mechanism by which the income from such specialized business could be shared equally by all the members.

The highly individuated structures of most taxi cooperatives may also limit their comparability to more centralized cooperatives and employee-owned firms. The discussion that follows will attempt to show that such comparisons are justified, however, on several grounds. Despite their loose structures, taxi cooperatives remain one of the most prominent instances of work organizations that are regularly owned and governed by their rank-and-file labor force. When they provide radio dispatching, these organizations can also form a quite powerful part of the daily work experience of their members. Taxi cooperatives merit comparison with producers cooperatives and other worker-owned firms, finally, by virtue of the fact that they are vulnerable to many of the same processes of degeneration that are characteristic of these firms.

These points will be made initially through an analysis of the history of one particularly long-lived cooperative located in Boston, Massachusetts. Like the scavenger companies, this organization had retained its democratic structure for more than fifty years by the time it was studied.

The organization is also clearly vulnerable, however, to many of the same processes of degeneration that were at work in the scavenger firms.

The Dynamics of Degeneration in Boston's ITOA

Boston's Independent Taxi Operators Association, ITOA, was formed in 1924. Its initial purpose was to wage a series of political struggles on behalf of the individual owner-operators who had founded it. These owner-operators had felt the need for a political union in order to gain access to the private cab stands then monopolized by the city's major taxi fleets. This battle was eventually won, but not until the new cooperative had begun to perform a number of additional services for its members. These additional functions included the purchasing and distribution of gas, and such marketing functions as the establishment of common insignia and colors, advertising, and the operation of a telephone dispatching service.

For much of its history Boston's ITOA showed an unusually high resistance to the degenerative processes that have undermined so many other worker-owned firms. Many of ITOA's founders had formerly been hired cab drivers on strike against the city's largest fleet, and they were determined that fleet-like labor relations would not be imitated in the ITOA. They therefore adopted a by-law barring any ITOA member from owning more than one cab. For decades, the ITOA also made no effort at all to limit the size of its membership, instead admitting all comers who were willing to pay a modest initiation fee. Through such policies, ITOA grew to include a peak of about 400 members by its fiftieth anniversary in 1974.

By the 1970s, however, several major signs of degeneration were clearly in evidence. Perhaps the most striking of these signs was a greatly increased reliance on the labor of nonmember drivers to operate ITOA cabs. Three processes appear to have contributed to this increasing use of nonmember labor: (1) it has long been ITOA policy to allow members to staff their cabs with nonmember drivers whenever they themselves cannot be in them, such as overnight or during vacations; (2) some members (recently around 35) never drive their own cabs, but staff them permanently with nonmember drivers—this includes two full-time officers, plus a number of other members who work in other jobs and own their cabs purely as investments; and (3) since the 1950s, ITOA has permitted its members to own more than one cab. When ITOA's traditional rule of "one member, one cab" was first relaxed, members were still limited to owning a maximum of three or four cabs. By the early 1960s, however, ITOA's rules were further amended to allow members to own an unlimited number of cabs. As a result, some ITOA members soon acquired so-called "minifleets" of as many as 10, 20, or even 30 cabs. When ITOA reached its peak size in

1974, its approximately 400 members together owned an estimated 800 cabs.

More recently, there have also been significant departures from the ITOA's traditional open membership policies. The initiation fee for new members, which as recently as in 1968 had amounted to no more than $25, was raised in 1974 to $500. By 1979, a series of internal divisions within the ITOA led to the defections of many members, reducing the size of the organization to 320 members and 525 cabs. In that same year, ITOA's leadership determined that many of the recent defections were due to the fact that the organization had grown too large in the past. As a result, the organization for the first time imposed a cap on the creation of new memberships, establishing 550 cabs as the organization's maximum permissible size.

It was also in 1979 that the present study of ITOA's "degeneration" was begun. The analysis that follows is based on interviews conducted in July, August, and November 1979, and in July 1980. These interviews included talks with ITOA officers, dispatchers, gas-pump operators, minifleet owners, single-cab owner-operators, and nonmember drivers. The cooperation of this wide range of respondents has made it possible to construct one of the most comprehensive accounts of the phenomenon of degeneration that has yet been reported for any cooperative or other worker-owned firm.

The Economics of Degeneration

Some of the leading analyses of the economic forces that contribute to the degeneration of democratic workplaces have already been discussed. The most influential economic theorist of this phenomenon is Jaroslav Vanek, who has emphasized the role of capital accumulation in causing the degeneration of these firms (Vanek, 1970, 1971, 1975, 1977). More recently, Avner Ben-Ner has argued that the temptation to degenerate is present even in firms that do not accumulate capital, whenever members have an opportunity to profit from the use of cheaper hired labor (Ben-Ner, 1981; 1984).

Even with the addition of Ben-Ner's recent work, however, the prevailing economic theories do not yet appear to have exhausted the full range of material incentives that contribute to the degeneration of cooperatives and similar worker-owned firms. Many of the forms of degeneration enumerated by Blumberg (1968: 3–4), for example, do not necessarily require the presence either of capital or of hired labor to produce them. It seems to be the basic nature of a market economy to provide numerous opportunities for worker-owners to enhance their incomes by engaging in

some or all of these "anti-co-operative" practices. A market economy encourages worker-owners to charge high premiums for memberships
whenever memberships for any reason become so attractive to would-be
members that they are willing to pay a high price for them. And this will be
true, regardless of the amount of funds that current members may or may
not have invested in the firm, or whether or not hired labor is being used in
the firm. And similarly, if a conventional buyer is motivated for any reason
to offer members an even higher premium to purchase the firm as a whole,
what is there to stop them from accepting the offer? It is fundamental to a
market economy to permit members faced with such choices to act in their
own interest, even if that interest conflicts with the interests of future
generations of would-be members.

When one seeks to explain the record of Boston's ITOA, each of these
three sets of economic considerations has at least some degree of relevance.
Following Vanek and Ellerman, it seems clear that a major influence retarding the degeneration of this cooperative is the fact that it does not accumulate capital. ITOA's cabs, and more importantly, the licenses to
operate them, are owned not by the organization itself, but by its individual
members. In 1931, the number of cabs authorized to operate in Boston was
fixed at 1,525, and the licenses or "medallions" associated with each cab
were declared freely transferable. Since that time, ITOA's members'
individually-owned medallions have appreciated significantly in value,
commanding prices of between $30,000 and $35,000 in 1979. None of this
appreciation, however, has accrued to the organization itself. The individual ownership of ITOA's taxis and medallions has thus had an effect in
some ways analogous to the "internal debt accounting" recommended by
Ellerman (1977).

While the capital structure of the ITOA thus made it unnecessary for
members to resort to any form of degeneration as a means of recouping
their capital, other aspects of ITOA's finances provided positive incentives
for them to maintain a policy of unlimited membership. This is because the
costs of running the ITOA are largely fixed, whereas its revenues are a
function of the size of the membership. ITOA members contribute to the
support of the organization via monthly payments of dues (which in 1979
amounted to $20 per cab per month), and via obligatory gas purchases at
ITOA pumps. In 1979, ITOA met approximately $500,000 in operating
costs by collecting $120,000 in membership dues, and another $380,000 in
profits from the sale of gas to members. ITOA members have thus usually
welcomed the admission of new members, because the additional revenues
contributed by these new members would help to curtail the growth of their
own monthly membership dues.

This same consideration also goes far to explain the ITOA members'
later decision to allow ITOA members to own more than one cab. As individuals, ITOA members have sought to own more than one cab for the

simple reason that by acquiring additional cabs, they could profit increasingly from the use of hired labor. But at no time in ITOA's history has more than a minority of its membership owned more than one cab. So why did ITOA's single-cab owner-operators abandon their former prejudice against hired labor and vote to allow a minority of their fellow members to acquire additional cabs? The answer once again begins with the finances of the ITOA. ITOA members voted to accept these additional cabs, largely because the additional cabs would mean additional gas purchases and additional contributions of dues, thereby lowering the average costs of membership to each individual member.

The two most recent steps in ITOA's degeneration appear to have been prompted by none of the considerations discussed so far, and owe much of their impetus instead to an altogether different market mechanism. Both the 1974 decision to increase the price of new memberships and the 1979 cap on the ITOA's total size were symptoms of a new economic logic that was unique to the 1970s. Each of these two developments occurred within a year after a major gas shortage, and appears to have been a direct response to the sudden new scarcity of gas. As a result of these gas crises, the fact that the ITOA had its own supply of gas suddenly caused ITOA memberships for the first time to acquire value in their own right. The increased initiation fee of 1974 appears to have been explicitly designed to profit from this fact. The subsequent establishment of an upper limit on the number of ITOA cabs was similarly tied to the availability of gas, as members argued that the ITOA should no longer admit more cabs than it could with certainty supply with gas.

The Loss of Community

The economic influences enumerated above go far toward explaining the phenomenon of degeneration, both in this and in many other cooperatives and worker-owned firms. But as was discussed earlier, the rise and fall of any experiment in worker ownership is rarely a matter of economics alone. It typically requires some unusually strong collective sentiments to establish these firms, and before a worker-owned firm can begin to degenerate, the salience of these special ties must often first be neutralized. In the scavenger companies, the persistence of ethnic and family ties between the Italian scavengers and their helpers appears to have acted as an important brake on the degeneration of their firms, and an increasing reliance on hired labor did not occur in these firms until they had begun to recruit a much more diverse labor force.

It may be characteristic of the various forms of solidarity and value consensus that have contributed to the success of so many democratic firms, however, that they cannot last forever. This may be the case simply because values cannot hold out indefinitely in defiance of self-interest. It is typical for collectivistic values to play a more prominent role in the founding of democratic workplaces than they later play in the minds of the firms' very same founders as they prepare to retire, or in the consciousness of future generations of members. Ethnic solidarity and other forms of homogeneity among members are also inherently short-lived, because both the passage of time and the growth of the firm tend to lead to the recruitment of an increasingly heterogeneous labor force.

Boston's ITOA, like many other successful co-ops, originated in a strong sense of solidarity among its founders. Many of them had come to know each other while working together as hired employees of Checker Cab, and they had formed the idea of creating their cooperative while on strike together against that fleet. One clear expression of their feelings about themselves as a group was the rule they adopted that no ITOA member should be allowed to own more than one cab. They were thus in agreement that the ITOA should be reserved for little guys, like themselves, and not fleets.

The solidarity that had united the ITOA's early members had clearly begun to wane, however, in the years after World War II. ITOA old-timers report that they began to feel increasingly estranged during this period from the "new element" that was then entering the Boston taxi industry. The "newness" of this younger generation of cab drivers was in part an ethnic phenomenon—whereas ITOA's older membership had largely been Jewish, the post World War II recruits to the industry had much more diverse backgrounds. More important than these ethnic differences, however, was the fact that ITOA's established members and the younger cab drivers had quite different work experiences, and took noticeably different attitudes to their jobs. The older members were by no means rich, but they owned their medallions free and clear, and thus felt free enough from material care to drive through the city streets with a certain amount of dignity and calm. The younger drivers, in contrast, were under heavy financial pressure, as they were either saving up to buy a medallion, or struggling to pay the mortgage on a medallion they had recently bought. As a result, these drivers often drove much more aggressively than the older ITOA members, darting in and out of traffic, cutting people off, and finding various ways to "hustle" themselves a living.

According to some ITOA old-timers, the concerns they had about the quality of these new drivers figured prominently in the decision to let members own more than one cab. To many of them, it seemed more desirable to let the existing members acquire additional cabs than to reserve the benefits of membership for a new generation of drivers who did not seem worthy of the privilege.

It has subsequently become apparent, however, that the decision to allow members to own more than one cab was in itself an even greater blow to the solidarity among the membership at the ITOA. The discord created by this move goes well beyond that fact that it permitted some ITOA members to grow richer than others, thereby arousing the envy of their less prosperous fellow members. In addition to giving rise to such petty jealousies, the creation of minifleets within the ITOA has split the ITOA membership into two competing classes whose interests conflict in numerous ways. The conflicts of interest between these two sets of members have in turn disrupted the formerly strong normative consensus among ITOA members at many crucial points.

One example of how the interests of single-cab and minifleet owners can come into conflict has to do with definition of what is fair treatment from ITOA's radio dispatching system. This is a sensitive issue, in any case, because it was estimated in 1977 that only 10% of ITOA taxis' business comes in over the radio, as compared to figures of 25%, 40%, or even 50% for cabs in some of the city's major fleets. Actually, the total amount of business taken in over ITOA's radio is quite comparable to the volume handled by these fleets; but since at ITOA, this radio business gets shared by a much larger number of cabs, the amount received by each cab is far less (Lloyd and Taft, 1978; Table 4). The impact of this low average volume of radio business per cab is further lessened by the fact that approximately 150 to 200 ITOA members have no radios in their cabs, preferring instead to find customers by the time-honored method of "playing the street." Other ITOA members keep radios in their cabs, but reserve them primarily as a means of summoning help in case of emergencies. Those ITOA cabs that make use of their radios can therefore expect to derive 20% or more of their daily business from the use of this dispatching system.

For ITOA's radio users, the organization has an elaborate set of rules and procedures designed to make sure that the allocation of radio business will be fair. Despite these rules, however, a significant proportion of ITOA's radio work ends up being meted out at the dispatcher's discretion. When a customer phones in an order to ITOA's radio room, that call is supposed to be assigned to the first ITOA cab in line at the taxi stand nearest to that neighborhood. But if there are no ITOA cabs waiting in line at the nearest stand, a telephone order is thrown open to "bids"— that is, any cabs in the area that want the business can simply request it. And when more than one cab makes a bid for a job, the dispatcher has a certain amount of freedom to choose which bidder will receive the assignment. In the exercise of this discretion by dispatchers, ITOA's officers privately acknowledge that "human beings cannot be impartial." A driver for one of Boston's large private fleets similarly expressed the opinion that "There is a certain amount of favoritism on all radios."

Insofar as ITOA's dispatchers do discriminate among drivers in the awarding of jobs, it is most typically the organization's nonmember drivers who are the victims of their preferences. This appears to be due in part to the fact that nonmember drivers tend to be inexperienced radio users who are less well-known to the dispatchers. It is also caused, however, by the perception that nonmember drivers are generally less reliable radio users and more likely to break the organization's radio rules. Nonmember drivers have often been known to "steal a job" from another cab, or to abandon a radio customer because they happen across another fare en route. One member of the commitee charged with enforcing ITOA's radio rules confided that such rule violations have increased dramatically as the role of nonmember labor within the ITOA has grown.

Many ITOA old-timers charge that the ITOA has lost a good deal of business over the years through the bad will created by these violations of its radio rules. As a result, dispatchers have been permitted to announce occasionally over the radio that a given job from a particularly valuable customer will be reserved for a "reliable man." Such discriminatory practices often upset ITOA's minifleet owners, however, because they make it harder for them to recruit nonmember drivers to take out their cabs. This issue of fairness in radio dispatching has thus become an increasingly sensitive source of tension between single-cab owners and ITOA members who own more than one cab.

An even more explosive issue creating conflicts of interest between these two groups concerns the finances of the ITOA. Here, the fundamental question is how the costs and benefits of ITOA membership can most equitably be shared. Such matters have become increasingly complex as a result of the growing differentiation of ITOA members into radio users *vs* nonradio users, and single-cab owners *vs* owners of more than one cab. In particular, single-cab owners and minifleet owners have repeatedly been divided over the issue of whether the costs and benefits of membership should be distributed per member or per cab. Such conflicts have recently had quite disruptive consequences for ITOA's internal politics, causing many ITOA members openly to wonder how much longer their organization's democratic institutions will be able to survive.

The Political Dynamics of Degeneration

In addition to the economic and social processes that contribute to the degeneration of worker-owned firms, it is also argued that these firms degenerate politically as well. That is, relations between members and their elected leaders are said to become increasingly less democratic over time, and this atrophy in their democratic institutions is seen as contributing to members' readiness to transform the firm into a conventional capitalist enterprise.

In a review of the history of some producers' cooperatives in the United States, Arie Shirom (1972) identified two major mechanisms that he saw as contributing to the decay of democratic practices in these cooperatives. One of these mechanisms appears to have been inspired by the elite theories of Pareto and Michels, and originates in the unequal distribution of managerial talent. As a result of this "unalterable fact of life" (Shirom, 1972: 545), leadership positions tend to be increasingly monopolized by the most qualified elites. The other mechanism identified by Shirom recalls the views of Weber and the Webbs, and originates in a perception that workplace democracy is inherently disruptive, stirring up dissension and undermining the enforcement of rules. Shirom argues that as a result of this perception, members become increasingly disillusioned with democratic decision making, and instead seek to entrust their firm to some permanent leadership stratum.

The ITOA's constitution gives the organization four executive officers (president, vice-president, treasurer, and recording secretary) and a board of directors. The board of directors is composed of the four executive officers, and seven directors elected at large. The president and treasurer receive full-time salaries; other officers and board members are compensated only for time actually spent on company business. Both officers and board members are required to be members of the ITOA, and have in the past been chosen by vote of the entire membership in elections held every two years.

For decades, the ITOA showed few signs of the oligarchical degeneration anticipated by Shirom. Board meetings are held twice per month, and board members insist that they, not the officers, really "run" the ITOA. ITOA members report that elections of officers and board members have often been vigorously contested, with candidates sending out letters to the membership, running ads in the local trade newspaper, and soliciting votes at the polling place on election day. Examination of past company records indicates that turnover in leadership positions has been quite common, and incumbents have by no means been sure of re-election. The current president, Max Dobro, is said to have won his office in the later 1960s by a margin of just four votes.

In the 1970s, however, ITOA's political institutions came under increasing strain as a result of the growing conflict between single-cab owners and the owners of more than one cab. While single-cab owners have consistently been a majority both within the ITOA membership and on the board, the minifleet owners have not been left totally without influence. In particular, since the organization depends heavily on the revenues brought in by the minifleet owners' additional cabs, ITOA's leaders are careful to avoid actions that would cause these members to take their cabs out of the ITOA. The policies that result have thus often been an uneasy compromise between the interests of these two categories of members, accommodating first one group and then the other.

One issue of chronic concern to ITOA's minifleet owners is the question of fairness in the ITOA radio room. Among Boston cab drivers who have used ITOA cabs, there appears to be a widespread consensus that you need to know a dispatcher to get good radio work from the ITOA. Some drivers also claim that it is necessary to do favors for the dispatchers, or give them gifts. They tell many stories of dispatchers quite openly soliciting gifts over the radio, asking for coffee, Christmas gifts, and the like, and it is widely assumed that drivers who do not respond to these overtures will lose out when they bid against other drivers for radio business. One dispatcher who became notorious for such practices was subsequently dismissed, but the impression remains among many drivers that the situation is largely unchanged.

In the early 1970s, one driver became especially embittered when he bought a cab and became a member of ITOA, but still felt he was not getting his fair share of the radio work. This driver's problem may have been due in part to the fact that English was not his native language, and he therefore had some trouble communicating with the dispatcher. In any case, he appealed for help to the minifleet owner he had formerly worked for, who in turn took his case to the company president. The argument came to blows, and the minifleet owner was subsequently fined for causing discord within the organization. Not long thereafter, the minifleet owner left the ITOA to form his own cab association, taking several other ITOA members along with him.

An issue that has created even more serious rifts within the ITOA in recent years has been the politics of its internal finances. These issues have been rendered increasingly more explosive as a result of the growing diffeentiation of ITOA members into radio users vs nonradio users, and single-cab owners vs owners of more than one cab. It has been proposed that radio cabs should be charged higher dues than the nonradio cabs, but this proposal has never been acted on. Several acrimonious debates have taken place, however, between the single-cab owners and the owners of more than one cab.

In the later 1970s, many single-cab owners left the organization in protest when a special assessment to combat a new bus line proposal was charged per member, rather than per cab. Although the amount involved was only $30, these members felt it was unfair to raise these funds by an assessment per member, as the issue would have a direct impact on the price and profitability of each cab. In 1979, it was the turn of the minifleet owners to be upset, as the ITOA established a $5,000 life insurance benefit for each member, and decided to pay for it via a two cent reduction in the rebate that ITOA members receive for each gallon of gas they purchase at ITOA pumps. Since owners of more than one cab have higher gas quotas and purchase more gas than members with only one cab, they felt that they were in effect being charged more for their life insurance policies than the other members were paying for that same benefit. The case was taken to court, but the court upheld the ITOA's right to finance the new benefit by this means.

Such internal disputes appear to have played a major role in the retrenchment of ITOA from its peak size of 400 members and 800 cabs in 1974 to only 320 members and 525 cabs in 1979. A number of other factors also contributed to this loss of members, including the fact that this was a difficult period for the Boston taxi industry as a whole, with the result that many members either lost their cabs entirely, or found themselves unable to pay their dues. In years when gas was plentiful, many members left because they found the requirement of buying gas at the ITOA too burdensome. This was especially true of nonradio cabs, who felt they derived little benefit from the organization's radio dispatching service in any case. Some members left the ITOA because they had reached the age of retirement. It was clear in many cases, however, that the internal problems outlined above also played a role in these defections.

Some members now feel that the ITOA's recent problems have been due to the fact that the organization is "too damn democratic." One company leader suggested that it is the democratic nature of the ITOA that makes it so difficult to enforce its rules. "This association gives people independence," he noted. "That's what the cab driver wants." As a result, "the rules are vague and flexible and it's easy to circumvent them." This same leader pointed out that the ITOA could attract and keep more radio customers if it didn't have to worry so much about being fair. Even if a customer specifically requests a driver by name, ITOA's rules require the job to go to the first cab in line. To this leader, such examples show that "in a business, there's no place for democracy."

There are signs that other members as well have reached similarly pessimistic conclusions about the value of democracy at ITOA. In 1978, the terms of office of ITOA's salaried officers were extended from two to four years. In that same election, all of ITOA's incumbent officers were easily re-elected, three out of the four having run unopposed.

Degeneration and the Nature of Work

Another often neglected set of circumstances that contribute to the preservation or demise of democratic workplaces has to do with the nature of the work performed in them. Democratic workplaces are more likely to appear and to succeed in labor-intensive industries rather than in capital-intensive ones. In part, this is due to the fact that workers typically lack the resources to finance a capital-intensive enterprise, and that capital-intensive businesses are typically more subject to Vanekian processes of degeneration than are labor-intensive ones. What is often overlooked, however, is that democratic workplaces are not merely labor-intensive, but make intensive use of labor of a very particular sort. Typically, democracies of producers perform work that cannot readily be supervised or machine-paced. As a result, job performance is highly sensitive to a worker's motivation, and some form of individual or collective self-employment is seen as necessary to induce workers to give the job their very best efforts. Conversely, it is precisely when techniques become available for making work machine-paced, or otherwise easy to supervise, that democratic workplaces are most likely to begin substituting cheaper nonmember labor for the labor of members. This latter point emerges with particular clarity from the experience of the scavenger companies.

In addition to the desirability of having jobs in which performance is sensitive to workers' motivation and in which nonmember labor cannot readily be substituted for the labor of members, a number of other aspects of the nature of work are relevant to the viability of democracy in the workplace. Frequently, workplace democracy appears to have arisen among workers who, like the scavengers, perform similar tasks, and thereby derive a sense of solidarity from their common work experiences. Typically, too, the most conducive occupations are those that tend to segregate their members from people who work in other occupations, giving them unique hours of work and a distinctive occupational culture. In the case of the scavengers, these shared occupational experiences appeared also to serve as valuable preparation for members' participation in democratic decision making, since it protected them to some extent from leaders' pretensions to higher levels of managerial expertise.

Many of these occupational considerations appear to have been important ingredients in the success of Boston's ITOA. When the ITOA was initially formed, the capital requirements for entering this line of work were quite modest, as Boston's taxi medallion system had not yet been established, and all a prospective member needed, therefore, was to own his own cab. Cab driving is also an occupation in which self-employed labor competes quite favorably with the labor of hired workers, since fleet owners have often found hired labor forces extremely difficult to motivate and control (Russell, 1983). The taxi business also does much to prepare cab drivers to participate actively in decision making in their workplace, since it encourages them to work autonomously, to handle money, to be articulate, and to confer with one another at many times throughout the day.

Before ITOA had begun to degenerate, moreover, some of these facilitating conditions had been significantly altered. Perhaps the most fundamental change was the creation of Boston's medallion system in 1931, and the subsequent appreciation of Boston's taxi medallions. What this development essentially did was transform a formerly labor-intensive industry into an increasingly capital-intensive one. As a result, Boston's taxicabs have tended to accumulate in the hands of individuals who can most effectively raise capital and profit from the rental of cabs, rather than those who do the best job of driving a cab.

A revealing study of Boston's medallion market was made public by the mayor's office in 1978. The study disclosed that climbing interest rates have recently forced would-be owner-operators to finance their medallion purchases on increasingly unfavorable terms. Many subsequently find that they cannot make ends meet, and are forced to give up their cabs. The 1978 study found, for example, that 101 of Boston's 1,525 medallions had changed hands five or more times between 1967 and 1977 (Lloyd and Taft, 1978: I-10).

In addition to transforming a labor-intensive industry into a capital-intensive one, Boston's medallion system has also contributed to a noticeable decline in the quality of owner-operator labor. That is, while owners of paid-up medallions continued to impress observers as conscientious drivers who "stick by the rules," Boston cabbies describe drivers with notes to pay as "hungrier" than the other cabbies and therefore also more likely "to cut in front of you." It is these drivers with the heaviest financial pressures who also seem most likely to come to blows over fares, or to refuse service to passengers who only want to take a short ride.

Thus, by the time that ITOA members had given their approval to the increased use of nonmember drivers, the labor of owner-operators had already lost much of its former superiority to the labor of hired drivers. This is not to discount entirely the perception of many ITOA members that the influx of nonmember drivers also had an even more deleterious effect on the ITOA's service standards and reputation in the tyes of the public. The problem is that the record of new members trying to pay off a mortgage on an owner-operated medallion was not all that much better. And since members who owned "free and clear" medallions seemed doomed to become a thing of the past, the advantage of reserving the ITOA solely for owner-operated labor had by the 1950s and '60s clearly ceased to outweigh its apparent costs.

Within the ITOA, these consequences of the medallion system were further exacerbated by a technological change. The introduction of radio dispatching in the 1950s not only created a powerful incentive to admit additional cabs, but also made it possible to adapt cab driving labor to a less experienced labor force. That is, the more business a driver receives over the radio, the less he has to go find for himself. Thus, the introduction of radio dispatching at the ITOA was in some ways parallel in its consequences to the introduction of centralized mail billing among the scavengers. That is, by centralizing certain entrepreneurial tasks, each innovation had the effect of adapting a more challenging set of work responsibilities to the needs of a cheaper and less skilled labor force.

Conclusion

As in the case of the scavengers, the so-called "degeneration" of democratic workplaces has been shown here to be a complex set of phenomena with more than one cause. Whereas published discussions of degeneration typically treat it as either an economic phenomenon, or a political one, the degeneration of Boston's ITOA is clearly both of these things, and a good deal else besides.

If one were forced to try to identify one single factor that is most responsible for the degeneration of Boston's ITOA, that factor would probably have nothing to do with the internal dynamics normally featured in the literature on the degeneration of worker-owned firms, and would consist instead of a development entirely external to the organization itself. This extremely significant external development was the creation of a medallion system for licensing Boston taxicabs in 1931. By establishing a fixed number of marketable licenses, this medallion system gave individual ITOA members both an opportunity and an incentive to acquire additional cabs. The subsequent proliferation of minifleets within the ITOA has tended increasingly to divide the ITOA membership into one class that lives by driving owner-operated cabs, and another that lives by renting cabs out. The disruptive consequences of this two-class sytstem for the organization's economic, social, and political life have already been reviewed.

The effects of local licensing arrangements on the stability or degeneration of taxi cooperatives will stand out more clearly when the fate of Boston's ITOA is contrasted to that of other taxi cooperatives in cities with different laws. The following section will show how the regulatory environment of two taxi cooperatives in Los Angeles created even stronger temptations to degenerate than were present in the case of Boston's ITOA. The effects of local licensing arrangements on taxi cooperatives in a number of other cities will be discussed in the concluding portion of this chapter.

The Role of Culture and Ethnicity in the Taxi Cooperatives of Los Angeles

The discussion that follows deals with the dynamics of two taxi cooperatives that were formed in Los Angeles in 1977. As in the case of Boston's ITOA, the story of these two cooperatives will do much to illustrate the impact that local regulatory bodies can have on cooperatives in this industry. Unlike Boston's ITOA, however, these cooperatives also provide a striking illustration of the contribution that ethnic and cultural factors can make to the stability or degeneration of democratic firms.

Like their counterparts in other cities, L.A.'s two taxi cooperatives emerged out of the shared needs of career owner-drivers, and owed much of their early growth and success to the common bonds that unite this occupational group. Within a period of two or three years, however, the character of these firms quite radically changed, as the result of a rapid transformation in the ethnic composition of their membership. A closely-knit group of Soviet Jewish immigrants quickly rose to prominence in both of these firms, simultaneously introducing a wholly new set of aspirations concerning the future of the firms. These changes in turn set in motion several processes of degeneration that might otherwise have taken many more years to unfold.

This discussion of these cooperatives is based largely on the results of open-ended interviews with approximately a dozen leaders and rank-and-file members of these two cooperatives conducted in May and July 1981. Interviews with Russian-speaking drivers were conducted partly in Russian, but mostly in English. These interview data were supplemented by newspaper accounts of the formation and subsequent history of the two cooperatives, and by copies of by-laws, budgets, and similar documents supplied by the cooperatives.

L.A.'s two taxi cooperatives owed their initial impetus to the bankruptcy of the city's Yellow Cab fleet in 1976. Until that time, the Yellow Cab company had held an exclusive right to operate cabs within the city of Los Angeles. The demise of this fleet threatened to leave the entire city without taxi service, and prompted a complete reorganization of its taxi industry in early 1977.

In this chaotic situation, two groups of former Yellow Cab drivers sought the right to become owner-operators of their own cabs. The city government was sympathetic, but feared that independent cabs would be difficult to regulate, and would also be unable to provide adequate radio dispatched service. Therefore, the city government voted in April 1977 to require the would-be independents to form cooperatives, each of which would operate a radio dispatching service, and would also bear responsibility for policing its own members' behavior.

While thus mandating the creation of these cooperatives, the city government nevertheless remained wary of the owner-operators and sought to limit their scope of action in several important ways. The city council restricted the use of nonmember labor within each cooperative by stipulating that owner-drivers could not hold permits to more than one cab, and must drive their own cab at least forty hours per week. In an attempt to prohibit their private sale, the city government also declared these licenses to be nontransferable. In addition, the city government granted to several privately owned fleets the right to operate an unlimited number of cabs, but limited the two cooperatives to a maximum of just one hundred members each.

Although authorized in April 1977, it was not until late spring or early summer that the city's new taxi cooperatives formally commenced operations. The first cab of the Independent Taxi Owners Association (ITOA) appeared on the streets late in May. The United Independent Taxi Drivers (UITD) did not begin operating until July 1977, and it was not until April 1978 that its 100th cab "hit the street."

Within a year of their creation, the two cooperatives were attracting enough radio business that they began to talk about the possibility of expanding the size of their membership. In large part, the motive for this expansion was to make more cabs available to respond quickly to the organizations' growing numbers of telephone customers. Some co-op members, however, also saw expansion as a way to share the benefits of co-op membership with other career drivers they had known at Yellow Cab. Thus the cooperatives petitioned the city government for permission to take in additional members. The one hundred cab limit was lifted, and by the end of 1980 the cooperatives had expanded their membership to a total of 200 cabs at United, and 201 at ITOA.

The new cooperatives also quickly showed signs of being quite democratic in practice as well as in structure. There are differences in the constitutions of the two organizations in this regard: at ITOA the board must refer more decisions to the membership than is the case at UITD. But in both organizations, board members and executive officers come up for election annually and incumbent officers have already failed to bids for re-election in each. In the UITD, the organization's first president was confronted with "an election catastrophe," being voted out of office at the end of his first term. He was voted back into office the following year. At the ITOA, a dissident minority took one group of leaders to court for taking action at a meeting in the absence of a quorum; this case led to a system of proxy voting, which eventually enabled this dissident group to take over the leadership of the ITOA.

Signs of Degeneration in the Los Angeles Taxi Cooperatives

After just four brief years of existence, the Los Angeles cooperatives had already shown several of the symptoms of "degeneration" that have so often been noted in other cooperatives and similar worker-owned firms. Perhaps the most striking of these symptoms has been the creation of a brisk market for memberships in the cooperatives. This private sale of cooperative memberships "has raised some eyebrows at city hall," according to a leader in one of the cooperatives, but it has been officially tolerated in part because it originated in a series of "hardship" cases to which city officials felt they could hardly object. The first sale of a membership in UITD involved a member from Texas who needed to return to his home state on urgent family business, and requested permission to sell his cab to another driver, along with his UITD membership. At ITOA, another cab driver lost his cab in a fire, and sought to sell his membership as a way to help recoup the loss. In the words of one informant, such hardship transfers in the first year or so of the cooperatives' operation "opened the door" to the subsequent development of a regular market for memberships in the two cooperatives.

By early 1980, memberships in the cooperatives were selling for about $12,000 each. A year later, they were bringing in $25,000. These prices have tempted a number of the founding members in each cooperative to sell their memberships "just for profit." Many of these former members remained in the organizations as nonmember drivers of other members' cabs. An informant in the UITD estimated that perhaps forty of the original one hundred members and perhaps another twenty to twenty-five of the members brought in during the organization's subsequent expansion had sold their memberships. A similar number of transfers appears to have taken place at ITOA.

The creation of this market for memberships has led both cooperatives to rethink their policies toward expansion. It now appears that to create new memberships in return for only modest affiliation fees is essentially to give away something for nothing. To discourage speculation in memberships, both cooperatives have instituted rules barring members brought in under expansion from selling their memberships for two years. There has also been sentiment in the cooperatives that the affiliation fees charged to new members ought to be increased. At UITD, these fees rose from $250 for the first 100 members to $500 for the 76 "add on" members brought in 1978–79 and then to $1500 for the last 24 members added in October 1980. Such fees of course still fall far short of the actual market value of a membership in the cooperative. In partial recognition of this fact, both cooperatives decided in late 1980 to freeze their membership at the current level of about 200 cabs per organization.

This decision by the cooperatives to freeze the size of their membership was prompted not only by the rising values of co-op memberships, but also by the perception that the streets of Los Angeles were being flooded with too many cabs. Between 1980 and 1981, the number of cabs authorized to operate in Los Angeles increased from around 1,000 to approximately 1,400 in less than a year. The source of most of these new cabs was not the cooperatives, but privately owned fleets. By 1980, many of these private fleets had begun to expand rapidly by selling "leases" to cabbies who then became drivers of owner-operated cabs affiliated with the fleets.

Members of the two cooperatives soon complained to the city government that the private fleets were selling these leases to far more taxicabs than the existing volume of passenger traffic could reasonably support. They also reminded the city government that only the two cooperatives were authorized to license owner-operated cabs. In July 1981, the city government reaffirmed this policy, and ordered the fleets to stop issuing licenses to owner-operated cabs. Even after that ruling, however, co-op members complained that the private companies were continuing to circumvent this regulation by a variety of inventive subterfuges.

While thus struggling to preserve their monopoly over the right to drive an owner-operated cab, members of the two cooperatives have in fact tended to spend less and less time behind the wheels of their own cabs, and instead to rely increasingly on the labor of nonmember drivers. Both cooperatives have long permitted their members to lease out their cabs when they cannot be in them. There is also growing sentiment in the cooperatives that members should be permitted to lease out their cabs one hundred percent of the time, especially if age or ill health make it difficult for them to keep driving their cabs. In some cases, cooperative members have permanently leased out their own cabs to another member of the cooperative, who in turn operates the cabs as a "minifleet." Since this violated the city's requirement that owner-drivers must spend a minimum of forty hours per week in their cabs, three or four owners received 15-day suspensions when this practice came to light. Co-op members acknowledged in private, however, that the practice continued on a more discrete basis.

Most recently, the members of the ITOA voted in the early spring of 1981 to permit their members to own more than one cab. Although the Los Angeles city ordinance of 1977 prohibited owner-drivers from operating more than one cab, ITOA's members perceived a loophole in this law, in that it applies only to cabs operated within the city of Los Angeles. Thus, it does not prohibit ITOA members from operating additional cabs under licenses from such nearby cities as Beverly Hills, or from the government of the county.

The rapid development of these processes of degeneration in the two taxi cooperatives of Los Angeles stands in striking contrast to the experience of Boston's much older and larger ITOA. Formed in 1924, it was not until the 1950s that the Boston cooperative permitted its members to own more than one cab. And for a full fifty years, Boston's ITOA made no effort to limit the size of its membership, and instead took in all comers willing to pay its modest affiliation fee. Only in the 1970s did this organization initiate steps to limit the size of its membership, raising its affiliation fee to $500 in 1974, and establishing 550 as the maximum number of cabs in 1979.

The most important key to the vastly different rates of degeneration in the cooperatives of these two cities appears to lie largely in the different regulatory environments in which the cooperatives operate. In Boston, governmental authorities license not companies, but individual cabs. The owners of Boston's 1,525 medallions have then been left free to operate their cabs under any arrangement they like, either as solo owner-operators, or as affiliates of a cooperative or fleet. Boston's medallion owners are also free to sell their medallions to any other buyer. As a result, in Boston it is these medallions, rather than any organizational memberships, that constitute the indispensable occupational resource, and that appreciate in value. By the 1970s, the price of a taxi medallion in Boston had risen to between $30,000 and $40,000, and represented by far the most formidable prerequisite for membership in Boston's ITOA.

In Los Angeles, in contrast, the city licenses not cabs, but companies. Individual taxi permits cannot be sold, and have no market value. Memberships in the cooperatives, on the other hand, can be marketed, and constitute the only legally recognized way to become an owner-operator of a taxi in Los Angeles. It is not surprising, therefore, that these memberships should have so quickly become objects of value, bringing all the consequences that result from that fact.

These unique features of the local regulatory environment thus clearly constituted an economic "time bomb" (Ellerman, 1977:2) that was inherent in the structure of the two Los Angeles cooperatives. That economic time bomb might have taken many more years to "explode," however, were it not for the fortuitous presence of a powerful cultural "detonator." This detonator came in the form of an extremely dynamic group of drivers who had recently immigrated from the USSR. The efforts of these Soviet immigrants to acquire memberships in the two cooperatives acted as a catalytic force within these organizations, bringing to rapid fruition a set of processes that might otherwise have taken many more years to make themselves felt.

The Role of Soviet Immigrants in the Cooperatives

Although no Soviet immigrants were part of the original membership of either cooperative, there are now estimated to be 70 Soviet immigrants among the members of ITOA, and 50–60 in the UITD. In their eagerness to buy into the two cooperatives, it has been largely these Soviet immigrants who have caused the price of memberships in them to appreciate so rapidly. And as they have gathered numerical strength, the Soviet immigrants have also played an increasingly prominent role in setting the cooperatives' policies in many other areas as well.

Several factors appear to have helped induce L.A.'s Soviet Jewish immigrants to enter the taxi industry in such large numbers. It has often been noted that immigrants in general, and Jewish immigrants in particular, have tended to be overrepresented in occupations that provide better than average opportunities for self-employment (Bonacich, 1973). Recent Soviet immigrants to Los Angeles have established their own businesses in a number of other fields besides cab driving, including approximately fifteen jewelry stores, several dental laboratories, and a variety of other retail establishments and repair facilities. They have flocked in greatest numbers to the taxi industry, however, because they find it to be the easiest field to enter. Language problems, in particular, are less of a barrier in the taxi business than they are in many other fields. As one informant explained, recent Soviet immigrants who seek to start their own businesses in other fields are typically handicapped by the fact that "we have lack of communication, knowledge of law, and so on." Thus a major attraction of the taxi industry is that "it's a give a great opportunity to one single person to make a living without a lot of knowledge of the industry." Another spokesman summarized these advantages of the taxi industry by saying simply that "it's a way into a new country."

In flocking to the taxi industry in such large numbers, these Soviet Jewish immigrants are to some extent repeating a pattern established by other Russian and Eastern European Jewish immigrants one or two generations earlier. L.A.'s Soviet Jewish cab drivers are aware of many of these earlier precedents; but insofar as they have been influenced by the example of others, the most important role models were probably the recent immigrants from the USSR who entered the L.A. taxi industry immediately before them. Most of L.A.'s new Soviet immigrants live in a closely knit enclave in the Fairfax district of Hollywood, renting rooms in the same apartment buildings, patronizing businesses owned by their fellow immigrants, and following each other into the same businesses. When newly arrived immigrants start driving cabs, they also make it a point to use cab stands frequented by other Russian-speaking drivers. That way, they not only keep each other company, but also exchange practical information about their new job — before taking a passenger to an unfamiliar location, an inexperienced driver will run over to a gathering of Russian-speaking drivers to ask them the best way to get there. One L.A. cab stand is now such a well-known immigrant hang-out that the local press has dubbed it "Little Moscow" (*Los Angeles Times*, June 19, 1980, p. II-4).

Once they have entered the taxi business, L.A.'s Soviet Jewish immigrants have impressed many observers with the speed and determination with which they acquire ownership of their own cabs. Like other successful immigrant small businessmen, they appear to owe much of their success to their tendency to work long hours, while taking only small sums out of the business for themselves. An American-born leader in one cooperative also attributes some of the immigrants' success to the fact that they are generally well educated, and often have professional backgrounds. The Soviet drivers also argue that their lack of formal business experience has been less of a handicap than might otherwise be expected, because coping with the shortages and black markets common throughout the Soviet economy was in itself an important form of business training. "In Russia," said one, "everything was business."

In May and June 1980, a controversy developed in Los Angeles over whether the Soviet immigrants' success in acquiring memberships in the city's taxi cooperatives was due not only to their own hard work, but to outside help. It was widely assumed both inside and outside the cooperatives that various Jewish organizations were providing loans to the Soviet immigrants to help them buy their cabs. If true, it was felt that such loans would be placing black and Hispanic drivers at an unfair disadvantage, since it would make it more difficult for them to outbid a Soviet immigrant for any cab up for sale. After complaints were made to the city government, the mayor formed a special task force to find out where the Soviet immigrants were obtaining their credit.

The investigation soon disclosed that with rare exceptions, no formal organizations of any kind had assisted the Soviet immigrants in the purchase of their memberships. On the other hand, the Soviet immigrants had not made these purchases without help; but in most cases, it turned out that the immigrants had helped each other to buy their memberships, through a variety of informal means. "One immigrant helps another," explained one spokesman. An American-born leader from another cooperative observed that "they are the type of people that help each other out; . . . they lend each other small sums."

The Soviet immigrants tell many stories of the way they have helped each other with small loans. One told of seeing an immigrant loan $50 to a perfect stranger who came from his own home town. Some stories draw pointed contrasts between the immigrants' willingness to make loans and the greater caution of Americans. If a Russian has $800, said one driver, he will loan you $800, not $700 the way an American would. This same driver reported that when he was buying his ITOA membership, an American relative had promised to loan him the money, but reneged. So he telephoned some fellow immigrants from Odessa and raised $9,000 in only ten minutes. Some of these lenders, he added, were people he had met only in Los Angeles and had known less than a year.

Some patterns of financing commonly used by the Soviet immigrants appear in many ways similar to the "rotating credit" institutions that have been observed within other immigrant communities, such as the Chinese in California and New York's West Indian blacks (see Light, 1972). Such institutions appear to have played an important role in the rapid growth of numerous populations of immigrant small businesses in a variety of occupations (Bonacich, 1973; Light, 1972). Among the Soviet immigrants, drivers who receive loans from their fellow immigrants to buy their memberships often later make loans to other immigrants to help them in turn buy cabs. One reported that to buy his membership he "got a private loan of $8,000." He added, "now I give it to somebody [else]," meaning that he had recently loaned another immigrant $5,000 to help him buy his own membership.

While the loan arrangements described by this immigrant appear to involve only a general obligation that one immigrant should help another, without implying any necessary reciprocity between a particular borrower and lender, another system of financing popular among the immigrants is much more tightly structured. In this system, two Soviet immigrants pair off, and pool their money to purchase a cab for just one of them. They then operate the cab together, and rapidly save up enough money to buy a cab for the second member of the team. One feature of the agreements binding partners in such schemes is that the first cab owner is obligated to share the cost of the second cab, regardless of how high the cost of memberships may have risen since the purchase of his own cab. The immigrant leader quoted above tells other immigrants that you "have to have a partner" to succeed in this business, especially now that the price of memberships has risen to $25,000.

As in studies of other immigrant communities (Light, 1972) these credit institutions developed by the Soviet immigrants appear to have been facilitated by many more ties than the mere fact of common national origins. Like other immigrants, many of these Soviet cab drivers developed habits of mutual aid while coping with the economy of the country they came from. In Russia, said one driver, borrowing among friends was not simply a custom, but a necessity of life—"Today I'm broke, tomorrow you're broke." And here in this country, the immigrants' mutual assistance is embedded in a dense network of residential, occupational, and regional ties. Most of L.A.'s Soviet cab drivers come from either Kiev or Odessa, and like Light's Chinese immigrants, they seem most inclined to help fellow immigrants who come from the same city or region back home.

As Light found in his work, the greatest disadvantage from which the nonwhite cab drivers suffer in their competition with the Soviet immigrants is not primarily a matter of discrimination, but rests rather in the absence of similarly strong ties within their own ethnic communities. And in this regard, their chief liability is that their own communities are too much like the rest of the society that surrounds them—that is, they are too diverse and individuated for their members to render each other much help in starting businesses. After discussing the success of the Soviets in his cooperative, one leader commented that "the Mexicans don't help each other at all," and the blacks too suffer from this "same situation." One promising sign, however, is that two Mexican drivers in the other cooperative have recently formed a partnership to acquire two memberships "by the Russian style."

Their experiences as immigrants and the effort they have made to buy into the cooperatives have given the Soviet drivers quite different attitudes toward their memberships from those of the founding members. Their cooperative memberships take on a different meaning, first of all, because they have to pay so much to acquire them. As one immigrant leader noted, "We didn't have the free cabs. No Russian has a free cab. Maybe one or two in United [UITD], no one in ITOA. All Russians bought their cabs." Since the Russians were forced to pay high prices for their memberships, they look forward to selling them for even more. Thus, whereas the cooperatives' founders saw their memberships as a "job" or as an "income," the Soviet immigrants are more inclined to describe them as a "business" or an "investment" that will appreciate in value.

This expectation of reaping capital gains from the sale of their memberships is intensified among the immigrants by their tendency to see cab driving not as a career, but as a merely temporary expedient. Many Russian-speaking cab drivers are quick to point out that they are "not in the U.S. to drive cabs." As one of them put it, "With two college degrees I'm not going to be a cab driver all my life." For these Soviet immigrants, like many others (Edelman, 1977; Jacobs and Paul, 1981), the fact that they have not yet been able to find jobs comparable to those they were trained for remains a sore point that they are eager to correct. It is thus common to meet immigrant cab drivers who attend classes in local colleges when they are not in their cabs, and many immigrant drivers express the intention of leaving the cab business as soon as they can acquire the educational credentials or the capital necessary to set themselves up in othe fields.

These aspirations among the immigrant cab drivers have periodically been fortified by the examples set by other drivers who have already completed the transition to other occupations. At UITD, a former dentist and a soil engineer sold their memberships as soon as they had been certified to enter these occupations in the United States. Other drivers have sold their memberships and used the capital to open businesses in other fields—one opened a coffee shop, and another bought himself a truck.

Thus the influx of the Soviet immigrants into the two cooperatives has brought with it an entirely new set of attitudes toward memberships in the cooperatives. Whereas the founding members saw the cooperatives as a means of securing their cab driving careers, the Soviet drivers are more likely to view their memberships as merely short-term investments. The immigrant members thus find themselves in a chronic clash of worldviews between what one of them describes as "the business people" and "the—well, I won't call them 'lazy'—people who settle for less." To illustrate this contrast, the immigrants tell many stories of co-op members who used to rent out their cabs at low rates to old friends from Yellow Cab, or who managed their affairs so poorly that they eventually sold their memberships and went to work as hired drivers for the immigrants who bought their cabs.

The American-born drivers, for their part, are often just as critical of the immigrants. A former president of ITOA is said to have even written to the Los Angeles city government to ask its help in preventing these immigrants from "taking over" the local taxi industry. A current American-born leader in UITD described the Soviet immigrants as "not 'greedy,' but 'ambitious.'" He also predicted a hardening of resistance to the immigrant influence within his cooperative, now that "the profit seekers are gone." That is, he believes that founding members who seek quick returns from the sale of their memberships have taken their gains and left, while those that remain are career cab drivers more concerned with the quality of their jobs than with the market value of their memberships.

It may be too late, however, for such members to challenge the immigrants' influence, because the Russian-speakers' close-knit organization has already made them a powerful political force in both cooperatives. In the ITOA, the Soviet immigrants appear to have become politically active as early as 1978 or 1979, when there were not more than a dozen of them in the organization as a whole. One of the first issues to concern them was the expansion of the ITOA. Since most of the Soviet drivers had paid large sums for their memberships, they were reluctant to see new memberships almost given away. The Soviets soon joined an opposition group led by an American-born member who had been the first treasurer of the ITOA. This group felt that the policy of expanding the ITOA was not backed by the majority of the members, and took the leadership to court. Out of this court case emerged the system of proxy voting that soon enabled this opposition group to come to power. Its leader became the president of the ITOA, and a Soviet immigrant was elected chairman of ITOA's board.

The next major political milestone for the immigrant cab drivers occurred early in 1980, when the Russian-speaking members of the two cooperatives formed the so-called "Club of the Spinning Wheels." As before, the motives prompting the immigrants to become politically active were primarily defensive, and again followed the logic that once the immigrants had invested large sums in their memberships, those investments would have to be protected. This time, the threat came from an effort by a new group of cab drivers to get the city government to allow them to form a third cooperative. Since many of these drivers were former co-op members who had sold their memberships at high prices to the immigrants, the Russian-speakers were scandalized. Since a third cooperative would have undermined the investments of Soviet drivers who had bought into the UITD, as well as ITOA, the Russian-speaking members of both cooperatives were quickly roused to join the new organization.

After it had quickly helped to kill the idea of a third cooperative, the Club of the Spinning Wheels remained as a powerful caucus for influencing the affairs of both cooperatives. In both organizations, the club had contributed to an impression that the immigrants engage in "bloc voting" on most important issues. ITOA's immigrant leader insists that the other Russian-speakers "don't go behind me like a ram," but does grant that he can usually count on their votes. In 1981, immigrants' votes helped elect this leader to the vice-presidency of the ITOA, and enabled Soviet drivers to capture five out of the eleven seats on ITOA's board. At the UITD, Soviet immigrants hold no executive officers, but have won nine of the sixteen at-large seats on UITD's board (UITD's four executive officers are also *ex officio* members of its board).

The newly won power of the Soviet drivers in the two cooperatives has encouraged them to shift from simply defending the value of their investments in the cooperatives to actively enhancing it. Thus it was largely at the initiative of its immigrant members that ITOA recently permitted its members to acquire more than one cab. The leader of ITOA's Soviet drivers acknowledges that "I was at the head of that movement." And while UITD has not yet taken this latter step, several of its Russian-speaking members have begun raising the issue with the leadership.

The arrival of these refugees from Soviet socialism has thus done much to trigger the rapid degeneration of both of L.A.'s taxi cooperatives. It was the immigrants' readiness to buy into these organizations that initially prompted their memberships to appreciate so quickly in value. Later, it was their need to protect the value of their investments that brought an end to the cooperatives' policies of creating new memberships. Most recently, their desire to realize more income from their memberships and to sell their memberships for high capital gains has led at least one cooperative to allow its members to own more than one cab.

Conclusion

It is clear that in these cooperatives, as in the scavenger companies and other worker-owned firms, ethnic and cultural ties within the work force have acted as a double-edged sword. On the one hand, such ties have served as powerful ingredients in the formation and early successes of these and many other democratic workplaces. But on the other hand, the dynamics of ethnicity and culture have also contributed rapidly to the degeneration of these very same firms.

In these two taxi cooperatives, as in other such firms, the design features that foreordained their later instability were ultimately of an economic and political nature. In this instance, the most fateful choice was a decision by the local government to issue licenses not to individual owner-operators, but to the cooperatives themselves. This decision gave the cooperatives a virtual monopoly over the right to own one's own cab in this city, and it was not long before co-op members learned to profit from the sale of this privilege.

But while this structural circumstance created unusually strong incentives for these cooperatives to degenerate, it was not these incentives alone that caused the striking transformation of these firms. For these potentialities to be brought to such rapid fruition required the addition of a powerful ethnic catalyst. And in the end, it was not individual maximizing behavior that was the undoing of these cooperatives, but a special form of solidarity — the quite intensive cooperation of a closely-knit group of outsiders who were determined to help one another buy into these firms.

The influence of ethnicity on these cooperatives lay first of all in the different values and aspirations of the two groups that figure so largely in their history. The men who founded the cooperatives were career cab drivers looking primarily for a way to save their jobs. They were slow to take advantage of the possibilities inherent in their cooperatives' structures, and if they alone had been involved, the cooperatives might have taken many more years to embark upon their present path. The Soviet immigrants, in contrast, had not driven cabs in the USSR, and did not wish to drive cabs for the rest of their lives here in the United States. For them, cab driving was merely a temporary expedient, something that could give them the time and the capital to prepare themselves to go on to bigger and better things. This outlook made the Soviet immigrants more alert than the others for opportunities to transform their cooperatives into institutions that would be less democratic, but far more profitable.

The history of these cooperatives cannot be explained, however, solely with reference to the contrasting values of these two groups of members. It is also necessary to take into account the dynamics of contact between the two groups. In particular, the experience of these two cooperatives calls attention to the interplay of ethnic and cultural features at the boundaries of a cooperative, in the contacts between present and would-be members of the firm.

Apparently, the condition most conducive to the stability of a cooperative is the presence of strong ethnic or cultural ties linking those inside the cooperative with those who want in. This condition seems to have lent stability to the scavenger companies and to many other celebrated successful democratic workplaces, and appears also to have been present during the first two or three years of these cooperatives' existence. Thus, many members of the new taxi cooperatives voted to expand and take in new members for a nominal charge, because they were happy to be able to help fellow cabbies from their days at Yellow Cab.

Soon after that, however, a situation arose that appears to be most threatening to the stability of a democratic firm — the presence of one solitary group inside, and a distinctly different group outside seeking admission to membership. In the scavenger firms, it was this condition that contributed to the decision to stop allowing new employees to become partners, and that led several companies to be confronted with discrimination suits. In Los Angeles, the taxi cooperatives offered very few of their "free" cabs to the Soviet immigrants, but did not bar them entirely from gaining membership in the firm. Instead, the Soviet immigrants were permitted to become members, but only if they were willing to buy their way in.

Thus the Soviet immigrants found themselves in the position of being forced to bid for a privilege that other cooperative members had acquired virtually for free. And almost overnight, the transactions between those who bought in and those who sold out totally transformed the meaning of membership in these cooperatives. Having started out as little more than a guarantee on a career cab driver's right to earn a living, a co-op membership had suddenly become an "investment," and one moreover that could rapidly appreciate in value. Once that discovery had been made, it was not long before Soviet and American-born members alike began to search for new economic strategies that could more rationally maximize the return on their investments.

Once memberships in these cooperatives had been put up for bid, it is also not surprising that the Soviet immigrants so thoroughly came to dominate the market for memberships. Like many other immigrants, they were willing to work long hours while taking only modest incomes for home consumption. And like other immigrant groups, the Soviet drivers also showed an unusual capacity to pool their capital resources to help each other achieve the goal they shared. Thus in the end, these minor experiments in workplace democracy have served largely to illustrate the superior dynamism of what historically has been a much more powerful force — the entrepreneurial capacities of immigrant ethnic groups.

Taxi Cooperatives and Local Governments

The degeneration of taxi cooperatives in Boston and Los Angeles, like that of the worker-owned scavenger firms, has been shown here to be a complex process resulting from a variety of influences. Among the forces shaping this process, however, the most prominent in each of these cases have been the actions of local regulators. In this concluding section of this chapter, the effects of local regulatory environments on the prospects for taxi cooperatives will be made still clearer by comparing the fates of taxi cooperatives in a number of cities located throughout the United States.

The prospects for taxi cooperatives in any city are shaped by the actions of local regulators in diverse ways. As already indicated, the means chosen by local governments for limiting access to their taxi industries can be the most important influence on the rate at which taxi cooperatives degenerate. Quite frequently as well, local licensing arrangements prevent taxi cooperatives from being formed at all, because local governments grant exclusive franchises to one or a few large fleets. This has been true in Philadelphia, and in Los Angeles before 1977.

Economists have often debated why local governments choose to limit the number of cab companies or taxicabs that can operate within their cities (Beesley, 1973; Schreiber, 1975; Abe and Brush, 1976; Coffman, 1977; Williams, 1980). It is frequently argued that without such limitations, a city's streets would become congested with too many cabs, and excessive competition among cab drivers would make it impossible for any of them to make an honest living from their trade. City governments have also been motivated to grant exclusive franchises to small numbers of fleets because of the many problems they encounter when they try to regulate a numerous taxi labor force all by themselves. By granting franchises to just a few fleets, city governments in effect delegate a portion of their regulatory responsibilities to the owners of these fleets. The holders of such franchises are expected to police their drivers' behavior and to take good care of their cabs, and city governments reserve the right to cancel a franchise if these expectations are not met.

While these arguments make a certain degree of sense, the historical record suggests that entry restrictions in the taxi industry were originally initiated not by city governments, but by the industry itself. Many local ordinances limiting entry into the taxi industry were adopted in the decade after 1929, when the fleet-dominated National Association of Taxi Operators had first urged its members to seek entry controls (Kitch et al., 1971: 317). Eckert (1970, 1973) has also suggested that city governments often granted exclusive franchises not in response to any clear public need for them, but merely to suit their own administrative convenience.

No matter which of these considerations were uppermost in the minds of any particular group of regulators, their net result has been that virtually every American city has at some time or another imposed limitations on entry to its taxi industry. The only prominent deviation from this pattern is Washington, D.C., but even this exception is more apparent than real. In Washington, local authorities have several times recommended that entry limitations be adopted, but these recommendations were thwarted as a result of opposition from Congress (Eckert, 1973:93). Thus this city, too, would have adopted entry restrictions, had it truly been self-governing.

In the 1970s, new developments in the taxi industry caused many city governments to reconsider their traditional means of licensing taxi companies and cabs. The root cause of these developments was a prolonged period of hard times for the American taxi industry. Since the 1960s, freeways and rental cars have reduced the demand for taxis in many cities, while rising prices for gasoline and insurance have dramatically pushed up costs.

The squeeze on incomes from cab driving that has resulted from these trends has been particularly hard on fleets, because it has made it difficult for fleet owners to attract enough drivers to man all their cabs. Many fleets have gone out of business as a result. Other companies have survived by cutting the size of their fleets, often divesting the unwanted cabs to their employees or to other owner-operators. In such cities as Seattle and Houston, major taxi fleets have gradually come to be composed entirely of owner-operated cabs.

Of the cabs that have continued to be owned by fleets, most are now made available to drivers under a rental or lease basis, in place of the old "commission" system in which fleets would pay drivers some fixed percentage of taxi fares. Under the rental system, a driver pays the cab owner some fixed rate per shift, and is then free to pocket every dollar he takes in. Lease rates vary from owner to owner and season to season, with each owner setting his rates at whatever level necessary to attract drivers for most or all of his cabs.

Advocates of leasing often argue that this system succeeds where the commission system fails because it is a superior form of incentive. Since the lease driver gets to keep every dollar he takes in, the argument goes, he works harder than the commission driver, and therefore earns more money.

There are other attractions of leasing, however, that have nothing to do with its value as an incentive. Since 1971, the Internal Revenue Service has ruled that while a commission driver is an employee of a fleet owner, a driver who rents his cab is not. Therefore, the fleet owner is not obligated to withhold income taxes for the rental driver, or to pay Social Security taxes for him, or to provide him with disability or unemployment insurance. These all constitute substantial savings, and go far toward explaining the popularity of leasing among fleet owners.

The legal consequences of the leasing system also have much to do with its popularity among drivers as well. Lease drivers may regret the absence of Social Security and disability coverage under leasing, especially when they see some of their colleagues beaten or murdered while driving their cabs; but for most of them, this disadvantage is outweighed by the fact that their incomes are not reported to the government. An IRS audit of tax returns filed in 1976 and 1977 found that 65% of the rental drivers investigated had not reported *any* of their cab driving income (U.S. Congress, House Committee on Ways and Means, 1979: 24). It is also whispered that many lease drivers also receive unemployment compensation, welfare benefits, retirement pay, or other incomes that would be endangered if their incomes from driving a cab were to become widely known.

Old-timers therefore now complain that leasing is "degrading" the American taxi industry. It is said to do this, first of all, by turning cab driving into an occupation suitable only for a labor force of temporary or part-time workers who intend to cheat on their income tax. Secondly, the lawless spirit encouraged by the tax consequences of leasing is further exacerbated by a lack of contact between the owner and driver of a cab. The IRS is only willing to consider lease drivers as independent contractors if the fleet owner agrees to make no effort to control them while they work. Finally, leasing seems also to affect labor quality by requiring the driver to make a significant investment "up front" before he can take out a cab. As a result of this ante, a lease driver is prone to become desperate and irritable toward the ends of a shift, as he begins to fear that his take for the day may scarcely suffice to cover the expenses of renting and operating the cab. It thus comes as no surprise that lease drivers in Chicago are said by city officials to receive many more complaints from customers than drivers who work on commission (Lloyd and Taft, 1978: D-3).

Owner-operators, in the meantime, have had troubles of their own, as the purchase of a cab and a medallion had by the 1970s become an extremely hazardous step. The appreciation of taxi medallions has made the taxi industry increasingly capital-intensive, and most cab drivers find it hard to obtain the needed capital. Climbing interest rates have forced cab drivers to finance medallion purchases on increasingly unfavorable terms. Many subsequently find that they cannot make ends meet, and are forced to give up their cabs.

One consequence of the difficulty of medallion purchases is that the labor of would-be owner-operators is now often of even lower quality than that of drivers who rent their cabs. Some cabbies say that these drivers more than any others are the ones most likely to come to blows over fares, or to refuse service to passengers who only want to take a short ride. Many of these medallion purchasers set grueling schedules for themselves, spending sixteen or more hours per day inside their cabs. Of men who fail to meet their payments, it is said in Boston that "Some are just skeletons when they pull them out of the cab."

The troubles of the fleets, coupled with the discrediting of medallion systems, have created an unusually favorable set of circumstances for forming cooperatives in the United States today. Many American cities have begun to reconsider their traditional policies toward limiting access to their local taxi industries. In San Francisco, the private sale of taxi medallions was abolished in 1978. Other cities have eased restrictions on the entry of new providers into their local taxi industries, as the decline of fleets has made it harder to argue that a city's streets are crowded with too many cabs. While members of taxi cooperatives have often been as vocal as fleet owners in objecting to this trend toward less restricted competition, they may in fact have less to fear from it than do the fleets. Washington, D.C., is the most prominent American city that has never imposed restrictions on access to its taxi industry, and it is also the home of what is probably the nation's largest taxi cooperative. Formed in 1941, the Capitol Cab Cooperative Association consisted in 1984 of 800 members and 900 cabs.

While the role of well-established taxi cooperatives in cities like Washington is not widely known, cooperatives have received much more attention in cities in which prominent large fleets were either sold or went bankrupt, and new cooperatives emerged to take their place. The Yellow Cab bankruptcy that led to the formation of two taxi cooperatives in Los

Angeles occurred simultaneously in several other cities, and spawned a whole new generation of taxi cooperatives in the American West. The case of the cooperative that emerged to take the place of Yellow Cab in San Francisco is particularly instructive, because it underlines many of the lessons that emerged from the study of the taxi cooperatives in L.A. That is, in its sudden eagerness to promote a taxi cooperative, the San Francisco city government, like that in L.A., ended up by mandating a form of organization that was doomed to self-destruct.

To San Francisco's city officials in 1977, the most important reform that appeared to be necessitated by the Yellow Cab bankruptcy was the abolition of the city's medallion system. In the fall of 1977, the city's Board of Supervisors voted to achieve this end in a quite ruthless fashion, by simply declaring that all outstanding licenses would henceforth be non-transferable, and would revert to the city upon the license holder's death. Thus, owner-operators who had worked long hours to obtain their licenses at a price of up to $20,000 or more per cab would suddenly find themselves as poor as the day they had started out. The mayor vetoed this measure, but it eventually became law as the result of a city-wide referendum that took place in June 1978.

The demise of San Francisco's medallion system was so timed, however, that it did not affect the sale of Yellow Cab's permits, which became final in December 1977. Even without this measure, some city officials had argued earlier in 1977 that Yellow Cab's permits should be declared null and void, since the company could be construed as having forfeited them when it pulled its cabs off the streets in December 1976. But these arguments were ignored, and Yellow Cab's permits were put up for auction in May.

A few months before that auction took place, San Francisco's police commissioner announced that independent owner-operators would not be allowed to bid for Yellow Cab's permits, because he wanted "a responsible company" to replace Yellow Cab (*San Francisco Chronicle*, 7 January 1977). Of the groups that were permitted to bid on Yellow Cab's assets, two announced an intention to operate the fleet as a cooperative. One of these two groups eventually emerged as the winner in this bidding, and purchased 250 of Yellow Cab's permits at $15,000 apiece.

Thus was born San Francisco's New Yellow Cab Cooperative, Inc., which also incorporated a number of novel organizational features into its design. The organization was unique in accepting non-cab-driving employees as members of the cooperative, including a mechanic and several managers. The New Yellow Cab Cooperative also owns and operates its cabs in common. Members are free to own their own cabs, but they must let the company maintain them, work regular shift hours, and pay a rental charge like any other driver for the right to take their own cabs out. Members profit from their memberships by receiving a portion of the income the organization earns in renting out their cabs. This income is not taxed at the organizational level, because the company is recognized as a cooperative by the IRS.

Despite its official recognition as a cooperative, this organization's structure bears many scars from the circumstances under which it was formed. Having been created not to help drivers operate cabs, but to raise capital, San Francisco's New Yellow Cab Cooperative is a cooperative not of cab owners, but of investors. Many of its members have no other tie to the company at all, either because they have never been in the San Francisco taxi industry, or because they have long since ceased to drive cabs. Members not only have no obligation to drive cabs, but do not even own or maintain them, letting the organization do this for them. Thus the return on their cooperative memberships purely represents profit from the ownership of licenses. Some members of the New Yellow Cab Cooperative own more than one membership share, while most drivers who rent cabs from the co-op own no shares at all. While older taxi cooperatives like Boston's ITOA have shown a tendency to gradually drift in this direction, the circumstances of this cooperative's birth caused it to be designed this way from the start.

By one published report, a total of 125 out of this cooperative's 187 members were still working as owner-drivers at the start of 1979 (*Taxicab Management*, February 1979: 22). This number is almost certain to decrease, however, as another consequence of the way in which San Francisco's medallion system was abolished. That is, since the city's permits still have the power to yield current income, but can not be sold, members tend to hang onto their memberships and permits long after they retire or leave cab driving for another line of work. Thus the regulatory environment of this cooperative has clearly provided another formula for rapid degeneration.

A more promising taxi cooperative was established in Denver in April 1979. The conditions surrounding the formation of this cooperative were unusually favorable in a number of important respects. First of all, the private fleet that it took over was not bankrupt, or in a crisis, so crucial decisions did not need to be made in a breathless rush. Secondly, the transfer from fleet to cooperative ownership came as the culmination of a long-term, gradual process. A previous owner had discussed the possibility of an employee buyout with the drivers as early as 1973. The last owner had already instituted an owner-driver program in the fleet, and was in the process of transferring 100 cabs to the ownership of their drivers. Finally, the transfer was greatly facilitated by some unique aspects of the union that represented the Denver drivers. For one thing, the union had cut its ties to any national organization back in 1969, and was therefore free to make whatever move it wished. More importantly, the union had a strike fund, which it could use to provide the down payment for the sale.

The role of this union in organizing the Denver buyout appears to have helped to give the Denver Yellow Cab Cooperative an unusually democratic structure. All drivers are required to be members of the cooperative. "Inside" workers like telephone operators and dispatchers are also free to join, although so far only a few of them have. The cooperative owns most of its cabs in common, with the exception that owner-drivers continue to hold title to 100 of the cooperative's approximately 400 cabs. Common ownership of cabs has encouraged the cooperative to go after various types of specialized business, including a recent government contract to provide transportation for the elderly. For tax purposes, drivers in the co-op are independent contractors, not employees, but they are also covered by disability insurance and a pension plan provided by the union.

Denver's cooperative clearly provides an attractive model, but it too has its share of structural problems. The presence within the membership of both owner-drivers and nonowning renters, "inside" workers and other diverse categories, all seem to create bases for future conflicts of interest among the members. The Denver co-op also seems vulnerable to a basic conflict of interest that has spelled the ruin of so many cooperatives before — the conflict of interest between present and would-be members of the firm. In particular, since the cooperative enjoys a near monopoly on the provision of taxi services in Denver, it is hard to imagine how members can indefinitely resist the temptation to take advantage of this fact. There are numerous subtle ways in which present members could begin charging future drivers for the right to acquire memberships — for example, simply imposing higher rental rates for less experienced drivers would nicely accomplish this result. There also appears to be nothing in the way this cooperative is regulated to prevent it from seeking to increase its members' incomes simply by decreasing the number of cabs they place on the street, and thereby increasing the demand for each cab. And yet, both the theory and practice of worker ownership make it abundantly clear that worker-owners are not saints, and that if you hand them a monopoly, they can exploit that position as well as anyone else.

The experience with taxi cooperatives in thse various cities suggests that in the case of taxi cooperatives, it may be that the government governs best that governs least. Even when a government tries to encourage taxi cooperatives, its regulations may just get in their way. But if a government makes no effort at all to restrict the providers of taxi services in its city, cooperatives spontaneously appear, as in Washington, D.C.

Since 1965, a total of twelve American cities are known to have abolished restrictions on entry to their taxi industries (Paratransit Services, 1983). In several of these cities, such as Seattle and San Diego, taxi cooperatives were already in existence at the time this deregulation occurred. In at least two others (Milwaukee and Sacramento) new taxi cooperatives have been formed in response to this change. In many other cases, open entry has taken place too recently for its consequences to be assessed.

There are signs, however, that this period of experimentation with deregulation in the taxi industry is coming to an end. Of the twelve cities that have eliminated entry restrictions since 1965, four cities have already returned to some form of entry controls, including both of the cities (Atlanta and Indianapolis) that took this step prior to 1979.

The cities that have abandoned open entry seem to have found that unlimited entry really did cause their cities to have too many cabs, and really did make their taxi industries more difficult to control. Open entry has caused taxis to be too numerous not in the sense of creating traffic problems on city streets, but in the sense that it leads more and more cabs to compete for an essentially unchanged number of fares. As a result, there are fewer passengers for each cab. Department of Transportation studies of the effects of open entry in Phoenix, San Diego, and Seattle found that the average number of trips per cab per day declined by between 34% and 48% in each of these cities (International Taxicab Association, 1984:6). This decline in cab ridership has had a correspondingly depressing effect on cab drivers' incomes, which were already low when these regulatory reforms began.

There are also a number of ways in which unlimited entry has made the taxi industries of many cities more difficult to control. Several cities appear to have issued new licenses to numerous owner-operators and small companies without taking steps to make sure that their cabs would be properly insured. As more and more cabs have competed for the same limited number of fares, cab drivers have also been increasingly inclined to overcrowd airports, to fight over passengers, to refuse short rides, and to overcharge their fares. When city officials have pursued complaints about any of these matters, the individuals involved have often been quite difficult to find, as they may not have supplied the city with a current business address. As a result, cities like Atlanta have had to assign additional police to taxi industry work, and have incurred other additional administrative expenses as well (Paratransit Services, 1983).

All of these events have left both the taxi industry and local officials responsible for regulating it in a somewhat confused and demoralized state. Much more is known about what does not work than about what does. Medallion systems have been discredited, and open entry appears also to have failed. On the other hand, fleets that employ and directly control their own labor forces are also largely a thing of the past. Thus cab drivers in the future, as in the present, are likely to be self-employed; but whether these self-employed drivers will be allowed to own their own cabs or will be required to rent their cabs from a fleet or a cooperative remains a much more difficult matter for local governments to decide.

It is nevertheless becoming increasingly difficult to justify policies that totally bar taxi cooperatives from any city's streets. Taxi cooperatives are currently operating in virtually every large American city in which local authorities permit these organizations to be formed. They are absent only from cities in which cooperatives are illegal, because local governments have granted monopolies to competing ownership forms. In recent years, these alternatives to cooperatives have suffered many setbacks, with the result that the prospects for cooperatives in the American taxi industry have dramatically improved.

CHAPTER 5

Group Practices In The Professions

The previous two chapters have dealt with worker-owned scavenger companies and taxi cooperatives. The present chapter will discuss an even more numerous population of workplaces in which ownership is routinely shared: the partnerships and incorporated group practices that are common in a wide range of professional fields. In such professions as law, medicine, and accounting, these forms of organization have long served as the standard models for practices of any significant size. In many cases, these organizations dominate their respective fields. In law, a list of the nation's two hundred or two hundred and fifty largest law firms is featured prominently in *The National Law Journal* every fall; all of these firms are partnerships or closely related organizational forms. They range in size from around twenty to more than two hundred partners each. In accounting, a mere handful of partnerships is even more dominant; known collectively as "The Big Eight" firms in their field, these firms have close to a thousand partners each (Stevens, 1981; Sammons, 1984).

Clearly, partnerships are common and play an important role in many professional fields. It may be more controversial to suggest, however, that these organizations deserve a place in a work that deals with worker-owned scavenger companies, taxi cooperatives, and other organizations that have stronger claims to be described as "employee-owned." I will nevertheless argue that these can indeed be viewed as employee-owned organizations, in at least the following two senses of this term. These are organizations, first of all, in which only individuals who work in the organization may participate in the ownership of the firm. That is, no outside stockholders or other absentee owners share in the ownership of these firms. This feature clearly differentiates professional partnerships from the conventional corporate form. Second, large professional partnerships are also all organizations in which ownership is widely shared. That is, instead of having one, two, or a handful of proprietors or partners, these organizations are owned

143

and controlled by large numbers of individuals from within their labor force. This clearly differentiates these partnerships from the conventional sole proprietorship or family-owned firm.

Thus large professional partnerships meet at least a modest definition of an employee-owned firm. It is typical for only a minority of their employees to be owners, but they are employee-owned nonetheless. This purely definitional fact would be of little interest, however, if it did not also carry some important additional implications as well.

These large partnerships and other professional group practices essentially provide us with an example of an economic sector in which employee-owned institutions are not the exception, but the rule. They are perhaps the most prominent instance in the American economy of organizations that want their employees to be owners not in response to tax incentives or other forms of external encouragement, but because this strikes them as the best way to organize a business in their fields. Thus a major theme of the present chapter will be an effort to understand why professional group practices are organized the way they are, and why they continually admit additional employees to the ranks of co-owners in thier firms. This discussion will also not ignore the fact that large numbers of employees have no chance at all to become owners in these firms; it will instead seek to explain both why certain categories of employees are offered opportunities to become owners in these firms, and why other employees are not. This analysis will thus hopefully provide some useful insights into both the vitality and the limitations of employee ownership in the American economy today.

In addition to these theoretical points, group practices in the professions offer a wealth of more immediately practical information as well. These organizations have been coping successfully for decades with many problems that newly-created employee-owned institutions have only begun to address. These problems include the issue of how income in an employee-owned organization can most fruitfully be shared; how expert, specialized management and democracy in the workplace can most effectively be reconciled; and how employee-owned institutions can be prevented from "degenerating" over time. Throughout the professions a great number of trade journals, management consultants, and knowledgeable individuals often prove to be virtual gold mines for information of this sort.

The internal operations of professional firms are so well documented, in fact, that I need to insert a few words here about the sources of information on which this chapter is based. Although I did conduct a small number of interviews in the early stages of this research, the most important outcome of those interviews was to steer me to the vast literature on these firms.

Thus most of the information reported in this chapter was obtained from published sources, rather than from interviews I conducted myself.

Of the professional fields that are dealt with in this chapter, the one whose group practices are perhaps best documented is the law. The literature on law firm management begins with such classic descriptions as Reginald Heber Smith's 1940 articles on Boston's Hale and Dorr, and Robert T. Swaine's history of New York's Cravath firm, published in 1948. By the 1970s, analytical articles on law firm organization had begun to appear regularly not only in bar association journals and in law reviews, but also in such newer and more specialized legal periodicals as *Law Office Economics and Management* and the *American Bar Foundation Research Journal*. Also in the 1970s, news of internal developments in particularly prominent firms began to be included regularly in such new journals as *The National Law Journal* and *The American Lawyer*. More recently, Steven Brill of *The American Lawyer* has begun publishing *The American Lawyer Guide to Leading Law Firms*, which provides a great deal of detailed information about the internal structures of the nation's most prominent firms.

This rich trade literature on law firm organization has also been supplemented by some quite informative journalistic, sociological, and fictional works. The journalistic sources include books by Joseph C. Goulden (1972), Paul Hoffman (1973, 1982), and James B. Stewart (1983). Valuable sociological contributions include Erwin O. Smigel's classic study of *The Wall Street Lawyer* (1969), and studies of the New York and Chicago bars conducted by Jerome Carlin (1966) and by John P. Heinz and Edward O. Laumann (1982), respectively. Last but not least, fictional works by Louis Auchincloss (*Powers of Attorney*, 1963, and *The Partners*, 1974) and by John Jay Osborn, Jr. (*The Associates*, 1979), have probably done as much as any of the preceding works to reveal the inner dynamics of the large law firm.

With regard to group practices in other professions, the sources are not quite this diverse, but most fields have trade literatures that provide information at least partially parallel to that available for the law. On the organization of collective practices in medicine, some particularly valuable sociological studies have been written by Eliot Freidson (1975, 1979), David Mechanic (1978, 1979), Paul Starr (1982), and Charles Derber (1983b). On the "Big Eight" accounting firms, the most useful sociological study I could find was that of Paul Montagna (1968); more current and quite insightful information about these firms appeared in Mark Stevens' journalistic work *The Big Eight* (1981), and in a recent article in *Inc.* (Sammons 1984). Group practices are also quite common in a number of other professions, including architecture, engineering, and management consulting, but to provide an exhaustive survey of the role of group practices in all the professions is beyond the scope of this work.

On the Origins of Group Practices in the Professions

Why do so many professionals work in partnerships or analogous organizational forms? This entire chapter will be relevant to answering this question in full; but a few of the most fundamental considerations will be briefly outlined here.

The predominance of employee-owned organizations in the professions originates in certain features of the work that professionals do. Professionals generally provide highly skilled and personalized services to individual clients. The nature of these services makes clients quite vulnerable to their practitioners in a number of ways—the problems that lead clients to consult a professional are commonly ones in which their health or fortunes are seriously at risk; these problems are also usually so complex and subtle that it is difficult for the client to tell good advice from bad; and in the course of rendering their services, professionals also frequently become privy to confidential information about their clients that could prove costly or embarrassing if divulged. For all of these reasons, clients are likely to welcome the involvement of organizations or other third parties that can help bring individual practitioners more effectively under control. Some of the same circumstances that make clients so vulnerable, however, also greatly limit the usefulness of conventional employment relationships for this task.

The first major disadvantage suffered by conventional employment relations in these fields is the inherent difficulty of supervising any professional's work. Supervision of professionals is difficult, even for other specialists in their fields, because a professional's recommendations in each instance must always be tailored to fit the idiosyncrasies of a particular case. In their classic article on information costs, the economists Alchian and Demsetz observed that "detailed direction in the preparation of a law case" would essentially require "that the monitor prepare the case himself" (1972:786). These authors also suggested that these problems in "metering" the work of professionals were largely responsible for the relative absence of conventional employment relations in these fields.

Conventional employment relations are handicapped in the professions in a number of other ways as well. In many occupations, conventional organizations derive much of their power over employees from the fact that employees have nowhere else to ply their trades. The professions, in contrast, are largely labor-intensive activities that place few barriers in the way of employees who wish to leave their current employers and create new businesses of their own. Medicine provides one important potential exception to this pattern, as the practice of medicine has become increasingly capital-intensive in recent years; Starr has noted, however, that the access doctors have to the medical equipment in their local community hospitals essentially safeguards their opportunity to form new practices of their own (1982:218). Given the highly personal nature of the relationship between professionals and their clients, departing professional employees are also capable of taking a significant portion of a firm's reputation and clientele away with them as they leave to strike out on their own.

For all of these reasons, conventional employment relationships have been quite slow to establish themselves in the professions, and self-employed practitioners have tended to predominate in these fields. These practitioners have sought to allay clients' concerns about their competence and discretion by creating licensing authorities that promise to prevent unqualified or unethical individuals from practicing their trades. The ethical standards that have been promulgated by these professional bodies have in turn erected additional barriers to the spread of conventional employment relations in thse fields. Until recently corporations were barred from most professions, on the grounds that the "commercialism" associated with incorporation was considered inconsistent with professional norms. Most professions have also sought to prevent their members from advertising or from competing on the basis of price; such policies have still further discouraged the formation of organizations in which small numbers of more aggressive professionals might have put many more of their less entrepreneurial colleagues to work.

Considerations such as these have made the professions safe havens for the self-employed. The question remains, however, whether professionals will choose to be individually or collectively self-employed. A number of factors have frequently caused at least some professionals to make the latter choice, and to practice their professions in partnership with other members of their fields.

Data from a number of fields suggest that professionals can often earn more money together than they can on their own. In dentistry, practitioners in partnerships report incomes almost one third higher than those in solo practice (American Dental Association, 1963:554, 1964:499). In law, national studies have repeatedly shown lawyers' incomes to increase uniformly with firm size (Blaustein and Porter, 1954:11; Weil and Roy, 1981:227); recent figures are shown in Table IV.

What produces these advantages of size? In some cases, employee-owned firms may be doing little more than capitalizing on conventional economies of scale. That is, employee ownership allows otherwise self-employed individuals to pool their resources, share overhead expenses, and gain some of the advantages that come from specialization, delegation, and a generally more rational division of labor. Such economies of scale have been particularly well documented for group medical practices (Graham, 1972; Lorant and Kimbell, 1976).

These economies of scale appear to have important limits, however, in at least some professional fields. In medicine, the income per physician peaks in practices consisting of between five and seven physicians, and decreases

Table IV. Lawyers' Receipts and Income by Size of Firm

Size of Firm	Gross Receipts per Lawyer	Average Income per Lawyer
2 to 6 Lawyers	$ 71,033	$37,568
7 to 11 Lawyers	83,678	50,816
12 to 19 Lawyers	91,200	55,912
20 to 39 Lawyers	102,036	63,203
40 or more Lawyers	111,910	68,204

Source: Weil and Roy, 1981:227

with further increases in size (Derber, 1983b:597; see also Newhouse, 1973). Starr has offered some interesting reasons as to why this should be so. Starr argues that some of the nation's oldest and largest group medical practices have developed in smaller cities where hospital facilities are limited, and a major function of collective practice is to enable doctors to afford to buy the latest medical equipment. In larger cities, this equipment is available in hospitals, and physicians in private practice have no need to shoulder these expenses themselves (Starr, 1982:212). Starr also notes that economies of scale in the professions are generally limited by the fact that occupational licensing laws make it unfeasible to assign nonprofessionals to do any por-tion of a professional's work (1982:206). Thus, in medicine, the most com-mon form of group practice is simply a small number of specialists who share a common office and take turns being on call for emergencies (Center for Research in Ambulatory Health Care Administration, 1976:12, 23–26). When group medical practices grow larger than this, their purpose may not be to reduce costs, but rather to make certain large or expensive equipment purchases affordable.

In other fields, organizations have also tended to grow large in order to meet the needs of their large clients. The legal and accounting professions provide the most outstanding examples of this. The legal profession has long been recognized as having a two-tiered structure, with solo attorneys addressing themselves to the legal needs of private individuals, and part-nerships serving the more complex needs of the business community (Laumann and Heinz, 1979). One survey of the legal profession conducted in 1972 found that sole proprietorships derived 71% of their receipts from individuals, and only 24% from business clients. Partnerships, in contrast, obtained half of their receipts from business clients (Bower, 1977). Firms large enough to take in more than a million dollars per year derived 71% of their receipts from businesses (see Table V).

Table V. Law Firm Incomes in 1972 by Size and Source of Receipts

| Size of Receipts | Source of Receipts: | | | |
	Individuals	Businesses	Governments	Other
Over $1,000,000	24%	71%	3%	2%
$500,000–$999,000	41	54	2	3
$300,000–$499,000	52	43	2	2
$100,000–$299,000	61	34	3	2
$50,000–$99,000	73	23	3	2
$30,000–$49,000	78	17	4	2
$20,000–$29,000	80	14	4	1
All Establishments	52	43	3	2

Source: Bower, 1977

Why do large clients require large law firms in order to meet their needs? Why do they not retain individual attorneys with the specific qualifications that they need on a one-by-one basis? The problem is that large clients commonly become involved in complex cases in which large sums of money are involved, and they therefore often put large numbers of attorneys to work on the very same case. If the client were to hire all of these attorneys one by one, numerous cumbersome transactions would be required, and it would be extremely difficult to sort out what each attorney had contributed to winning a given case, or to assign responsibility for mistakes. It is thus more preferable for the client to hire a group of attorneys *en masse* by retaining a firm whose attorneys accept collective responsibility for each other's behavior, and who can sort out among themselves what share each will be entitled to collect from the client's full fee. Leibowitz and Tollison also note that large clients are often willing to pay a premium to firms that have acquired particularly good reputations and that are known to screen labor inputs more effectively than any layman possibly could (1980:383).

The link between the size of professional partnerships and the size of their clients is even more pronounced in accounting than it is in law. Stevens notes that together, the Big Eight accounting firms audit ninety percent of all the corporations listed on the New York Stock Exchange, and adds that "This is their exclusive territory because they alone are big enough to serve it" (Stevens, 1981:7). To illustrate why large businesses require large accounting firms to audit them, Stevens gives the example of Deloitte Haskins & Sells, which uses fourteen hundred accountants to conduct its annual audit of the General Motors firm. Stevens comments that "Big business needs big auditors," and concludes that the Big Eight accounting firms have grown large in order to meet that need (Stevens, 1981:8).

Sharing Income in Professional Firms

Most major professional group practices are organized as partnerships, rather than corporations, because it was long held to be both unethical and illegal for corporations to practice in these fields. Since about 1960, many of these barriers to incorporation have gradually been removed, and many partnerships in fields like medicine and dentistry have converted themselves into corporations in order to take advantage of the tax and legal consequences associated with this form (Center for Research in Ambulatory Care Administration, 1976:13–15, 109–116; Schmedel, 1983). In law and accounting, however, group practices have been slower to incorporate, and the largest firms have been particularly reluctant to take this step. These firms appear to be concerned that if they were to give up the partnership for the corporate form, this might easily disturb the delicate relationships between the firms and their clients, and among the professionals within the firms (Beck, 1972a; Bodine, 1979). What some large firms have done instead has been to allow their partners to incorporate as individuals, but to retain the partnership form for the firm as a whole (Gerson and Berreby, 1981; see also Beck, 1981).

Whether group practices are organized as partnerships or corporations, perhaps the most complex issue that needs to be decided among them is how they will divide up the income of their firms. Unlike the scavenger companies, professional firms do not compensate their partners with fixed annual salaries, because firm incomes are too unpredictable from one year to the next. Unlike taxi cooperatives, on the other hand, group practices cannot solve this problem by simply allowing each member to keep all the income from business that he or she is personally involved in. Because a number of professionals often become involved in any given case in a wide variety of ways, deciding which of them deserves how large a portion of each piece of business is a complex matter to decide. So most professional group practices normally pool all of their income, deduct the firm's costs, and then divide the net income among the members in a tremendous variety of ways.

One sign of the great diversity of compensation arrangements in professional group practices emerged from a recent effort to gather statistics on this topic within the legal profession alone; the researcher subsequently reported that "I've got 25 responses to questionnaires on how firms share income, and each one is different" (Granelli, 1978:1). We are not entirely in ignorance about income division in the professions, however, because this is also an issue about which professionals frequently seek advice. A good deal of information about this topic is therefore now available in the trade journals of many of these fields. This is particularly true of the legal profession, which has produced a quite extensive literature on sharing income in recent years (see, for example, Hunt, 1970; Moldenhauer, 1971; Cantor, 1974, 1978; Orren, 1974; Granelli, 1978). A parallel but somewhat more modest literature offers advice on this topic to group practices in medical fields (Zirkle, 1972; Beck, 1972b; Beck and Kalogredis, 1977a, 1977b).

Within all the complexities of these arrangements for sharing income, a few general patterns stand out. The most important is that partners' compensation is largely a direct or indirect function of the hours they bill and the business they bring in. In some firms, partners' compensation may also be affected by their seniority, public service, or service to the firm; but while these criteria come and go, partners are virtually everywhere rewarded for the business they originate and for the billable hours they work.

Of these criteria, professional firms often seem most embarrassed about the credit they give partners for the business they bring in. There is a danger that public awareness of this practice might inject a note of commercialism into their image that they would rather not admit. The need to reward partners for the business they attract, however, reflects a fundamental fact of professional life (see Reed, 1983). If good business getters were not rewarded adequately for this service they perform for their firms, they might easily be tempted to take their clients elsewhere, causing a great loss of income for their firms. Thus firms may offer high incomes to partners who do little apparent work, but whose presence in the firm is crucial for the attraction or retention of particularly lucrative clients.

While criteria such as these provide the basic ingredients, firms have many choices as to how these criteria will be combined to determine each partner's relative share of the income of the firm. Both in law and medicine, the trade literature on compensation describes a basic choice between "formula" and "percentage" systems for dividing the income of a firm. In formula systems, individual partners are rewarded for each specific contribution that they make to the firm. In the classic "Hale and Dorr" formula system described by Reginald Heber Smith in 1940, each partner's income was determined by assigning a weight of "6" to all the work that he did, a weight of "3" to all the business he brought in, and a weight of "1" to a factor that reflected the relative profitability of all this work (Smith, 1940). Such formula systems are also sometimes referred to as "point systems" or "productivity division."

In nonformula or percentage systems, each partner receives a simple, fixed percentage of the firm's total income determined before the year begins. Although superficially quite different from formula systems, percentage division is in many ways similar to them in practice. In determining any partner's percentage, for example, the most important criteria will normally continue to be the business partners' bill and the clients they attract.

An additional source of diversity in compensation systems among professional firms is that many firms do not rely solely on either formula or percentage systems for dividing up their incomes, but instead try to combine the two. Many firms use calculations based on formulas as tools for negotiating their fixed percentages (Cantor, 1978). Other firms divide one portion of their incomes by formulas, and another portion by percentages (see, for example, the "Preti" formula described in Moldenhauer, 1971).

There is one other aspect of income division in group practices that is worthy of note. This is the way that capital is accounted for within these firms. Although the professions are generally labor-intensive occupations, it is often the case that some or all of the members will have contributed some form of capital to the firm. In medical groups, some or all of the doctors may own the medical equipment that is used in their practice. In many law practices and accounting firms, it is often customary for newly made partners to be required to contribute "working capital" to their firms. New partners who make these contributions are often said to be "buying in" to their firms.

In most cases, however, these working capital contributions are relatively modest, in that they rarely amount to more than a fraction of the annual compensation of a partner in these firms. These capital contributions are also not usually allowed to become a major factor in dividing the profits of a firm. Group practices often go to quite elaborate lengths, in fact, to prevent members' capital contributions from interfering with the organizations' intention to divide up firm income solely on the basis of members' professional contributions to the firm. In many firms, members' capital contributions are carefully calculated so that an individual's relative share of the working capital fund will be closely commensurate with the share of firm income that he or she is slated to receive (Boughner, 1962: 237; Gibson, 1968:39; Stevens, 1981:31). In the Big Eight accounting firms, these capital contributions do not even earn interest, and are simply refunded to partners when they retire (Stevens, 1981:32). In some law partnerships and many medical groups, members' capital accounts earn income, but these interest or rental charges are treated as costs to the group practice and are accounted for separately before the professionals' net income is divided up (Gibson, 1968:39; Cantor, 1978:6; Starr, 1982:213).

Professional Partnerships as Communities

Judging solely from the ways in which they divide up their incomes, it would be easy to view professional partnerships as mere aggregations of rationally calculating, profit-maximizing individuals; but these organizations are a good deal more than this. Professional partnerships also typically engage in a variety of efforts designed to encourage partners to be loyal to and respectful of the traditions of their firms, and to be responsive to the needs of their profession and the community as well.

A common focus for group loyalties and traditions in many professional firms is the respect they show for founders and other major figures from the history of their firms. Imposing oil portraits of many of these giants can often be seen hanging in reception areas, firm libraries, or rooms in which important meetings are held. The names of these pioneers are also commonly commemorated in the names of their firms. In the early years of a professional partnership, it is common for the name of the firm to change as prominent individuals are added to or depart from the circle of major partners in the firm. Over time, however, firm names have a tendency to stabilize, even though most or all of these "name partners" are now dead. This stabilization in the name of a firm appears to symbolize the fact that the firm has become an institution whose existence is at least partially independent of the individuals who may or may not be working in it at any given time.

New generations of professionals are also taught respect for their firms' traditions through the process by which they become partners in their firms. Professional partnerships tend to recruit new members by hiring them as salaried "associates" directly as they graduate from professional schools. Partnerships in law and in a number of other fields also maintain "up-or-out" policies that require associates to leave their firms if they cannot become a partner within a period of from five to seven, or at most ten years. These "up-or-out" policies essentially define associates as partners-in-training, rather than as hired employees. Most associates also appear to understand that their chances of becoming a partner will depend at least in part on their ability to adapt themselves to the traditions, public image, and social climate of their firms.

What are the values that professional firms try so hard to encourage their members to uphold? There are differences from firm to firm in each profession and between professions as well, but a few themes seem to cut across both firm and professional lines. The values of these firms are the same as those of the professions themselves, but carried one step further. In fields like accounting and the law, the large partnerships seek to be the elite of their professions, to be the best and the brightest, the most competent and hardest working, the most scrupulously ethical, and the most generous in their support of the profession and the community at large. Thus they encourage their members not only to work tirelessly on behalf of their clients, but also to be leaders of their profession, to make themselves available for public service, to serve on the boards of the best charities, and to belong to the best clubs.

It is hard to know what to make of the aspirations of these large partnerships to embody the highest standards of professionalism in their fields. Satow (1975) takes their ideals at face value, and argues that these organizations provide the most outstanding example of "value-rational authority" in modern economic life. I find it hard to resist the temptation to debunk these ethical pretensions, since they are clearly so deeply rooted in the material interests of these firms. Partners are encouraged to engage in public service and sit on the boards of prestigious charities not simply for the public good, but more importantly because this is one of the best ways to drum up new business for their firms. More generally, these firms project an image of moral and professional excellence because such reputations are the primary mechanisms with which they attract and hold an elite clientele to their firms.

Although their values are thus self-serving, there is also ample evidence that they have real effects on the behavior of the professionals who work in these large firms. In his survey of lawyers' ethics in New York, Carlin found that many common breaches of ethics do appear to occur less frequently in large firms than among attorneys who practice on their own (Carlin, 1966). One major reason why large firms have been able to achieve this superior record is that these firms maintain a policy of turning away any business that has the potential to bring unfavorable publicity to the firm. Thus they prefer to refer divorce or criminal cases to other attorneys, even when these cases involve some of the most important clients of the firm. Such practices led Everett C. Hughes to conclude that there is a "moral division of labor" within the legal profession, in which the large corporate law firms reserve the most prestigious (and lucrative) clients and cases for themselves, while delegating the moral "dirty work" to less fastidious firms (Hughes, 1971:306).

There are also signs that the large firms' emphasis on high professional standards is not just for public consumption, but also has some important internal effects. Magali Sarfatti Larson has noted that professionals in general have a tendency to be taken in by their own propaganda, and to become prisoners of an ideology that requires them to be dedicated to their work (Larson, 1977; see also Derber, 1983a, 1983b). Professionals in large partnerships certainly press themselves hard, and many complain that their jobs force them to work longer hours than they would prefer to, if they thought they had a choice. Gareth Jones (1983) has also argued that professional partnerships depend heavily on their value systems, traditions, and long periods of socialization in order to coordinate the efforts of a labor force that might otherwise prove impossible to control. Jones notes that the shared values and loyalties uniting the professionals in these firms not only make them more conscientious in their work, but also discourage them from leaving the firm and taking important clients with them when they go.

The dependence of group practices on external respectability and on internal consensus have had similar effects on the kind of personnel that they like to recruit. Both traditionally led them to prefer white Protestant males from elite social and educational backgrounds. Such policies helped to sustain the image of these organizations as elite professional firms, and also increased the likelihood that new recruits would "fit in" socially with clients and with the professionals already working in these firms.

For many years the most prominent victims of these preferences were Catholic and Jewish males. In the legal profession, individuals with these backgrounds were generally excluded from the large prestigious firms, and have instead made up a disproportionate share of the attorneys who practice on their own (Ladinsky, 1963; Carlin, 1966; Heinz and Laumann, 1982). In some cases, Jewish and Catholic attorneys overcame these barriers by forming group practices of their own, and building up a clientele from within their own ethnic groups. By the 1960s, some Jews and Catholics had also begun to gain admittance to many of the traditionally Protestant firms; complaints persisted, however, that associates with these backgrounds had less chance to become partners than those whose backgrounds more closely matched the traditional preferences of the firm (Carlin, 1966; Hoffman, 1982:203–207).

In the 1970s, new assaults on the recruitment practices of the large law firms were launched by women and blacks. In several cases, female job candidates successfully pressed charges of sex discrimination against some of the nation's most elite law firms (Epstein, 1981:184–188, 195–196; Hoffman, 1982:209–212). These prominent cases caused a notable change in hiring practices throughout the legal profession, and many firms have at times appeared to go out of their way to attract women and minority job candidates (Epstein, 1981; Segal, 1983). While women and blacks thus now have a foot in the door in many major firms, concerns remain that they will find it more difficult to become a partner than the white males with whom they compete. Cynthia Fuchs Epstein notes that women attorneys on Wall Street are reputed to be less successful than males in attracting business to their firms; given the importance of this criterion in most firms, this reputation could make it difficult for women attorneys ever to play more than a mere token role in most large law firms (Epstein, 1981: 205–206).

Decision Making in Professional Firms

The political life of many professional firms is active, to say the least. In law, it is common for all the attorneys in a firm to meet together once a week (Burke *et al.*, 1978). In addition to these firm-wide meetings, there are also less frequent meetings reserved for partners or shareholders alone, plus committee meetings, departmental meetings, and meetings that bring together all the attorneys working on the same case.

What is the purpose of all of these meetings? Given that attorneys' time is so valuable to their firms, it seems unlikely that so many meetings would be held if they did not produce important benefits for their firms. According to the trade literature on this topic, the most prominent goal of most of these meetings is to allow information to be exchanged (Burke *et al.*, 1978; McLendon, 1978). Much of the time at firm-wide meetings is spent discussing the details of each potential new case. These discussions are time-consuming, but they serve two purposes at once: (1) they invite all attorneys present to pool their expertise in finding the most promising strategy for winning the case; and (2) they protect the firm against the embarassment of inadvertently attempting to represent both sides in the very same case. Other topics discussed at firm-wide meeting include recent changes in the law, newly established contacts that may lead to future business for the firm, plus various matters of firm management and personnel.

Although frequent meetings thus meet an important informational need, the literature on firm meetings also acknowledges that they serve other purposes as well. Several sources appear to agree that frequent firm meetings are good for morale — they help weld the organization into a unit and provide an arena for airing and smoothing out differences between individual professionals and the firm. A managing partner in one law firm notes that firm meetings help develop an "esprit de corps" among the professional personnel (Burke *et al.*, 1978:8). An article in an osteopathic journal observes that professionals are too jealous of their independence to work for long where they are denied a voice in the management of the firm (Zirkle, 1970:1054). Reginald Heber Smith was perhaps most explicit in ascribing to his firm's meetings a cooptative use. He wrote in 1940 of Boston's Hale and Dorr that

> . . . the few disciplinary rules we have, have been adopted by the men themselves after discussion and vote. It is a very poor sport who will not comply with a rule of his owning making (Smith, 1940:16).

Although group practices are generally careful to allow their professional personnel to have a voice, some voices speak much more loudly than others within this set of firms. Many key decisions are not made by the entire professional staff, but are usually reserved for partners alone. This includes such major matters as hiring, firing, job assignments, and compensation. Among the partners, authority for making many of these decisions is frequently delegated to a managing partner, executive committee, or more specialized committees of various types.

It is thus said of many professional firms that despite their democratic structures, much of the actual decision-making power within them is concentrated in a small number of hands. Managing partners and executive committee members tend to acquire many of the same political advantages enjoyed by managers in other types of firms, including patronage, access to confidential information, and constantly accumulating experience and expertise. Added to these familiar advantages are certain other assets more unique to the politics of professional firms. For example, managing partners tend to be recruited from among and/or to govern in close association with the most senior and prestigious professionals in their firm. Firm founders and name partners, if still active in the firm, are included within this governing circle, and add luster to its ranks.

In coping with the political power of the ruling circles of their firms, rank-and-file partners have some important assets of their own. One of these is their vote. Even in organizations as large and as centralized as the Big Eight accounting firms, rank-and-file partners have the power to give their leaders some nasty electoral shocks. Stevens describes major "partner revolts" that occurred in two of the Big Eight accounting firms in 1979 (Stevens, 1981:33–36, 61). One case involved Peat, Marwick, and Mitchell, whose partners rejected their outgoing chairman's handpicked choice of a successor in what was later described as the "Battle of Boca Raton" (Stevens 1981:33–36). After this defeat, the outgoing chairman later acknowledged that "We are a partnership, and there are one thousand and forty-four persons who have the vote" (Stevens, 1981: 35).

In some firms, the voting power of rank-and-file partners is limited by constitutions in which many matters are not submitted to the members for votes, or in which partners' voting power is weighted by their proportionate shares in the income of the firm. Even then, however, rank-and-file partners have important sources of informal power. Like professionals everywhere, low-ranking professionals in these group practices often derive a good deal of *de facto* power merely from what they know and who they know (Miller, 1980; Blau and Alba, 1982). In these firms, disgruntled professionals always have the power to leave their firms, taking their knowledge and possibly some of their clients with them when they go.

One illustration of the potential for low-ranking professionals to influence the policies of a group practice in which they hold little formal power was reported in the *National Law Journal* in 1979. The story involved five junior partners and three associates who had left a major Chicago law firm to establish a new practice of their own. The attorneys had decided to leave the firm largely out of disaffection with "the secretive fashion in which the firm was run." The firm's managing partners had refused to release figures on the billable hours each attorney had put in, thereby fueling suspicions that junior partners and associates were doing the lion's share of the work without being adequately paid. The departure of the eight attorneys hurt the firm badly, not only because it brought the firm bad publicity, but also because the departing attorneys took away some clients as they left. Although it was too late to keep those eight attorneys from leaving the firm, the firm announced that in the future, figures on the billable hours worked by each partner would be made public throughout the firm (Margolick, 1979).

On a more routine basis, revolts and splits like these do not normally occur, because most firms' decision-making procedures work tolerably well. In Hirschman's terminology, professionals in most of these organizations choose not to "exit," because they are "loyal" to the organization and therefore chose to take advantage of their opportunity to exercise "voice" instead (Hirschman, 1970). Reginald Heber Smith also noted that the relative success of democratic decision making within these organizations should not be viewed as a surprise. Smith wrote in 1940 that

. . . if democracy cannot be trusted to work among a small group of well-educated men who are bound together by a community of interest, it is hard to see how it can work anywhere (Smith, 1940:16).

Partnership and the Nature of Work

This chapter has already had many occasions to refer to various links between the organization of group practices and the work that professionals do. It has been hard to look for very long at any aspect of the operation of these group practices without perceiving the persistent influence of some unique features of the work performed within them. Thus, I have already argued that conventional organizations are largely absent from these fields because they are ill-suited to controlling professional work. The way group practices share income, socialize their members, and make decisions, are all related to the difficulty of controlling this work. The present section will attempt to bring some of these diverse points together, and arrive at a more general perspective on how the structure of professional organizations is related to the nature of professional work.

The preceding three sections have hopefully made it fairly easy to see how the organization of group practices helps to motivate partners in the course of their work. Being a partner or shareholder in these organizations simultaneously confers a share in the profits, full membership in an occupational community, and a voice in the organization's affairs. All of these benefits of partnership, however, are mediated by the value of a partner's contributions to the firm. If a partner works long hours and brings lots of business into the firm, he or she will gain simultaneously a higher income, the respect of peers, and a more influential voice in the councils of the firm. If a partner's productivity is low, that partner will have a lower income, will receive less respect, and his or her views will also have less impact on the governance of the firm. It is hard to imagine a system of shared ownership more single-mindedly calculated toward motivating co-owners to maximize their efforts on the organization's behalf.

In these organizations, ownership motivates not only the partners or shareholders, but their hired associates as well. This effect is particularly encouraged by the "up-or-out" policies that apply to associates in so many of these firms. As a result of these policies, these firms have few permanent associates who work for salaries alone, and most associates seek avidly to become partners, both in order to obtain the rewards that go with this rank, and because this is their only way to keep their jobs.

Associates are also generally made aware that their chances to be made partners will be based upon the same criteria that partners are rewarded for. One article on law office management recommended that the following wording should appear in the employment contract of every young associate:

Your opportunity to become a partner of our firm will be based entirely upon your progress as a lawyer and your ability to establish the standing and contacts which create a personal following of clients. In the event you have not established your capacity for partnership when you have served us for three or four years, that fact will be communicated to you, and you will be permitted to seek employment elsewhere (Reisner, 1978:12).

When associates respond successfully to this challenge by working hard, learning their trade, and taking good care of clients, then conferring partnerships upon them not only becomes a reward that they will feel that they deserve, but also becomes increasingly necessary to protect the interests of the firm. This is because associates who learn the appropriate job skills and gain the confidence of their clients thereby acquire assets that their firm will be increasingly reluctant to lose. Rather than allowing those skills and contacts to be taken out of the firm, these organizations make their proven associates partners and thereby discourage them from leaving the firm.

Some valuable insights into these uses of shared ownership to control professionals' work can be obtained with the aid of a typology of employment relationships recently offered by Oliver Williamson (1981). Williamson generated a total of four alternative employment relationships by crossing two dichotomous variables: the presence or absence of site-specific "human assets," and the ease or difficulty of "metering" or supervising the performance of employees. When Williamson's two dichotomous variables are crossed, a total of four possible situations result. Williamson argues that a characteristic set of employment relationships is associated with each of these four combinations (see Table VI). When human asset specificity is absent and metering is not difficult, a "spot market" for labor is what typically results. That is, labor is hired only as the need for it arises, typically on an hourly or daily basis, and no special effort is made to tie the worker's interests to the interests of the firm. When metering of individual performance is difficult, but learning by doing is not involved, the typical result is

Table VI. Williamson's Typology of Employment Relationships

Difficulty of Metering \ Human Assets	Nonspecific	Highly Specific
Easy	Spot Market	Obligational Market
Difficult	Primitive Team	Relational Team

Source: Williamson, 1981:566

what Williamson follows Alchian and Demetz in calling a "primitive team." When human assets are significant, but metering is not difficult, Williamson predicts that an "obligational market" will result. That is, the firm will offer nonvested retirement benefits, job security, returns to seniority, and other inducements for experienced employees to stay on. Finally, when both human assets are present, and metering is difficult, a firm will strive to establish a "relational team." Williamson describes this last employment situation as one in which "the firm . . . will engage in considerable social conditioning, to help assure that employees understand and are dedicated to the purposes of the firm, and employees will be provided with considerable job security, which gives them assurance against exploitation" (Williamson, 1981, p. 565).

It is not clear from Williamson's discussion how widespread these relational teams are supposed to be. Williamson notes that relational teams "are very difficult to develop and it is uncertain how widespread or sustainable they are" (Williamson, 1981b, p. 565). Following Ouchi (1980), the only examples of relational teams that Williamson himself could offer were "some of the Japanese corporations" and "certain utopian societies," and Williamson had misgivings even about these. Thus Williamson leaves us in doubt as to whether any "relational teams" can be found in the American economy at all.

It may very well be that these group practices in the professions provide some of the best contemporary American examples of Williamson's "relational teams." Their structures are designed to create the strongest possible bond between the individual and his firm; and the conditions that give rise to them appear in many ways similar to those that Williamson uses to predict the occurrence of relational teams. The difficulty of metering the work of professionals has already been commented on. These firms also encounter human asset problems of an unusual type. To label these firms as relational teams, however, requires a slight extension of Williamson's discussion of the forms of human asset specificity that have an impact on the choice of governance structures for a firm.

For Williamson, the most typical instance of human asset specificity is the knowledge that an experienced employee has acquired about his or her own unique job. Such knowledge is both employee-specific, because it is locked inside an individual employee's head, and firm-specific, because it is a form of knowledge that would be of less value in any other organization than in the one in which it was acquired. Williamson contrasts these specific skills to the general skills of doctors and lawyers, which although they are formidable are also widely distributed within their fields. As has already been noted, however, professionals also acquire certain quite important employee-specific assets in the course of their work, such as their personal ties to clients, their knowledge of particular cases and procedures, and their experience in specialized aspects of their fields. These assets are often employee-specific, but not firm-specific; and it is precisely because employees can so easily take their clients, reputations, and experience elsewhere that the structures of their firms must include incentives that discourage turnover and weave seasoned employees into the very fabric of the firm. The importance of these human assets is further enhanced by the relative insignificance of capital in these fields; thus employees in these fields are owners, because their employee-specific assets are the most important assets of their firms.

Several authors who have recently sought to account for the prevalence of partnerships in the professions have independently seen some combination of metering difficulties and human asset considerations as the most important determinants of the unique structures of these firms. Jones (1983), for example, sees interaction between metering problems and mobility of labor as most responsible for the genesis of partnerships in professional fields. He argues that because metering in these fields is difficult, differences in quality among employees reveal themselves only over rather long periods of time; but since professional skills are transferable to other firms, employees may be tempted to leave their firms before differences in quality among them can be sufficiently made known. Partnerships are therefore likely to develop, as these structures discourage turnover and promote collective efforts to monitor and socialize the labor force (1983: 463–464). Dealing solely with the origins of partnerships in the law, Nelson (1981) calls attention to the autonomy of professional work and to the personal ties between lawyers and their clients—especially because of the latter, he observed, "lawyers are less dependent on their firm than they otherwise would be" (1981:127–128). In his discussion of the development of group practices in medicine, Starr (1982) notes how difficult it is for third parties to supervise and motivate a physician's work (p. 206), but also lays special emphasis on the doctor-patient tie. His remarks are sufficiently relevant that they are worth quoting at length:

> The physician had a resource that the ordinary worker lacked. Patients develop a personal relation with their physicians even when medical care takes place in a hospital or clinic . . . . If, as often happened in group practice, the doctor threatened to leave, he might take his patients with him. This was the problem the group practices faced in dealing with their discontented young physicians. The older doctors might have brought capital to the enterprise in the beginning, but the younger doctors accumulated a kind of capital in the process of serving patients. They acquired reputations, devoted patients, and skill and experience. To substitute another physician, even if he were equally competent, might not succeed in holding the first physician's patients. . . . The younger physicians generally had to be given a share in the partnership because they had the alternative of individual practice and, by virtue of their relations with patients, had acquired some of the group's capital (Starr, 1982:217).

Williamson's variables also help to explain who does not get included in the ownership of professional group practices as well as who does. Secretaries and paraprofessionals make important contributions to the success of their firms, but their work does not present the kinds of governance problems that cause professional employees to be incorporated into the ownership of these firms. Thus, although professional offices depend heavily on typing skills, the work of typists is sufficiently commodified and easy to supervise that these services are readily obtainable through a spot market. Other office skills are more firm-specific, but metering them is less problematic, so they can be dealt with via a conventional obligational market, rather than by including office employees in the ownership of the firm. Inclusion of nonprofessional employees in professional partnerships would also be prohibited on occupational licensing grounds, as this could be viewed as permitting unlicensed individuals to practice these professions; but this prohibition is not the most important reason why this is not done. Professional firms are not tempted to share ownership with their nonprofessional employees in the first place, because they have no need to use ownership to govern their work.

These same considerations also help explain why the mix of partners and associates varies from firm to firm and from one profession to another. The ratio of associates to partners is much higher in the Big Eight accounting firms than it is in large law firms. Within the Big Eight, associate-to-partner ratios range from a low of 5 to 1 at Touche Ross to a high of more than 10 to 1 at Arthur Andersen and Price Waterhouse; the most typical ratio appears to be 7 to 1 (calculated from figures that appear in Sammons, 1984:82). In large corporate law firms, these ratios are frequently below one, and rarely climb higher than 3 to 1. The cause of this difference appears to lie in the fact that both the marketing and actual conduct of major corporate audits are much more centralized activities than the ebb and flow of case work in the law. This is not true of Big Eight tax work, which Stevens describes as a "partner intensive" activity (1981:147); but when 1400 auditors work together on an audit of General Motors, most of them are engaged in quite standardized activities, and there is little danger that any handful of associates will be able to steal their client away from their firm. Here is how Stevens describes the work involved in an audit of a typical Big Eight client:

> As in most practice areas, the great bulk of the audit is performed by staff accountants. These underlings — most of whom are green recruits a year or two out of college — do 90 percent of the interminable grunt work that goes into an audit. Their days are spent much like those of the squinty-eyed bookkeepers in Dickens' novels — the old handwritten ledgers replaced by computer printouts. Pouring over reports, checking and rechecking calculations, they are near robots, forced to adhere to an exacting audit plan and to perform a long list of set chores (Stevens, 1981:77).

Since the Big Eight firms have so many more associates than partners, most of their associates also realize that they have little prospect of becoming a partner, and are instead motivated largely by their salaries and by the unique professional training that their jobs provide.

Similar distinctions appear among large firms within the legal profession itself. Associate-to-partner ratios have traditionally been highest in the large law practices of New York. In 1983, associate-to-partner ratios in the 44 largest New York firms averaged 2.3 per firm, while the comparable figure for the 204 largest traditional practices located outside New York was 1.4 (calculated from figures published in the *National Law Journal* September 19, 1983; excludes legal clinics). Apparently, the New York firms are able to make more use of associates because they are the nation's most prestigious firms, have a generally loyal clientele, and include many nationally prominent attorneys among their senior personnel (Hoffman, 1973, 1982, and Stewart, 1983). There are thus significantly fewer opportunities for associates to interpose themselves between the organization and its clients in these firms than in those outside New York.

These higher associate-to-partner ratios in the New York firms also appear to be associated with different strategies for controlling associates' work. Associates in New York firms have less chance to become a partner than those in other cities, but they are also much better paid. In 1983, salaries of new associates in the 44 largest New York firms averaged $43,600, versus $34,400 for the 204 largest firms elsewhere. In recruiting associates, the New York firms like to emphasize not only the chance to become a partner and the high salaries they pay, but also the unique training their jobs provide (Swaine, 1948, excerpted in Stewart, 1983:367–375). It is also said that many of these firms make it a point to isolate their associates from meaningful client contact by not allowing them to sign letters to clients and permitting them to meet with or telephone clients only in the presence of a partner. Stewart quotes an associate in one New York firm who said of such practices that "they were afraid that the clients would develop an attachment to some of the associates who did most of their work. Then if the associate didn't make partner . . . and left to go elsewhere, the client might leave too" (Stewart, 1983:313). It would be a mistake, of course, to think that these fears and these precautionary measures occur only in New York firms; but they are particularly likely when associates have little chance of making partner in their firms.

Do Group Practices in the Professions Degenerate over Time?

A recurrent theme in previous chapters has been the persistent tendency for employee-owned workplaces to degenerate over time. Does this same tendency show up in the professions as well?

Interestingly, some of the economic forces that have appeared most responsible for the degeneration of other employee-owned firms are either absent or at least partially neutralized in these firms. Capital plays only a minimal role in these firms, and insofar as it is involved it is usually accounted for in ways that prevent it from affecting the internal structure of a firm. The way group practices share income provides at least a partial solution to Ben-Ner's problem as well. That is, the arrangements for dividing income among partners make it unnecessary for members to use hired labor in order to profit from the labor of other professionals in their firms. Even if other partners do the work on a case that a given partner has brought in, the partner who initially attracted this business is assured of getting a share.

While partners can thus make plenty of money from each other's work, they can make even more money by using associates, since associates' salaries are far lower than what most partners are paid. Among watchers of the legal profession, in fact, it is a popular passtime to try to calculate just how much profit the large partnerships are making from each associate they employ (Hoffman, 1973:128–129, 1982:197–200; Stewart, 1983:376–377). This awareness that associates are highly profitable also fuels speculation that major law firms have tendencies to increase their associate-to-partner ratios over time, and to lengthen the probationary periods that associates must pass through before they are made partners. In the late 1970s and early 1980s, such speculation had a strong basis in fact. Between 1975 and 1979, the ratio of associates to partners in the *National Law Journal's* listing of the 200 largest law firms increased by more than 50% (calculated from data reported in Lavine, 1979:1). In the early 1980s, various reports also began to suggest that many firms were stretching the number of years required for associates to become partners, and were inviting some associates with long service to become permanent associates instead of partners (Burke, 1981; Galante, 1983).

While this trend seems clear enough, it is not easy to determine whether it reflects a long-term change in law firm structure, or is merely the result of a variety of short-term trends. As has already been indicated, the choice of whether or not to make an associate a partner is not a simple function of organizational policy, but is also affected by the individual associate's career progress and his or her bargaining power vis-a-vis the firm. In the 1970s, unprecedented numbers of young attorneys were graduating from the nation's law schools, and the major law practices hired many of them, because thanks to the so-called "litigation explosion," large numbers of their clients were being sued. This influx of fresh law graduates into the large law firms was in itself responsible for a significant short-term increase in the ratio of associates to partners in these firms. By the end of the decade, moreover, the economy was in recession, and many firms claimed that they were becoming slower to make associates partners as a means of coping with this slump (Lavine, 1979:1). If the associates had been in a better bargaining position, the large firms might have had to find some other way to respond to the business decline; but with the economy in recession, and so many young attorneys already in private practice, this was not a good time for associates to start practices of their own.

It remains to be seen whether these recent increases in the ratio of associates to partners reflect a permanent change, or will be reversed when prosperity returns and the glut of young attorneys from the "baby boom" generation has finally been absorbed. Some historical materials on large law partnerships suggest that associate-to-partner ratios have been subject to similar fluctuations before, but have tended not to stray far from their levels of recent years. In his history of the Cravath firm, Robert Swaine noted that the period of time required for an associate to make partner lengthened in some cases to well over ten years under the impact of the Depression and World War II (Stewart, 1983:371). Nevertheless, when Smigel studied Wall Street lawyers in 1957, the partners he interviewed had spent an average of 8.5 years as associates (Smigel, 1969:93), and associate-to-partner ratios ranged between two and three in all but one of New York's twenty largest firms (1969:34–35). These figures are not very different from those that apply to this same group of firms today.

If time itself is not necessarily harmful to the institutions of the nation's major law firms, another threat may have been created by their recent dramatic growth. Nelson notes that in the epilogue to Smigel's revised edition of *The Wall Street Lawyer* that appeared in 1969, Smigel could identify only 20 law firms in the nation with more than 100 lawyers per firm (Smigel, 1969:359; Nelson, 1981:97–98). By 1983, however, 183 law firms exceeded that size, and 18 law firms had more than 200 attorneys per firm (*National Law Journal*, September 19, 1983). Several firms were a good deal larger than this; biggest of all was Baker & McKenzie, with 658 lawyers in 1983. Baker & McKenzie was not only the largest, but also one of the most rapidly growing law firms, as it had included only 27 attorneys in 1960, and 116 in 1970 (Nelson, 1981:105).

Firms like Baker & McKenzie had grown in two ways at once. They had both increased the size of their home office, and opened branch offices in other major cities as well. Multistate law firms are something that the American Bar Association traditionally had frowned on, but in 1970 it reversed itself and gave these organizations a green light (Travostino, 1980). Since that time, many firms have rushed to open branch offices in Washington, New York, and other major cities, and other multistate law firms have been created through mergers among firms. By 1983, 207 of the nation's 248 largest law firms had offices in more than one city, and firms with branch offices had an average of three branches per firm (calculated from figures published in the *National Law Journal*, September 19, 1983; excludes legal clinics).

The dramatic growth of multistate law firms has led to a great deal of speculation over whether the legal profession is now following a path taken earlier by the accounting profession, and is now on the verge of giving rise to its own "Big Eight" (Iezzi, 1981; Nelson, 1981:131–132). Insofar as their internal structures are concerned, however, the new giants of the legal professional remain quite distinct from accounting's "Big Eight." Among the nation's two hundred and fifty largest law firms in 1983, for example, associate-to-partner ratios for firms with more than one hundred partners were not higher, but lower, than those for firms with less (see Table VII).

Why do the structures of the large new multistate law firms not look more like those of the Big Eight firms in accounting? First, it shold be noted that even the largest of today's law firms remain closer in size to the traditional corporate law firm than they do to accounting's Big Eight. Big Eight accounting firms employ between 5,000 and 12,000 professionals per firm (Sammons, 1984); the largest law firms are now barely approaching a mere tenth of those figures. More significantly, size appears to be far less important in determining the structures of group practices than the nature of the services a practice offers and the way those services are marketed to clients.

This last point is particularly well illustrated by a recent innovation in the marketing of professional services that has indeed had a major impact on the structure of some large professional firms. This was a 1977 Supreme Court decision that made it permissible for professionals to advertise their services. So far, the established group practices that cater to a corporate clientele have been reluctant to take advantage of this opportunity, out of fear that advertizing would offend their traditional clients. A new type of professional practice, however, has recently begun to use advertising to reach a wholly new clientele. In the law, such new "legal clinics" as Hyatt

Table VII. Associate-to-Partner Ratios in the 248 Largest Law Firms, 1983*

Firm Size by Number of Partners	Number of Firms	Branch Offices Per Firm	Average Ratio of Associates to Partners
100 or more	19	6.0	1.44
50 to 99	122	2.6	1.49
Less than 50	107	1.7	1.61
All Firms	248	2.5	1.54

*Based on figures that appeared in the *National Law Journal*, September 19, 1983. Excludes the Hyatt Legal Services and Jacoby & Meyers legal clinics, which are discussed separately in the text.

Legal Services and Jacoby & Meyers have relied heavily on advertising to provide low-cost legal assistance to individuals who in many cases had never consulted an attorney before (see Harper, 1982).

It appears that building a practice through advertising creates an entirely different ownership structure within a firm. In these organizations, whoever controls the advertizing controls the clientele, and there is no need for the professionals who actually see clients to be included in the ownership of the firm. Thus Hyatt Legal Services has only 4 partners, and its remaining 270 attorneys are listed as salaried associates of the firm. Jacoby & Meyers, similarly, has only 3 partners, and employs 132 attorneys as associates (*National Law Journal*, September 19, 1983).

The example provided by these new organizations is clearly instructive, but it probably has little to tell us about the future of the more traditional professional firms. These legal clinics do not represent the degeneration of an established organizational form, but rather the creation of entirely new organizations to serve a completely different market. As for the older group practices themselves, they look remarkably unchanged, despite their recent flurry of growth. Thus these group practices in the profession are not only the largest and most successful employee-owned organizations in the United States today, but are probably the most stable as well.

CHAPTER 6

Sharing Ownership In
The Services

The three preceding chapters have described a diverse range of organizations that are at least to some extent employee-owned. This chapter will now attempt to make comparisons across all three of these populations of organizations, in order to see what lessons can be derived from looking at them together, rather than one by one.

To clarify what I hope to gain from these comparisons, it may help to explain how all these studies came to be done. I began studying the scavenger companies at the invitation of Stewart Perry, as has already been discussed. When that research was finished, what I most wanted to know was whether the scavengers had been just a one-time fluke, or were part of a more general phenomenon. So I then went searching for other organizations to compare the scavengers to.

In this search for comparable cases, I had two criteria primarily in mind. First, I wanted populations of organizations that were numerous, because I feared that if employee-owned organizations came only in handfuls, then they might not be worth studying at all. Secondly, I wanted to find organizations that were old. The experience of the scavengers had clearly demonstrated many of the most common tendencies that cause employee-owned workplaces to degenerate over time, but it had also shown that these tendencies can in many cases be held in check. Finding other such organizations that had long histories would provide additional opportunities to see these processes at work, and to identify more methods for keeping them under control.

These are simple criteria, but not easy ones to meet. Among organizations that have already been described in the American literature on worker ownership, only the plywood cooperatives can meet these tests. Since these organizations have already been thoroughly studied in other works, I did not include them here. To these lonely examples of well-established,

169

employee-owned workplaces, however, this research has now added three more.

Objections could be raised that by deliberately looking for cases in which employee ownership has been an unusual success, I have unfairly stacked the deck on its behalf. I would nevertheless argue that the weight of scholarly opinion about employee ownership that provided the background for this study justifies this approach. Employee ownership was already a well-known phenomenon in the nineteenth century, and many nineteenth and early twentieth century social theorists were agreed that if these experiences had taught us anything, it is that employee-owned institutions either do not work or do not last. In later generations, these assertions have become so commonplace that scholars frequently repeat them without making any effort to offer evidence in their support (e.g., Drucker, 1974:190; Williamson, 1980:33).

In the organizations examined here, employee ownership does work, and in at least some cases it also lasts. Theoretically, that makes this study an exercise in "deviant case analysis" that is in many ways parallel to what Lipset, Trow, and Coleman attempted in their work *Union Democracy* in 1956. As they asked in that study, I am asking here, "Given that workplace democracy has encountered serious obstacles almost everywhere else, why is it doing so well here?" Such analyses can do two things. First, they are in themselves sufficient to discredit categorical overgeneralizations to the effect that workplace democracy has never worked or could not possibly work. Secondly, these cases may also make it possible to identify clues to why the democratic institutions established here were able to overcome the obstacles that have limited their usefulness everywhere else. If such facilitating conditions can be identified, this information might clearly be helpful to other democratic workplaces that are now starting up.

In attempting to derive lessons from these cases, however, it will be important not to suggest that only organizations that resemble these should be democratically organized or employee-owned. These three sets of organizations actually have a great deal in common, and it is not surprising that they do. Given the many factors that have traditionally inhibited the spread of employee ownership in the American economy as a whole, it required an unusual combination of circumstances for these organizations to be formed, and these circumstances show up within these populations again and again. But as has already been discussed in Chapters 1 and 2, employee ownership is now spreading into many new economic sectors by many new means. The goal of the present analysis is not to discourage these new experiments, but to offer them practical help. The hope is that this effort to learn from the successes of employee ownership as well as its failures will serve as a more constructive way to avoid repeating the mistakes of the past.

Why Are These Organizations Employee-Owned?

Organizations in these three populations are owned by their labor forces first of all because the nature of work performed within them is unusually conducive to employee ownership in a number of ways. The conduciveness of these occupations begins with the fact that all of these are labor-intensive rather than capital-intensive lines of work. When large amounts of capital are an important requirement of work, investor-owned organizations rather than worker-owned organizations are what most commonly results. In such organizations, two consequences of capital-intensity help to subordinate workers to capital's control: (1) in the form of machinery, capital paces work and makes it in other ways subject to "technical control" (Edwards, 1979); and (2) as a prerequisite for starting a business, capital prevents workers from leaving a given employer to start businesses of their own. When work is labor-intensive, in contrast, workers are more free to start their own businesses, and any employee-owned organizations that do get formed are also less likely to transform themselves into conventional capitalist organizations with the passage of time.

In the three sets of occupations examined here, other factors beside the absence of capital help to make labor unusually difficult to control. All three involve the sale and delivery of personalized services directly to the public. Both the marketing and performance of these services is extremely sensitive to the quality of the labor involved. If clients are well cared for, they will become a source of repeat business and new referrals for the individual service provider or firm. If they are not, an organization's reputation can quickly slide downhill. Thus, each of these occupations is in its own way a "hustle" business, and requires a certain degree of tact, initiative, and salesmanship throughout its labor force. It is very difficult, however, to impose these qualities on a labor force from above, or even to supervise this work in any meaningful way. As a result, these are all entrepreneurial occupations in which conventionally employed labor has had a difficult time competing with labor that has the motivational advantage of being self-employed.

These two conditions—the relative absence of capital, and labor that is difficult to control—apply to all three of the occupations considered here, but to a different extent in each case. They fit the professions best of all, which helps to explain why partnerships are so dominant in those fields. The work of the scavengers and of taxi drivers does require some capital, in that both require vehicles, and taxi drivers must often pay for licenses as well. This fact may help to explain why capitalist organizations can often compete successfully with labor-owned organizations in both of these fields. Alchian and Demsetz noted, however, that vehicles are a form of capital that is particularly difficult for anyone but the user to control, and is therefore quite frequently employee-owned (1972:792). The nature of other control problems that promote self-employment in each of these occupations requires some additional comments as well.

We do not normally think of refuse collection as an entrepreneurial occupation, as most of us live in cities in which the local government makes the arrangements to have our trash picked up. That was certainly not the case, however, in the San Francisco Bay area when the scavenger companies were being formed. Back then, it was every scavenger for himself, with each scavenger selling as many services to as many customers as he possibly could. Even after the scavenger companies were formed, scavengers were still expected to sell optional extra services to their customers, and into the 1960s were also responsible for collecting bills from their customers at night. It was partly as a result of these unique entrepreneurial responsibilities of the scavengers that their companies were structured as worker-owned firms.

The taxi industry is another occupation that has by no means been universally dominated by labor that is self-employed; but fleet owners that have sought to employ labor in this field have also traditionally complained that their hired drivers were not sufficiently diligent in seeking out fares. For years, fleet owners paid their employees with commissions that amounted to 40–45% of their metered fares; it was hoped that this method of payment would motivate hired drivers to seek business as actively as if they owned their own cabs. In practice, however, commission drivers often seemed less "hungry" for business than the owner-drivers they competed with. Many of them also began to offer passengers "off-the-meter" discounts at the cab-owner's expense. In New York, this problem became so serious in the late 1960s that owners installed "hot seats" to record electronically each time a passenger entered an employee-driven cab (Vidich, 1976:34–36, 128). By the 1970s, many American taxi fleets had adopted a more permanent solution to their employee-driver problem: they stopped hiring drivers entirely, and instead began renting out their cabs to self-employed drivers who paid them a flat fee for each shift, and then kept every dollar they took in. Other owners sold their cabs outright to the drivers who operated them, thereby converting their firm entirely into owner-driven fleets.

Once the circumstances just described have created basic opportunities for self-employment, employee-owned organizations have arisen in all three of these occupations when otherwise independent service providers have decided to work together in an organization that they will collectively own. Since we know that this step was taken, it would be easy with hindsight to underestimate how big a step this was. Reference was made earlier, however, to the general rarity of cases in which workers voluntarily choose to pool their own resources to create an employee-owned firm (Aldrich and

Stern, 1983). In these occupations, there are also reasons why workers could be expected to be especially reluctant to take this step. Given that they can usually make adequate livings on their own, why should they give up their independence to work with someone else? Moreover, how much cooperation can be expected from the members of occupations whose practitioners normally work independently and compete with each other for customers or fares?

Apparently, members of all three occupations agree to join forces only when the attractions of independence are outweighed by unmistakable advantages of size. Thus they pool resources in order to reap clear economies of scale, or when it seems that large organizations have the best opportunity to attract the business of corporate clients whose demand for their services is equally large. In many cases, the needs that drove otherwise independent practitioners together were not solely economic, but political as well. Thus the providers of these services have often joined forces to deal more effectively not only with clients, but also with the state.

Governments seem to become involved repeatedly in the delivery of these services for many of the same reasons that cause conventional employment relationships to be inappropriate for these lines of work. The basic problem is once again that these tasks are very difficult to control. With no employer to screen service providers and guarantee their work, clients are left vulnerable to unqualified or unscrupulous practitioners in a number of ways. As a result, governments insist on some form of occupational licensing in all of these fields.

Given that all of these occupations require licensing, what form is that licensing to take? Here there are a number of possible alternatives, and the making of such choices has had a crucial impact on both the formation and subsequent development of employee-owned workplaces in all three of these fields. At the risk of some oversimplification, the alternatives are these: (1) governments can go to the trouble of issuing licenses to each individual provider of a service; (2) governments can grant to associations of service providers the right to regulate their members in the government's place; or (3) governments can grant exclusive licenses to one or a few large employers, and then encourage those employers to use this monopolistic advantage as a way to keep their labor force in line. In this last alternative, in other words, governments essentially delegate their licensing authority to a large capitalist firm. It is in many ways an attractively simple solution, as it drastically reduces the number of service providers with which governments are required to deal. As a result, governments have often leaned toward this latter solution, and many of the worker-owned institutions described in this book have emerged out of efforts to persuade governments to consider a different alternative instead.

San Francisco's worker-owned scavenger companies were formed, for example, when that city government began seeking one large company that could be licensed to meet all of the city's refuse collection needs. When no such large company stepped forward, the city government divided the city into districts in 1921, and allowed smaller firms to bid on those district franchises. The worker-owned scavenger firms emerged in this period essentially as consortia of formerly independent scavengers in order to help those scavengers bid more effectively for these new district franchises. By 1935, two of these firms had accumulated all of these district franchises, and by 1940, these same two firms were being accused of playing far too big a role in local officials' re-election campaigns. Since then, the scavengers have played a more discrete role in San Francisco politics, but they have also not forgotten the importance of good "public relations" for the survival of their firms.

While the scavengers are to some extent unique in their own industry, the taxi industry offers many parallels to these events. In the 1920s, fleets were requesting exclusive franchises from local governments in many American cities, and owner-operators often felt that they had to organize in self-defense. Where they were strong enough, medallion systems rather than franchise systems were the typical result. More recently, when Yellow Cab fleets went bankrupt in San Francisco and Los Angeles, government officials in both cities made it clear that only "responsible companies" would be allowed to apply for the right to replace Yellow Cab. Thus would-be owner-operators in both cities were required to organize themselves into cooperatives, in order to have any hope of obtaining licenses at all.

The relationship between taxi cooperatives and local governments is by no means always as passive as these illustrations might imply. In many cases, the taxi cooperatives themselves have taken the initiative and have appealed to local governments for help against what they consider to be unfair competition from fleets. Boston's ITOA was formed in 1924 in order to seek a government ban on the exclusive arrangements that various hotels were making with large fleets. In granting these concessions to fleets, these hotels were going something quite similar to what governments in other cities had often done: they were creating a situation in which a single employer would have both the incentive and the power to screen cab drivers and to be answerable for their conduct. The large fleets, moreover, were ready to pay for this privilege. For owner-operators, however, these arrangements meant that they would be denied access to a source of business that is a staple in their trade. Thus Boston's ITOA fought this practice vigorously, and in the 1930s prevailed upon the city to establish a system of public taxi stands. This process was repeated in Washington, D.C., when that city's Capital Cab Cooperative Association led a successful campaign to outlaw exclusive contracts between hotels and fleets in 1981.

These struggles are merely illustrations of the numerous political issues that taxi cooperatives must routinely face. Others include the regulation of taxi fares, controls over access to airport traffic, and the competition among taxicabs, limousine services, and bus lines. Taxi cooperatives also regularly stick up for their members when they become involved in minor disputes with the local police. One member of Boston's ITOA summed up the organization's political functions by suggesting, "Without the ITOA, we'd lose any kind of rights, any clout we have. We'd be pushed by outside forces." When asked why owner-operators join the ITOA, another member answered simply, "In unity there is strength."

In the professions, group practices do not play this kind of overtly self-defensive role. This is partly a result of the fact that these occupations won the right to be self-regulating a long time ago; but in many cases, today's most prestigious group practices emerged at the same time and in response to the same concerns as many of the other self-governing institutions and practices that make the professions so unique. It appears that members of these occupations saw both big business and big government coming quite early in their development, and they organized both their professional bodies and their group practices in ways that would enable them to deal with both of these giants on their own terms.

Collins (1979) notes that the university-based system of professional education that became standard in the United States in the early twentieth century protected the professionals from two hazards at once. It fended off threats to their autonomy that might come from above, and it also insulated them from competition from below, in the form of the numerous upwardly mobile immigrants then seeking admissions to professional ranks. The fact that professional education would be university-based and that the best professional schools would require applicants to have baccalaureate degrees meant that newly trained professionals from elite social and educational backgrounds would be able to carry those advantages with them into professional life.

This professional system ran largely on credentials and prestige, and group practices in these fields have sought from the very beginning to corner the market on both. Group practices in law have always made a point of recruiting the most elite graduates of the most elite law schools. In Smigel's study of the 20 largest New York law firms conducted in 1957, he also found that 30 percent of the 468 partners in these firms were listed in the *Social Register* at that time (Smigel, 1969:39–40).

In law, accounting, and other professions as well, the relationship between group practices and their corporate clients is to some extent similar to the arrangements between fleets and hotels that independent operators find so objectionable in the taxi field. In each case the client will require the services of a large number of service providers over an extended period of time, and delegates to the fleet or group practice the responsibility for putting together an appropriate team.

Viewed from this perspective, all three of the forms of shared ownership examined in this work are variations on an essentially similar theme. All represent "collective conquests" (Larson, 1977) of sheltered markets by otherwise independent practitioners of regulated fields. The fact that all of these occupations require licenses means that there are many advantages to be won by united action or to be lost by inaction. The efforts that gave rise to these firms were sometimes defensive and sometimes offensive, and sometimes a little of both. In the case of the scavengers, a set of developments that were initially intended to erect barriers between the scavengers and their markets eventually allowed the scavengers to appropriate these market advantages for themselves. Before that could happen, however, the scavengers had to organize themselves into worker-owned firms.

This process is also partly economic, partly political, and this is another distinction that it may be fruitless to try to draw. Is Boston's ITOA an economic or a political organization? It operates a radio-dispatching service, purchases gas and insurance for its members, and represents its members' interests at city hall. So clearly, it is both. And despite their pride in their autonomy, group practices in the professions are also frequently creations not only of the corporations, but of the state. Stevens (1981) notes that the Big Eight accounting firms derive most of their business from efforts to help clients cope with regulations established by the SEC and the IRS. Stevens also quotes one accountant who quipped that the Employee Retirement Income Security Act of 1974 had brought the professions so much new business that it was jokingly referred to as the "Accountants, Lawyers, and Actuaries Retirement Income Security Act" (Stevens, 1981:140).

Thus through a process that is partly defensive and partly offensive, partly economic and partly political, shared ownership occurs in these occupations when individuals who practice them find reasons to give up at least a part of their independence to pursue common goals. Organizing efforts within these occupations are also often facilitated by many of the same features that make these occupations so unique. Since individual practitioners throughout these occupations commonly handle their own accounts and have direct contact with clients, many of these people have a good understanding of the economics of their business and are quite skilled at dealing with others. All of these lines of work also have a tendency to gather their practitioners into distinct occupational cultures with common hours and places of work and play and with widely shared backgrounds, work experiences, and occupational norms.

In many of the instances examined here, these occupational sources of solidarity were supplemented by strong ties of ethnicity among the service providers who organized these groups. Thus the early scavengers were not only Italian, but came from the north of Italy rather than the south; in this country, they lived in Italian neighborhoods, joined Italian clubs, and participated in numerous other Italian-American cultural events. The founders of Boston's ITOA included many Jewish immigrants from Eastern Europe, and a new wave of Jewish immigrants is now a prominent part of the taxi cooperatives of Los Angeles. Group practices in the professions were for many years the exclusive preserve of white Protestant males, and have only belatedly and reluctantly admitted members of other groups.

The ethnic and occupational cultures that these organizations were embedded in not only helped make it possible for them to be formed, but also greatly facilitated their diffusion once their initial prototypes had begun to emerge. Thus the organizational model established by the San Francisco scavengers was soon borrowed by other groups in cities like Stockton, San Mateo, and San Jose, and scavengers in these other cities continue to look upon the San Francisco companies as their industry's leaders up to the present day. The scavengers' system did not spread to any part of Southern California, however, where the refuse collection industry was in largely Armenian hands.

Group practices in the professions provide an even richer set of examples of how success formulas established in just one or a few innovative firms were later imitated by many others. Thus the Mayo Clinic in medicine (Starr, 1982:210–211) and the Cravath firm in law exerted an influence that was felt throughout their fields. Hoffman notes that many organizational practices that are now common to hundreds of large law partnerships can be attributed to the influence of a very small number of individual pioneers. In the late nineteenth century, Walter S. Carter earned himself a reputation as a "collector of young masters and progenitor of many law firms." (Hoffman, 1982:214). Hoffman also credits Emory Buckner with being the first person to begin referring to nonpartner attorneys in law firms as "associates" instead of "clerks" (1982:214). The widespread influence of such organizational innovations should not come as a surprise, given that the professions in particular show many of the occupational conditions that DiMaggio and Powell (1983) have identified as unusually conducive to the diffusion of organizational forms.

In the taxi industry diffusion has played a less prominent role, in part because there is less contact among cab drivers who work in different cities than there is among the practitioners of these other lines of work. Within a given city, however, former members of one taxi cooperative have been known to create new cooperatives of their own. Boston's Red and White Cab Association was organized by individuals who had formerly been members of the ITOA. There may also be some inter-city diffusion of cab cooperatives as well. It seems unlikely that the Los Angeles city government would have encouraged former Yellow Cab drivers to organize themselves into cooperatives in 1977, if local officials had not been aware that taxi cooperatives were already functioning in other cities at that time. Since the Denver Yellow Cab Cooperative was established in 1979, efforts to organize taxi cooperatives that are at least partly patterned on the Denver model have occurred in such cities as Minneapolis and Sacramento.

In most industries, such imitative processes normally help to make conventional capitalist organizations the universal organizational types. When worker-owned organizations do appear in these other industries, these processes also help to transform them back into conventional organizational forms (DiMaggio and Powell, 1983:151). In the case of the scavengers as well, a major threat to their stability occurred when these organizations broadened their horizons beyond their own San Francisco Bay area, and began to identify themselves with the nationwide solid waste management "agglomerates." Throughout most of their histories, however, such mimetic processes helped to strengthen rather than to weaken the scavengers' unique institutions. Within the professions, these processes have played an even more effective role in helping to make group practices in those fields the most dominant organizational types.

The capacity for an early success to spawn many imitators also had a lot to do with the spread of cooperatives throughout the plywood industry of the Pacific Northwest. The success of cooperatives in the plywood industry originates in many of the same features that were earlier identified as having been conducive to the formation of worker-owned organizations in the occupations being examined here. For example, although the plywood cooperatives are engaged in manufacturing, rather than a service, capital requirements in their industry were relatively modest when the cooperatives were being formed, and productivity was quite sensitive to the motivation of the labor involved. The founders of many of these cooperatives were also united by a common Scandinavian descent. Although more than 30 of these cooperatives would eventually be formed, there would probably be no cooperatives in the plywood industry today if 125 workers had not decided to organize their new Olympia Veneer Company as a cooperative in 1921. The remaining firms in this group were all established after 1939, in explicit efforts to emulate this single pioneer's success (Berman, 1982:162–163).

This discussion should thus help to make clear both why these occupations have been so unusually productive of employee-owned firms, and why these firms are generally so rare. Members of these occupations had both strong reasons and good opportunities to establish employee-owned firms, and also had mechanisms by which innovations successfully developed in a few pioneering organizations could be rapidly spread to other firms. In other lines of work, conditions conducive to both the creation and diffusion of employee-owned firms have been much more scarce, and the few isolated experiments in employee ownership that have occurred have been allowed to wither on the vine. In the United States, opportunities for the spread of employee ownership have recently been much improved, with consequences that will be reviewed in the next chapter. The remainder of this chapter will be concerned with the fate of employee ownership in these three sets of organizations after they have been formed.

The Politics of Sharing Income

Many of the same circumstances that caused employee-owned organizations to be formed in these occupations also caused some unusually democratic structures to be adopted by these firms. These organizations required democratic structures first of all because only with such structures could firm founders be induced to give up their independence and enter these organizations at all. These organizations also felt a need to extend full membership to individuals who entered them after they were formed, because conventional employment relationships did not work for them any better than they did for anyone else. It thus did not seem possible to introduce high proportions of hired labor into any of these organizations without suffering a loss of labor quality and of clients at the very same time. As the Sunset scavengers put this, "it was not to be expected that a hired scavenger would work as well and as willingly as one who is a shareholder."

For such reasons, organizations were created in which ownership is widely shared throughout the labor force. Admittedly, this sharing of ownership and the workplace democracy associated with it are imperfectly realized in all of these institutions. In all cases, only a subset of the labor force shares in the ownership of the firm, and in many instances only a minority enjoys this privilege. Typically, whole categories of employees are completely excluded from ownership, such as secretaries and other auxiliary employees. Employees who have a chance to become owners are often expected to serve some period of apprenticeship before they can be considered fully eligible for this privilege. This is true of associates in law firms and of "helpers" in the scavenger companies.

Despite these limitations, these firms offer rare examples of organizations that have been significantly employee-owned for quite substantial lengths of time. They are thus in a position to help us answer many questions about the impact of employee ownership and workplace democracy on the governance of a firm. Can workplace decision making really be democratized? Does workplace democracy help or hinder the economic performance of a firm? These are some of the questions to which at least partial answers can be provided by the example of these firms.

Before attempting in any way to generalize from the experience of these firms, it is important to bear in mind the many ways in which they are unique. Many of the conditions that fostered the creation of these firms also help to make their democratic institutions unusually strong. For example, work that requires both experience and initiative means that worker-owners will show up at meetings relatively well prepared to take part in discussions about the future of their firms. That worker-owners do similar work, participate in a common occupational culture, and often have ethnic ties as well, all predispose them to communicate effectively with each other and to share common sentiments toward their firms. These circumstances thus duplicate many of the features that have been classically identified in previous studies as giving democracy the best chance to work (see for example, Weber, 1968:I, 289–290, and II, 948–949, and Lipset, Trow, and Coleman, 1956).

Other conditions that appear unusually conducive to the success of workplace democracy can be discerned in the structures of these firms. All of these firms are relatively modest in size, with the largest organizations in each group ranging from several hundred to about a thousand employee-owners per firm. All of these organizations have mechanisms for screening potential new members, and for ejecting members whose continued presence in the organization would be detrimental to the group. In group practices and the scavenger firms, newly hired employees must complete relatively long probationary periods before they can become owners, and in all three sets of organizations, new owners must "buy into" the organization by making some form of capital contribution to the firm. Thus, many analogues to the "commitment mechanisms" discussed by Kanter (1972) and by Bradley and Gelb (1981, 1982a, 1982b) are present in these firms.

It would be a big mistake, however, to conclude that these organizations were tailor-made to make workplace democracy work. They also have some unique problems that democratic workplaces in other industries would be less likely to have to face. One of these problems is the relative ease with which members can leave these organizations and go into business for themselves. This is not a serious problem for the scavengers, due to the exclusive licenses they hold, but it is for many taxi cooperatives and for group practices in the professions. These centrifugal possibilities seriously limit the ability of these organizations to discipline their members and often threaten the integrity of the organizations themselves.

In addition, these organizations also face a fundamental dilemma in determining how the rewards and costs of worker ownership can most equitably be shared. On the one hand, the members of these organizations do similar work, and commonly also have equal voting power when their organizations' owners meet. These circumstances encourage these organizations to adopt policies that require both the rewards and costs of ownership to be allocated on a strictly equal basis. On the other hand, however, the entrepreneurial nature of the work performed in these firms encourages these firms to establish strong direct links between individual effort and individual reward. That is, work effort in all of these fields has traditionally depended not on machine pacing or hierarchical supervision, but on the direct interest of the worker in the material outcome of the work. It is this fact that did so much in the first place to make self-employed labor so successful in these fields. The motivational advantages of self-employment might easily be lost, however, if the incomes of the worker-owners in these firms were made solely dependent on an equal share of an income that was divided too many ways. Thus these organizations therefore often go to great lengths to maintain direct links between individual effort and individual reward, and these policies typically require that individual members will receive unequal rewards.

These common problems work together to produce many similarities in political life across these three populations of firms. The politics of sharing income appears to be the most volatile issue across all three sets of firms. In some cases, income sharing is equal, in others it is unequal, but in all cases a consensus is required that the existing compensation system is fair. When that consensus is lost, members are quick to express their sense of injustice either by storming out of the organization in a huff, or by fomenting revolution in their firms. More frequently, however, peace is preserved through the adoption of compensation systems that may vary tremendously from firm to firm, but are alike in being responsive to these fundamental problems of democracy in these firms.

These points can hopefully be made clear with the aid of a brief summary of how these themes are reflected in the political life of each of these three sets of firms:

WORKER-OWNED SCAVENGER COMPANIES. Some of these generalizations apply more weakly to the scavenger companies than to either of the other two sets of firms examined in this work. Several consequences of the way in which the scavenger firms are licensed make them more like conventional firms and less like the other two groups. For example, the fact that the scavengers hold exclusive licenses within the geograpical areas they serve makes it impossible for members to leave their organizations to set up rival firms. In addition, the fact that all residents are required to accept the scavengers' basic refuse collection service sharply limits the degree of entrepreneurship required of the men on scavenger trucks. As a result, it is feasible for shareholding scavengers to be compensated through a fixed hourly wage, and material incentives do not play a significant role in the scavengers' day-to-day work.

The scavenger companies' entrepreneurial origins and democratic organization have nevertheless left their marks on their reward structures in two major ways. The first involves the scavengers' traditional procedures for determining the size of their routes. Although residents were required to accept the scavengers' basic service, the scavengers still felt the need for some way to motivate crewmembers to sell extra services to the customers along their routes, and to be diligent in collecting bills from their customers at night. This was for many years accomplished with the aid of a policy that required all routes to be made equal not necessarily in the amount of work they involved, but in the income they produced.

This system worked for the scavengers for a number of years, but it also produced many strains. One chronic problem was the fairness issues that it raised. Many hard-working crews had good excuses for the low dollar yields of their routes, such as the poverty of the residents, or the presence of hills that made it hard to call on large numbers of customers in one day. In such cases, it seemed unfair to burden these unfortunate crews with any more work. More generally, the prospect of route adjustments was too remote and uncertain a consequence to inspire more than a handful of scavengers to approach their entrepreneurial responsibilities with any real zest. Many came instead to agree with the common opinion that "[bill] collecting is a pain." The deficiencies of this system thus created pressures for more and more of these "proprietary duties" to be reassigned away from the scavengers on the trucks, with consequences for these organizations' structures that have already been discussed.

While this tradition has waned, a remaining legacy of the scavengers' preoccupation with equality and fairness has been the shareholders' reluctance to allow company officers to earn higher incomes than the men who work on the trucks. Scavenger leaders tend to acquire a good deal of power within their organizations, both because they are good vote-getters, and because of the powers that their offices confer. Clearly, however, the issue of officers' compensation has so far marked the most important limit on the officers' power. It was an effort to increase officers' compensation without the consent of the members that cost Leonard Stefanelli's predecessor his job. Although Stefanelli himself believes that officers should be entitled to receive higher pay, his fellow shareholders did not agree with him, and voted in 1967 that "all directors and all executive officers shall . . . receive equal compensation as the corporation is paying from time to time to all of its stockholder members."

TAXI COOPERATIVES. In contrast both to the scavenger companies and to group practices in the professions, most taxi cooperatives have loosely organized structures in which members do not really share income, but merely share certain costs. That is, members pay dues to the organization in return for such services as radio dispatching, insurance coverage, and political representation; but when they drive their cabs, they keep every dollar they take in. This remains largely true, even in cooperatives like those in San Francisco and in Denver that own their cabs in common. In these organizations, members pay a rental charge to the cooperative for each shift in which they use a cab, but continue to pocket all their own fares. Thus throughout this group of firms, members' work incentives remain generally as direct and undiluted as those of any other cab driver who is self-employed.

Conflicts nevertheless frequently arise within these organizations over the question of whether any given arrangement for allocating the costs and benefits of membership is completely equal and/or fair. One chronic source of trouble is the distribution of radio-dispatched work. This distribution can never be made equal, as some radio orders will always be more lucrative than others, and luck, if nothing else, will therefore always cause some drivers to get better radio work than others. If radio dispatching cannot be made equal, it can at least be made fair; and so every taxi cooperative has procedures designed to make sure that each radio job will be given to the cab driver who is nearest to it, or who asks for it first, or who has been waiting longest in line. No matter how scrupulously these procedures are followed, at least some members are likely to suspect that they are being violated, even if they are not; and co-op leaders themselves acknowledge that "human beings cannot be impartial." This issue is thus a constant source of both real and imagined injustices throughout this group of firms.

A second major source of disputes within these organizations is the fairness of shift rental charges or dues. Should members who do not use the radio to get business pay the same fees as those who do? Should members who drive at night or on weekends be charged the same as those who drive during weekdays?

In many cab cooperatives, such inherently difficult questions are made even more troublesome by the presence of more than one kind of member within the same organization. In cities with medallion systems, like Boston and San Francisco, one often finds owners of single cabs and of "minifleets" as members of the same cab cooperative. In such cases, disputes are common over the question of whether any given cost or benefit of membership is to be allocated per member or per cab. In the two taxi cooperatives of Los Angeles, disputes also developed between members who viewed their memberships as investments, and those who saw their memberships as nothing more than a guarantee of their right to own their own cabs. In the Yellow Cab cooperatives of San Francisco and Denver there is also a potential for disputes in the fact that these organizations include both individually owned and collectively owned cabs. And in many of these organizations, there is another possible source of conflict in the fact that some members do not drive cabs at all.

It is issues and cleavages such as these that largely drive the politics of the taxi cooperatives examined here. At Boston's ITOA in the 1970s, disputes between the owners of single cabs and of minifleets over such issues as the fairness of radio dispatching and of dues contributed to the defections of hundreds of cabs. In other cities, local licensing arrangements have prevented disgruntled members from leaving their cooperatives, but these issues have been a major source of political controversy and of leadership turnover in such taxi cooperatives as the two in L.A. Denver's Yellow Cab Cooperative, after getting off to a promising start, has also experienced disputes between drivers of individually and collectively owned cabs, and among drivers who work different shifts.

PROFESSIONAL GROUP PRACTICES. Unlike taxi cooperatives, group practices in the professions generally pool all their income, and then redivide it in ways that reward partners for their various and often unequal contributions to the success of the firm. Choices about how this income division is to be accomplished probably constitute one of the most complex decisions that these group practices have to make, and they are certainly the most volatile decisions as well. These decisions are complex both in the large number of criteria that they may potentially include and in the many ways in which those criteria can be combined. They are volatile in that lack of agreement about these issues can so easily lead to the disintegration of a firm. In the legal profession, disputes about compensation are estimated to be responsible for about half of all law firm breakups (Granelli, 1978:1). Disagreements over income division have also frequently been cited as a major problem limiting both the success and the spread of group practices in medicine as well (e.g., Mechanic, 1978:385; Starr, 1982:215).

As was earlier discussed (Chapter 5), most group practices make a basic choice between "formula" and "percentage" systems for division of firm income. Although these two systems ultimately rely on similar criteria, they differ considerably in the ways in which they seek simultaneously both to stimulate productivity and to minimize conflict within a firm. Whereas formula systems aim directly at providing individual rewards for individual efforts, percentage systems offer more collective incentives. Since a percentage partner's share of firm income is fixed in advance, the only way a partner can increase his or her own personal income is by increasing the total size of the pie. Under formula systems, the possibility exists that partners will be tempted to hoard business, or will take little interest in each other's work. In percentage systems, in contrast, a partner derives an equal material benefit from every contribution he makes to the success of the firm, including advice to other attorneys and general contributions to morale. When asked why his firm does not pay its partners on a formula system, one San Francisco attorney summarized this advantage of percentage compensation by answering, "because we want them to cooperate."

Another way in which percentage systems can promote cooperation in a firm involves a second area of difference between formula and nonformula systems. This has to do with the tendency for compensation system to create ruptures in a firm. Both formula and percentage systems are potentially disruptive, but each creates dissatisfaction in different ways. Hypothetically, formula systems might appear to be the least disruptive of the two, because they ostensibly depoliticize the compensation issue, and make each partner's income a mathematical function of his measurable contributions to the firm. In practice, however, formula systems still leave plenty of room for disputes, over such issues as which criteria to use and what weights to assign to them. In addition, formula systems make it possible for partners' incomes to fluctuate widely from one year to the next, with the result that these systems are always capable of generating new sources of dissent.

It may be an important advantage of percentage systems, therefore, that they explicitly acknowledge income division to be a matter not for calculation, but negotiation. In establishing a percentage system, partners can raise all the criteria they consider to be relevant, and can keep talking until they find a distribution that they can all agree on. Once adopted at the beginning of a year, a percentage system produces no further surprises before the year is out. Percentage systems also seem to support, rather than disrupt, age grading and other types of stratification within a firm. They prevent older partners from suffering the embarrassment of being unexpectedly surpassed by younger attorneys. Many firms with percentage systems tend also to pay the same fixed percentage to all the attorneys who entered the firm in or around the same year.

This is not to suggest that percentage systems do not have disruptive consequences of their own. They can easily create the impression in many partners' minds that they earn less than partners who are less productive than they are. Charges are common that "Too often one partner's share may depend on whether he is a friend of a member of the committee which determines the distribution" (Moldenhauer, 1971:12). Smith believed that the use of a formula system at Hale and Dorr was chiefly responsible for the fact that no partner had left his firm for another in more than forty years (Cantor, 1974:162).

It is possibly because each system has its own advantages and disadvantages that neither has ever been able to demonstrate any clearcut superiority to the other. Two studies of the productivity of group medical practices found only weak and generally nonsignificant relationships between the use of formula compensation systems and the income of the firm (Kimbell and Lorant, 1973; Lorant and Kimbell, 1976). In law, statistical information about compensation systems is hard to come by, but what literature is available provides little evidence that either system is displacing the other. Qualitative studies often conclude that the desirability of one system or another is partly a function of such factors as the size and demographic structure of a firm.

In the absence of any data to suggest that either one of these compensation systems is decisively superior to the other, variations on both of them have continued to proliferate, and the design of a compensation system for any particular firm has been as much a political choice as an economic one.

The fact that no compensation system has been established as standard within the professions also virtually guarantees that this issue will long remain a chronic source of dispute.

It should be evident from this review that in none of these populations can workplace democracy be dismissed as a meaningless charade. There are many organizations in all three of these populations in which decision making is clearly democratic in content as well as in form, and in which the concerns of rank-and-file members have an important impact on the goverance of the firm.

It would also be easy to conclude, however, that workplace democracy exercises an ultimately disruptive influence in all three of these sets of firms. There are certainly both managers and rank-and-file members in all three sets of organizations who are quick to express this thought themselves. In many cases, these disruptive consequences of democracy may also be exacerbated by policies that require managers to be elected from among the worker-owners, rather than hired from outside. Such policies appear on the one hand to make managers too closely involved in the electoral politics of their firms, and on the other hand to make rank-and-file worker-owners more resentful of managers' compensation and power. Thus many of these firms might be better off with a more professional management that is hired by and answerable to a democratically elected board, as is customary among the worker-owned plywood firms.

However they choose to structure their democracies, and despite the problems that their democratic structures occasionally create for these firms, it remains highly doubtful whether these firms would function any better if the labor force were denied a say in the governance of the firm. In many cases it is hard to imagine how these organizations could exist at all if they were not structured in a democratic way. Where experienced workers have readily available opportunities to strike out on their own, it is hard to see what form of organization could hold them together more effectively than one that they themselves own and control. And given the difficulty of controlling so many of these tasks, these organizations would find it very difficult to function without a labor force that is both highly motivated and loyal to the firm. It is hard to imagine how this motivation and loyalty could be generated more effectively than through employee ownership and control of these firms.

On should also not expect either the strengths or the weaknesses demonstrated by workplace democracy in these three sets of firms to be necessarily duplicated in other types of employee-owned firms. Workplace democracy has had some unique assets in these firms, and has also faced some unique challenges. The practitioners of these occupations are an unusually independent lot, and democracy in these organizations has helped to forge some tolerably long-lasting alliances among them. In other occupations, workplace democracy might show far less vitality, both because it has less promising material to work with, and because it has far less to do.

On Degeneration: A Final Note

The widely noted tendency for employee-owned workplaces to transform themselves into conventional capitalist organizations has been a preoccupation of much of this work. The present section will attempt to summarize what can be learned about this phenomenon by comparing the experiences of these three populations of firms.

One of the most important lessons that can be derived from these firms is the confirmation they give to a good deal of current theorizing about the role of capital in promoting the degeneration of employee-owned firms. The relative absence of capital within these occupations thus not only made it possible for these firms to be formed, but has also helped to keep these firms stable over time. Insofar as these firms have nevertheless shown tendencies to degenerate over time, they appear to be largely attributable to ways in which capital does come to play a role in these firms.

Across the three categories of firms, degenerative tendencies are noticeably stronger in the scavenger companies and taxi cooperatives than within professional firms. Two forms of capital appear to be largely accountable for this difference. First, refuse collection and taxi driving have an important capital prerequisite that the professions do not in the form of the vehicles that they use. The refuse collection industry in particular has shown a pronounced tendency to become increasingly capital-intensive in recent years, as more and more specialized vehicles have been brought into wide use. Second, an even more valuable asset in both sets of firms has been the marketable licenses that they or their members own. It is these licenses that have probably done more than any other single factor to destabilize the insitutions of both of these populations of employee-owned firms.

The role of occupational licenses in promoting the degeneration of taxi cooperatives has already been discussed. It may be less obvious how licensing arrangements have contributed to the degeneration of scavenger firms as well. The scavengers' exclusive licenses to collect residential refuse in their cities have encouraged their degeneration in two major ways. First, by making it less necessary for scavengers to act as entrepreneurs, they have facilitated the use of hired labor in these firms. Second, it was largely the licenses they controlled that prompted the newly formed nationwide solid waste management firms to offer the scavengers such unexpectedly large sums to purchase their companies in the early 1970s. By the middle 1970s, several larger scavenger companies had learned to play this game as well, and had begun to buy up smaller companies in nearby communities themselves.

Thus both in taxi cooperatives and in the scavenger firms, marketable occupational licenses have played a role somewhat similar to the one played by capital equipment in manufacturing firms. As prerequisites for doing business, they make it difficult for late entrants to an industry to open new businesses of their own, and instead make it more likely that latecomers will become hired employees of firms or individuals who already have these prerequisites in their hands. In addition, the fact that these assets are marketable makes it possible for them to accumulate in fewer and fewer hands, and for outside investors to acquire the most important assets of the firm.

Professional firms, in contrast, have been less likely to degenerate because all of these forms of capital are either absent or have been neutralized in their firms. Professional licenses are neither marketable nor limited by number, but are instead granted to everyone who can meet the educational requirements and pass the examinations necessary for admission to these fields. As for other types of assets, the amounts of equipment and working capital required by professional firms are either insignificant, or are accounted for in ways that do not encourage the degeneration of these firms.

The way in which professional firms account for capital provides a particularly impressive demonstration of the value of financial arrangements of the sort that Vanek and Ellerman have recently recommended. Partners in professional firms appear to have long been aware of how easily capital can, in Holyoake's words, "steal like the serpent of Eden from the outer world into the garden of partnership" (Holyoake, 1906, vol. II:338). Thus, they are careful to account for their capital contributions in ways quite analogous to the "debt financing" and "internal capital accounting" favored by Vanek and Ellerman.

In addition to demonstrating ways in which the presence or absence of capital can promote the degeneration or stability of worker-owned firms, these firms have a number of other lessons to teach. There is a good deal of support in the experience of firms for those who argue that capital is not the only major cause of degeneration in worker-owned firms, and who see this phenomenon as a result of other processes as well. In fact, it is precisely because capital plays such a minimal role in so many of these firms that they provide such a good opportunity to see so many of these other processes at work.

The potential for degeneration that runs throughout these sets of firms originates in a simple economic fact, the implications of which have been most fully developed in the work of Ben-Ner. This fact is that worker-owned firms will be tempted to use hired labor, whether they own capital or not. Whenever possibilities exist for these firms to profit from the use of hired labor they can therefore be expected to respond to them, unless some additional factor or factors intervene to prevent them from taking this step.

Because of this fundamental economic fact, there is a certain symmetry between degenerative processes and formative processes within these sets of firms. That is, the influences that discourage these organizations from degenerating are generally parallel to the influences that initially caused them to become worker-owned. As long as these conditions remain in force, these organizations are likely to remain worker-owned; but insofar as these facilitating conditions are subject to erosion over time, then worker ownership is likely to become increasingly susceptible to decline.

Throughout these sets of firms, worker ownership derived much of its early impetus from the difficulty of controlling this work. This circumstance both made it possible for the founders of these organizations to be self-employed themselves, and encouraged them to allow later entrants to their organizations to become worker-owners as well. Thereafter, both the stability and limitations of worker ownership in these firms continued to be shaped largely by the nature of work. As the professional firms particularly demonstrate, work that continues to require ownership to control it remains the best defense against degeneration in these firms. At the same time, however, very few of these firms have ever shown the slightest interest in extending ownership opportunities to employees whose work could be controlled effectively by conventional means. Thus secretarial employees are almost universally excluded from ownership in these firms. In the scavenger firms, it was also changes in the nature of work that did most to facilitate the increased use of hired labor on scavenger trucks. As licensing arrangements and technological changes made it less and less necessary or even desirable for scavenger crews to act as entrepreneurs, the need to have worker-owners on scavenger trucks was corresponding lost. In taxi cooperatives, marketable licenses and the spread of taxicab leasing have had a similar tendency to transfer ownership away from individuals who are merely good at driving cabs, and into the hands of people who have learned how to profit from the control these licenses give them over access to this field.

In addition to these dynamics rooted in the nature of work, the stability or degeneration of worker ownership in these firms has also been influenced by the collective sentiments that help tie worker-owners to each other and to their firms. Both the formation and later success of these worker-owned organizations were due in part to strong occupational and often ethnic sources of solidarity among the worker-owners. Insofar as these ties have been shared by both present and would-be worker-owners in these firms, they have helped to preserve the structures of these firms, even when those structures are no longer strictly required by the material interests of their firms. Thus the scavengers long maintained their tradition of allowing helpers to become partners, because they enjoyed extending ownership opportunities to family members and to new immigrants from Italy. Conversely, later entrants to these firms who lack these ties to the existing worker-owners have had a more difficult time becoming owners in these firms. This has been true not only of the scavenger companies, but of many professional firms as well. Carlin, for example, found that in New York law firms with a religiously mixed composition,

> . . . the proportion of lawyers who are of an "out" religion increases as we move down the office status ladder . . . . These results, moreover, apply whatever the "out" religion happens to be—Protestant, Catholic, or Jewish (Carlin, 1966:106–107).

There is also at least some support in the histories of these firms for the classic claim that worker-owned firms degenerate politically as well. These firms do not, as the Webbs suggested, gradually abandon workplace democracy because they find that it just does not work. As they grow in size and complexity, however, these firms do show tendencies for leaders to become increasingly differentiated from the rank and file, for terms of office to lengthen, and for authoritarian patterns of leadership to emerge.

There is thus much in the experience of these firms to support the positions of the many social theorists who have predicted that insofar as the influence of capital can be removed from the workplace, this will not produce equality, but will instead cause various sources of inequality within the labor force to come to the fore. These sources of inequality include positions, affiliations, contacts, and status, as well as licenses, credentials, and skills. Given both the ubiquity and persistence of these bases of inequality, many of the phenomena that are commonly referred to as degeneration appear likely to be with us for many years to come.

While many forms and causes of degeneration thus seem unlikely to go away, we should be careful not to draw unduly pessimistic conclusions about worker ownership from this fact. It should be clear by now that the degeneration of democratic workplaces does not imply that these firms have "failed." In many ways, the institutions of these firms seem less vulnerable to economic stagnation than they do to economic success. In this respect, worker-owned firms do not seem very different from sole proprietorships, which have a similar tendency to transform themselves into capitalist corporations over time. When this happens to sole proprietorships, we normally do not take these transformations as a sign of failure, but of success. When similar changes occur in worker-owned firms, however, there is a wide tendency for advocates of worker ownership to lament the loss, and for its opponents to gloat. What often gets forgotten in all of these reactions is that the degeneration of these firms is less likely to result from economic failure than from economic success.

Even more importantly, many organizations have no need for these excuses, because they are still worker-owned. This is true of many of the organizations examined in this work, and of many other organizations around the world. In these organizations, worker ownership continues to derive stability from many of the same conditions that initially called it forth. As processes of degeneration have made themselves felt in these firms, many of them have also developed counter measures that promise to hold many of these degenerative tendencies in check.

A number of authors have written about the capacity of organizational democracy to renew itself in the face of oligarchical threats (e.g., Cafferata, 1982; Batstone, 1983). In labor unions, such mechanisms of democratic renewal have included the two-party system that Lipset, Trow, and Coleman attributed to the ITU, and the rank-and-file movements that emerged in such unions as the United Mine Workers in the 1960s and 70s. Within worker-owned firms, Eric Batstone has recently proposed a "life cycle" model of their democratic institutions in which oligarchical tendencies are repeatedly followed by efforts on the part of rank-and-file members to reassert and to formalize their right to be included in decision making in their firms. Using data on 60 French cooperatives, Batstone describes a number of developments in these organizations that are in some way parallel to and in other ways more far-reaching than the 1965 "revolution" in the Sunset scavenger firm (Batstone, 1983:149–152).

In and of themselves, such internal reform efforts are probably incapable of halting or reversing all of the processes of degeneration that affect these worker-owned firms. Increasingly, however, the worker-owned institutions of these firms have also received powerful support from without. In the scavenger companies and professional group practices, ethnic minorities and women who believe they have unfairly been denied opportunities to become owners in their firms have recently succeeded in taking their firms to court. As a result of their victories, ownership opportunities in many of these firms are no longer viewed as favors that the existing worker-owners may or may not bestow, and have instead now been transformed into legally enforceable rights.

An even more significant development in this regard is that the United States government is now actively encouraging the spread of employee ownership to many American firms. In order to induce as many corporations as possible to establish Employee Stock Ownership Plans, the federal government has offered a variety of tax deductions and tax credits to firms that set up these plans. The effects of these recent federal efforts to promote employee ownership will be examined in detail in the next chapter of this work.

CHAPTER 7

Making Workers Owners In The Contemporary United States

The preceding four chapters have dealt with populations of organizations in which employee ownership has often shown great richness and vitality, but is also quite limited in scope. The dynamics they illustrate have caused employee ownership to develop only in small numbers of firms, and have confined it to a subset of the labor force even in these.

This final chapter will shift its attention to mechanisms by which employee ownership has recently been spreading to far greater numbers of employees and firms. Some of the reasons why employee ownership has recently become more popular in the United States were discussed in Chapter 1; others will be included here. To the extent that the available data make possible such assessments, this chapter will also examine the impact of these new forms of employee ownership on industrial relations and decision making in the firms they touch.

Although the organizational innovations to be considered here are extremely diverse, they share one major theme. Whereas the previous four chapters have described employee-owned organizations that were generally created by and for the employee-owners themselves, this chapter will describe mechanisms by which the employees of conventional organizations are being converted into owners at the initiative of someone else. This unique circumstance of their origin raises certain common issues about these forms of ownership that did not arise in studies of the previous sets of firms. Since these ownership changes are being superimposed on conventionally organized firms, it is necessary to ask whether employee ownership has any real impact on the internal operation of these firms. And since workers have so little to do with initiating these changes, it is also necessary to consider whose interests they really serve, and to ask whether workers have as much to gain from these new forms of ownership as they potentially have to lose.

Efforts to turn employees into owners in the United States currently take three principal forms: (1) divestitures to employees of entire businesses or plants; (2) the establishment of Employee Stock Ownership Plans, or "ESOPs," in numerous incorporated firms; and (3) the displacement of employees by independent contractors and franchisees. The first section of this chapter will briefly assess the prevalence of each of these ownership forms. Later sections will then look more closely at some of the causes that have brought these changes about and at the impact they have had.

Devices for Making Workers Owners

Divestitures to Employees of Entire Businesses or Plants

In recent years, the United States has witnessed a number of well-publicized instances in which major industrial enterprises that were threatened with closure have been divested to their employees instead. In 1979 more than 2000 workers in Waterloo, Iowa, initiated steps that would soon make them the owners of the Rath meat packing plant (Gunn, 1980b). In the fall of 1981, 750 roller bearing makers in New Jersey purchased their Hyatt Clark plant from General Motors for $53 million (Moberg, 1981). On March 15, 1983, negotiations were completed on the nation's largest buyout yet: the 7,000 employees of a Weirton, West Virginia mill would purchase the mill from its parent firm, National Steel (*Fortune*, April 18, 1983). Even before the Weirton buyout, it was estimated that worker buyouts of closing plants had saved more than 50,000 jobs by 1982 (Rosen and Whyte, 1982:16).

Less widely publicized, but probably much more numerous, have been divestitures to employees of businesses that were not in any particular trouble at the time. In some instances, such as the 1972 conversion to fifty percent employee ownership of Washington, D.C.'s International Group Plans, these divestitures have had no other apparent motive than that the owner thought that employee ownership seemed like a good idea (Zwerdling, 1977). A much more frequent cause of these divestitures has been that the firm's owner was on the verge of retirement, and decided that it would be more desirable to sell the firm to its employees than to anyone else.

The Spread of Employee Stock Ownership Plans, or "ESOPs"

Employee Stock Ownership Plans have proliferated rapidly in the United States since the passage of the legislation that first provided tax incentives to companies for establishing these plans in 1974. As late as 1976, it was estimated that no more than 300 companies were offering these plans (Marsh and McAllister, 1981:553). By 1983, however, the National Center for Employee Ownership reported that over 6,000 American corporations had adopted these plans (*Wall Street Journal*, July 16, 1983).

It is harder to estimate the number of employees who are covered by these plans. According to one source, the typical firm with an ESOP has between 50 and 100 employees (Howitt, 1982). This in turn would suggest that approximately half a million employees are currently covered by these plans. Since many ESOPs have been established in some of the nation's largest firms, however, the true figure probably amounts to at least several million employees.

Displacement of Employees by Independent Contractors and Franchisees

Harder to quantify, because they have been less carefully observed, are the many ways in which American business firms have made it possible for self-employed individuals to do jobs for them that would otherwise be performed by hired employees. One such organizational device is franchising. In such franchised industries as sales of automobiles and gasoline and fast food retailing, nationwide firms spare themselves the trouble of hiring an employed labor force, and instead let self-employed franchisees own and operate each individual retail establishment. In itself, however, franchising has provided only a modest source of self-employment in the contemporary United States. In 1984, the U.S. Department of Commerce recognized only 461,849 business establishments as part of the franchised sector, and of these, only 374,152 were estimated to be "franchisee-owned" (U.S. Dept. of Commerce, 1984:24). The actual number of self-employed franchisees was even smaller than this, given that franchisees often own more than one unit each.

Of greater significance than franchising itself, however, are numerous other industries that share with franchising a preference for dealing with self-employed individuals instead of hiring their own employees. In the taxi industry we have already seen that the employed cab driver who was paid by commissions is now largely a thing of the past; most taxi fleets now rent out their cabs to self-employed drivers who keep every dollar they take in. Other fleets have sold their cabs entirely to a labor force of individual owner-drivers. Among hairdressers and barbers, similarly, commission work has largely disappeared, and most members of these occupations now operate as self-employed individuals who merely rent space from the owners of their shops. Construction, trucking, warehousing, logging, real estate, and sales are some of the numerous other industries in which such "independent contractors" are now prominently in use.

The exact numbers of these self-employed individuals are hard to calculate, because in many cases these independent contractor relationships are not reported to the federal government. It is not even possible to study a random sample of workers from this employment category because, as the General Accounting Office reported to Congress in 1979, "No one knows the total universe of independent contractors" (U.S. Congress, House

Committee on Ways and Means, 1979:429). IRS officials did estimate in 1979, however, that their pending actions applicable to this category would affect approximately 2 million workers (U.S. Congress, 1979:399). Some indirect insights into the numerical consequences of indirect contracting can also be gained by examining figures on the role of self-employment in the American labor force. Here, the evidence suggests that the present popularity of independent contracting is contributing to a reversal of the historic decline of self-employment in the United States.

Evidence that self-employment was making a major comeback in the American economy first drew serious attention in 1980. According to an article in the November 1980 *Monthly Labor Review*, the self-employed segment of the American labor force grew at a significantly accelerated rate from 1975 to 1979. This trend was especially pronounced in the nonagricultural sector, where self-employment grew by 17%, while wage and salary employment rose by 11%. In 1979, a total of 8.2 million American workers were officially listed as self-employed, constituting 8.6% of the total population at work. More than 2 million additional Americans identified themselves as self-employed, but were classified as wage and salary earners because their businesses were incorporated. Had these individuals been included, the growth of self-employment would have shown itself to be even more pronounced, because there were only 850,000 such individuals in 1967, when this group was initially reclassified out of the self-employment category. Moreover, another 1.5 million Americans in 1979 were self-employed at their second jobs, accounting for more than one-third of all the dual or multiple jobholders (Fain, 1980).

Since those figures were reported, the trend toward self-employment in the American labor force has continued at an even stronger pace. Between 1979 and 1983, self-employment outside of agriculture grew by nearly 18%, while nonagricultural wage and salary employment grew by less than 4%. Despite the fact that agricultural self-employment continued its historic decline, the total number of workers officially designated as self-employed grew by November 1983 to 9.4 million, accounting for 9.2% of the employed labor force (these figures are based on U.S. Department of Labor statistics reported in the January 1984 issue of *Monthly Labor Review*, p. 90).

Why All of These Efforts to Turn Workers into Owners?

Admittedly, these three sets of changes are extremely diverse. They nevertheless show some important similarities that greatly facilitate comparisons among the three. First of all, there is the similarity of result. In all of these instances, workers who yesterday were merely hired employees of the places in which they work are today being called upon to participate in the ownership of their firms. In addition, all three of these developments are quite similar in cause. In each case, employees are becoming owners not at their own initiative, but at the instigation of someone else. In addition, the specific considerations that have caused employers to promote these changes cut across all three of these mechanisms for converting workers into owners of their firms.

Any explanation of these recent efforts to convert workers into owners in the United States must begin with the fact that the economy has been stagnant over much of this time. In many instances employee ownership or the use of independent contractors has been introduced into firms only after they had reached the verge or gone over the edge of bankruptcy. More broadly, the recent period of economic stagnation has promoted the current popularity of worker ownership and self-employment in three general ways, each of which will be discussed at length below: (1) It has caused employers to search for new ways to obtain labor on more attractive terms. Employers currently seek a more motivated labor force, at either reduced costs or for wages that at least do not rise as steeply as they have in the past (Goldman and Van Houten, 1980). (2) Economic stagnation has also contributed to a capital shortage and capital flight. This in turn has made employers increasingly interested in their employees as potential investors in their firms, or as buyers of firms they wish entirely to divest. (3) These economic difficulties have also aroused the government to act, and the American government, even more than American employers, has increasingly been inclined to view employee ownership as a solution to our current economic problems. As a result, the American government now promotes the conversion of workers into owners through a variety of means.

Ownership, Morale, and Labor Costs: Beyond Bureaucratic Control

Some useful insights into current efforts to make workers owners in the United States can be obtained from Richard Edwards' analysis of capitalist strategies of control. Edwards (1979) divides these control strategies into three major types, which he labels "simple," "technical," and "bureaucratic" control. Simple control amounts to little more than face-to-face supervision. Technical control relies on machine pacing, plant design, and the authority of science; its purest expression is the automobile assembly line. Bureaucratic control involves the use of job security and opportunities for advancement to evoke workers' loyalty to an organization and its rules.

According to Edwards, these three categories constitute the three most successful control strategies that American capitalism has yet produced; Edwards nevertheless argues that historically, each of them has ultimately manifested defects that sharply limit its use. Simple control works well in small firms, but is less effective in large organizations, because it becomes attenuated when stretched across long hierarchical chains. Technical control works well in the short run, but has a tendency to make workers sullen and resentful, and therefore leads ultimately to union militance and spiraling labor costs. Bureaucratic control breeds better morale, but has costs of its own. Bureaucratic control becomes particularly expensive during periods of stagnation and decline, because firms are then forced either to retain and promote more employees than their current sales really warrant, or to lay off and otherwise frustrate and alienate large numbers of employees whose loyalties and job skills reflect an investment of many years.

It is in this context that the various means of converting workers into owners now present themselves as an alternative strategy of control. Like technical and bureaucratic control, ownership now appears to be another effective way to encourage rank-and-file employees to do what their managers would like them to do. Even more importantly, however, and unlike technical and bureaucratic control, these new ownership arrangements promise to achieve this result in ways that do not lead to constantly increasing fixed labor costs. Taken together, these two aspects of the use of ownership as a control mechanism do much to explain many of its most common applications in the United States today.

Consider first the current uses of ownership to motivate a labor force. What these efforts amount to is an attempt to subject rank-and-file employees to control mechanisms analogous to those that have already proven their effectiveness in motivating the small businessman and the corporate executive. This parallel is closest in cases in which former employees are converted into independent contractors or franchisees. After such conversions, each former employee becomes a self-employed small businessman, and derives his income solely from business that he makes himself personally responsible for. Matters are more complicated, however, when many workers each acquire only a small claim on the profits of some large business, and continue to receive most of their income in the form of fixed wages or salaries, as they did before. This is true of most instances of employee stock ownership plans in conventional firms, as well as worker buyouts of entire plants.

In these latter instances, employee ownership is unlikely to have much direct impact on the relationship between workers' individual efforts and their material rewards; but as was discussed in Chapter 2, there are stronger indications that employee ownership makes a more symbolic and diffuse contribution to increasing employees' loyalty and morale. Findings of this sort have been reported for firms that have a long history of being worker-owned (Russell, Hochner, and Perry, 1979; Russell, 1982; Greenberg, 1980; Rhodes and Steers, 1981); for newly created worker-owned firms (Long, 1978a, 1978b, 1980), and for employee stock ownership plans in otherwise conventional firms (Goldstein, 1978; Christiansen, 1980; Marsh and McAllister, 1981; Long 1982). Some of the specific morale consequences that have been associated with employee ownership include reductions in turnover (Long, 1978a, 1978b; Marsh and

McAllister, 1981), greater support for managers' authority (Russell, Hochner, and Perry, 1979; Long, 1979, 1981; Hammer and Stern, 1980; Hammer, Stern, and Gurdon, 1982); more cooperation among employees (Russell, 1982); and less tolerance among employees for co-workers whose performance is poor (Long, 1978a; see also Tannenbaum *et al.*, 1974:64–74).

Thus employee ownership promises to encourage in American firms something very much like the enthusiastic loyalty and team spirit that American managers currently admire so much about Japan. It is perhaps for this reason that these two topics are now often mentioned in virtually the very same breath. A 1982 New York Stock Exchange report entitled *People and Productivity* is typical in this regard — the report begins with a discussion of the Japanese challenge, and ends up talking about employee-owned firms (New York Stock Exchange, 1982).

While such research results and public discussions provide some indication of what employee ownership can potentially do to improve employees' attitudes to their workplaces and their jobs, it is hard to say how many employers actually turn to employee ownership in response to considerations of this sort. A survey of personnel managers in companies with ESOPs reported that these managers did place morale and motivational considerations high on their lists of reasons for adopting these plans (Marsh and McAllister, 1981:602–609). Corporations have had some quite different reasons for establishing ESOPs, however, that have clearly been paramount in a number of cases. Some of these other reasons for the spread of ESOPs will be discussed in later sections of this chapter; but there remains one additional aspect of the use of ownership as a control mechanism that must be included here.

In considering employee ownership as a strategy of control, it is necessary to examine not only its potential effectiveness, but also the comparative advantages it offers with respect to alternative forms of control. If improvements in morale were all that employers were after, they might have no need to give up bureaucratic control. Greater loyalty and motivation, after all, are precisely what bureaucratic job structures were originally designed to produce; and to this day, there are probably no more effective ways to evoke these attitudes from employees than by offering them a stable work organization with opportunities to advance. The great attraction of turning workers into owners, however, is that it promises to achieve similar results at a much lower cost. Unlike bureaucratic control, ownership as a control mechanism does not depend upon stable or expanding employment levels and on periodic increases in pay. It is thus well suited to a period of stagnation or decline, such as the one we are living through today.

What employee ownership essentially seeks is to strike a completely different bargain with a labor force than that represented by any conventional employment relationship. Employee ownership offers employees a source

$WD = \downarrow$ wages

of income that can only come through company profits and not at their expense. A hope of many of its advocates has therefore been that as employees
have more to gain in the form of profits, they will become less insistent
about maximizing their wage. This thought links nineteenth century
figures like Hewitt with such leading contemporary spokesmen as Louis
Kelso (Derber, 1970:62; Kelso and Adler, 1958, 1961; Kelso and Hetter,
1967; Mitchell, 1982).

A similar philosophy of compensation, by the way, has long been standard in Japan, and helps to give the Japanese workers' highly touted morale
a strong material base. Here in the United States, it is often assumed that
the apparently greater loyalty and motivation of Japanese workers are due
to cultural and social psychological differences; but employees of large
Japanese companies receive semiannual bonuses that often amount to the
equivalent of several months pay (Vogel, 1979:138–139). If American
workers stood to receive a similar boost in their incomes when their company had a good year, they might be equally as eager to help make sure that
it did, and they might also be less concerned about the size of their
guaranteed wage.

There has also long been evidence that organized labor might potentially
be as interested in striking such a bargain as anyone in management.
Walter Reuther of the United Auto Workers proposed an arrangement of
this sort as early as 1958, but got no response from management. The deal
he offered then sounds extremely relevant now. In Reuther's words:

> What we ought to do is to work out the equities in two stages in which we
> deliberately understate the size of the equity of the wage earner in our
> minimum demand, so that we will be certain it will have no inflationary im-
> pact. Give us a down payment now—represented by our minimum
> demand—and we will defer the realization of the balance of our equity until
> you've completed the year, the consumer has paid his price, and you've made
> your profits (quoted in New York Stock Exchange, 1982:34).

Despite the potential for employee ownership to provide the basis of a
new form of bargaining between labor and management, American labor
unions have had understandable misgivings about some of the terms on
which employee ownership has recently been offered to them. In a number
of cases, employee ownership has been presented to workers not as new
means of boosting their income, but as a basis for cutting their pay. This
has been true of the recent rounds of "concession bargaining" that have
taken place in such ailing industries as auto manufacturing, commercial
aviation, and trucking (Mills, 1983). Such talks have been particularly far-
reaching in the airline industry, where recent agreements have provided for
employees to acquire 13% of Pan Am, 25% of Eastern, and 32% of
Western Airlines (*Employee Ownership*, June, 1983, p. 9, and March, 1984,

pp. 8, 10). All of these stock purchases have come at the price of heavy wage concessions, and it remains to be seen whether the employees' shares of subsequent company profits will ever be sufficient to recover the income they have already lost.

Employee ownership has also been closely associated with pay cuts when workers have purchased closing plants. In some cases large firms have therefore been able to divest a subsidiary to its employees and then to continue to do business with it on much more advantageous terms. This is what happened when General Motors divested its Hyatt Clark plant in 1981. By selling this plant to its employees, GM was able to obtain the workers' agreement not only to a 30 percent pay cut, but also to major work modifications that sharply reduced the number of workers required to run the plant (Davy, 1983). In 1981, Ford tried to duplicate GM's Hyatt Clark success by offering the employees of its aluminum die-cast plant in Sheffield, Alabama, a choice between accepting a 50 percent pay cut and purchasing their plant. In this case, the employees refused to buy their plant (Moberg, 1981).

Conversions of employees into owners have been used to reduce labor costs not only in these instances, but in many others as well. The effects of independent contracting on labor costs have already been discussed. Firm owners pay no Social Security taxes and provide no disability or unemployment insurance protection for independent contractors that they hire. They are also not responsible for withholding federal income taxes or Social Security payments from independent contractors' pay. This absence of withholding means that for the workers involved, a conversion from employee to independent contractor status may produce major increases in their take home pay. It is only when these workers are injured on the job or begin to contemplate retirement that they realize that their incomes are not what they might otherwise have been. For their former employers, in the meantime, these savings in labor protection and withholding expenses do much to explain the popularity of independent contracting in the United States today.

American union leaders can also not help perceiving many efforts to turn workers into owners not only as assaults on wage levels and benefits they have fought for in the past, but also as threats to the organizational integrity of the labor movement itself. In many cases, employees who have become owners have left their unions at the same time. This was true of Boston cab drivers who switched from commission work to renting or leasing their cabs during the 1970s (Russell, 1983). Local unions that have bought out their businesses have often left their internationals at the same time, in part because the pay cuts they have agreed to have dropped their wages below nationally negotiated rates. In nonunion companies, there are also strong indications that employee ownership is being used now as it was in the 1920s (Derber, 1970; Edwards, 1979; Patard, 1982a) to help keep labor unions out. Several newly formed airlines that make much of the fact that they are employee-owned also employ a nonunion labor force at wages that run 40–50% lower than those paid by the unionized carriers (Northrup, 1983; *Employee Ownership*, December, 1983, p. 6; Rhodes, 1984).

Workers as Investors

So far, this analysis has concentrated on how converting workers into owners can help American employers secure well motivated labor at a bargain price. Making workers owners has another major attraction, moreover, that is probably even more important in promoting its popularity in the United States today. This is the capacity of employee ownership to open up new capital resources for a firm, either by inducing workers to replace their employer's capital with their own, or by providing sources of new capital investment for the firm.

The use of workers as a source of capital is most obvious in cases in which workers purchase an entire plant. In these instances, workers typically make it possible for the previous owners to extricate themselves from investments for which no other appropriate buyers can readily be found. Worker ownership facilitates these divestitures in two distinct ways—it both provides a buyer for the plant, and simultaneously transforms the labor force in ways that can greatly facilitate the sale. In the case of ailing plants, worker ownership may be the only way to induce workers to accept the pay cuts and work modifications necessary to keep the plant alive. Worker ownership has also played a similarly facilitative role in divestitures of moderately successful entrepreneurial firms whose founders are approaching retirement age. Conventional capital sources are often reluctant to invest in such firms, because they are uncertain as to what direction a firm may take after its founder is gone. If the firm's current employees can be induced to purchase the firm, however, that may be the best way to guarantee that the firm will stay on its present course.

The use of employee ownership as a source of capital has so far also been the most important factor behind the creation of ESOPs in otherwise conventionally owned firms. Insofar as employers are interested in employee ownership for no more than its motivational value, they in fact have no need to establish these cumbersome and expensive trusts; they can merely give or sell stock to individual employees through such long-established devices as stock bonuses, stock options, profit sharing, or employee stock purchase plans. When corporations go to the trouble of setting up ESOPs, therefore, it is normally to take advantage of one of several financial inducements that the federal government has offered to corporations to encourage them to set up these plans.

One popular way in which corporations use ESOPs to obtain capital on more attractive terms is the so-called "leveraged ESOP." In this situation, a corporation seeking a loan from a bank typically issues new shares of stock to an ESOP, and has the ESOP borrow the money on the corporation's behalf, using the value of its new shares as collateral. Then, as the corporation donates sufficient funds to the ESOP to repay the loan, federal regulations allow the corporation to deduct the full amount of these loan repayments from its income, including principal as well as interest.

While such a leveraged ESOP thus appears to be a relatively inexpensive way for a corporation to get a loan from a bank, it does have the defect of requiring the corporation to issue new shares of stock, thereby diluting the existing shareholders' claims on the profits of the firm. And if a corporation intends to raise capital by issuing new shares of stock, why should it have to take out a loan and pay interest at all? Why not just sell the stock for cash on the day it is issued?

There appear to be two answers to this question, one for closely held corporations, and one for publicly traded stocks. For closely held corporations, the creation of an ESOP may be the only way to find a buyer for their shares, since there are no regularly established markets for such stocks. For publicly traded stocks, a major problem with conventional stock issues is that they normally dilute the voting power of the corporation's existing leadership, and thereby increase the firm's vulnerability to a hostile takeover attempt. By selling stock to an ESOP, on the other hand, the firm's management increases the amount of capital that is in "friendly" hands. This is true first of all because employee stockholders can normally be expected to join with management in resisting efforts by avaricious conglomerates to gobble up their firm. Even more importantly, beneficiaries of leveraged ESOPs acquire voting rights to their stock only in proportion to the amount of the loan that has been paid off. Shares that are still being used as collateral, in the meantime, are voted by management-selected trustees.

This capacity of ESOPs to provide a source of friendly capital for managers has led to a number of instances in which ESOPs have been created in direct response to takeover bids (Weyher and Knott, 1982:14–15, 140–142, 167–179). Perhaps the most prominent of these cases was the 1981 effort to create an ESOP at Continental Airlines that would have been put to this use. While that effort failed, an ESOP was successfully used in 1983 to defeat a threatened takeover of Dan River, one of the nation's largest textile manufacturing firms. With over 12,000 employees, Dan River immediately became the nation's largest employee-owned firm (*Employee Ownership*, June, 1983, p. 7; Caudell-Feagan, 1983; Williams, 1984).

All of these are uses of the so-called "leveraged ESOPs." A possibly even more attractive set of financial incentives for the formation of ESOPs consists of the tax credits that the federal government offers to corporations that reimburse them for the entire cost of stocks that they donate to these plans. The maximum amounts of these tax credits have differed from year to year as shown in Table VIII. These tax credits may not be applied to stock that is leveraged, but only to stocks that are fully credited to employees' accounts in the year for which the credit is claimed. ESOPs formed to take advantage of these tax credits were initially called "TRASOPs," an acronym for "Tax Reduction Act ESOPs." In 1980, the TRASOPs were officially rechristened "tax credit ESOPs," but many people have continued to call them TRASOPs. Since 1983, tax credit ESOPs have also frequently been referred to as "PAYSOPs," in reflection of the fact that these tax credits are now "payroll-based." Whatever label one applies to them, these tax credits constitute major gifts from the federal government to American corporations, and have done much to stimulate the growth of ESOPs in the contemporary United States (Ludwig and Curtis, 1981; Weyher and Knott, 1982; Frisch, 1982).

Franchising and independent contracting have also frequently arisen as means of tapping new sources of capital for their firms. In troubled industries like the taxi business, the sale of business opportunities to former employees has provided a way for owners to divest enterprises that are no longer as profitable as they formerly were. Many fleet owners realized in the 1970s that they could make more money by selling cabs to former employees than they could by operating the cabs themselves; as one Boston fleet owner put this point in 1979, he realized that he "would rather be in the cab financing business than in the cab owning business." In more prosperous industries, on the other hand, franchising and independent contracting have provided an additional source of capital to help finance the growth of rapidly expanding firms.

In practice, it is often difficult to draw a hard and fast line between the uses of worker ownership as a source of capital, and its uses as a strategy of control. One of the great attractions of worker ownership as a form of investment is its capacity to kill two or three birds with one stone. That is, the same capital contributions that help a firm meet its financial needs also have the potential to make workers more motivated, more loyal, and less likely to press for a higher wage.

Table VIII. Tax Credits Available to ESOPs

Year(s)	Tax Credit
1975	1% of new capital investment
1976–82	Same, plus an additional 1/2% "matching credit" in correspondence with voluntary employee contributions
1983–87	1/2% of payroll

Regardless of which particular motives and devices are paramount in any given instance, there are several important reasons why workers should have serious misgivings about worker ownership as a form of investment. There is first of all the danger that workers will be motivated to invest their money in enterprises that have little chance of success. Secondly, when workers become owners of sound enterprises, there is a danger that their ownership will be purchased at too high a price. Finally, even if both of these dangers can be eliminated, worker ownership may still be an unwise investment strategy, because it exposes workers to the risk of losing their jobs and their life savings at the very same time.

At present, the danger that workers will put their money into unsound enterprises appears greatest when workers buy closing plants. When these buyouts are discussed, critics often charge that owners are merely dumping unwanted "lemons" or "turkeys" on their employees, offering them superfluous and technologically obsolete factories that have little chance of success (Zwerdling, 1979; Singer, 1982). In responses to such charges, it has been noted that employers do not divest only unprofitable plants; often, they will put profitable plants up for sale, if these sites are producing a lower rate of return than other ventures the organization is involved in (Zwedling, 1979; Stern et al., 1980; Bluestone and Harrison, 1980). Even when these plants remain marginally profitable, however, it is usually at levels that conventional investors find unacceptably low, especially given their risk. That worker ownership occurs in these plants at all, in fact, is because only workers desperate to save their jobs are willing to make these dubious investments and to shoulder these risks (Ross, 1980).

Advocates of these buyouts are typically well aware of the dangers involved, and urge workers to undertake thorough feasibility studies in order to minimize these risks. With the help of such precautions, worker buyouts compiled a surprisingly good record in their first few years. In 1982, it was reported that only two of these buyouts were known to have ended in failure, involving a total of only 50 employees, at the same time that buyouts were being credited with having saved more than 50,000 jobs (Rosen and Whyte, 1982). In 1983, however, three more of these firms were reported to have filed for bankruptcy, including Waterloo, Iowa's Rath meat packing plant (Employee Ownership, June 1983, p. 10, and December 1983, p. 6; Wall Street Journal, November 14, 1983, p. 29). While all of these are only preliminary and somewhat anecdotal results, the viability of these buyouts seems highly questionable, to say the least.

Some similar criticisms could be made about the employee shareholdings that are currently growing in such troubled industries as automobile manufacturing, commercial aviation, and trucking; in the cases of ESOPs, however, the greatest danger is not that employees are acquiring a worthless stock, but that shares contributed to ESOPs are being significantly overvalued. This in turn means that workers are receiving far fewer shares than are warranted by the size of the tax deductions and tax credits their employers are receiving for these gifts. This danger is particularly high in closely held companies, for which there is no regular market to determine the price of a share. In such firms the price of a share is set by consultants, who are selected by management and are free to choose from among a wide range of possible formulas in calculating the value of a share (Granados, 1980; Larson, Stanley, and Warren, 1981; Hughes, 1983). Opportunities for abuse are therefore rife, and some particularly prominent instances of unreasonably high share values have already come to the attention of the public (U.S. General Accounting Office, 1980; Granados, 1980:27–29). In one instance an IRS-sponsored appraisal concluded that stock sold to an ESOP had been overvalued by 632 percent (U.S. General Accounting Office, 1980: 16).

Even more likely to overpay for their ownership are the independent contractors and franchisees. The desire to own one's own business beats strongly in many American hearts, and millions of Americans therefore seem ready to pay dearly for this privilege. The discussion of the taxi industry in Chapter 4 has already made reference to a number of abuses to which this ambition can lead. In Boston, would-be owner-operators constantly bid up the price of taxicab licenses, or "medallions," and allowed their medallion purchases to be financed on what can only be described as predatory terms. Many drivers later discovered that they could not keep up their payments, and were forced to give up their cabs.

The possibility that workers will be tempted to pay too much for their ownership is also present when workers collectively purchase an entire firm. The potential for abuse in these cases is well illustrated by the record of the plywood cooperatives of the Pacific Northwest. Although the first of these firms had been worker-owned from the day they were formed, many of the later cooperatives were created as worker buyouts of conventional firms. Berman reports that in these cases, many former owners

> appear to have used sale to a worker-group as a way to obtain a price above the plant's true value, or to obtain a lucrative exclusive sales (or, less frequently, log-supply) contract for the cooperative's output. Although a sales-agency agreement could be initially helpful . . . the exclusive sales contracts forced on cooperatives by former owners proved detrimental in several cases, and disastrous for the cooperative's survival in at least one instance (Berman, 1982:163).

Berman goes on to note that a number of these cooperatives were established at the initiative of speculators who purchased mills with their own resources and then sold them to workers at a marked-up price. In some cases, these promoters required worker-owners to make continuing payments to them for management services, or to grant them exclusive rights to sell the firm's output. Berman reports that "some of these promotional arrangements imposed a lasting operating or financial handicap on the cooperative" (1982:163). In the case of two ventures, promoters were later convicted of fraud. Berman adds that in the aftermath of these scandals, "The widely publicized fraud trials cast suspicion on all worker-ownership projects and are probably partly responsible for the lack of subsequent additions to the cooperative group" (Berman, 1982:163).

Finally, there remains the argument that even when workers become owners of a viable company at an appropriate price, worker ownership constitutes an unwise investment strategy from the worker's point of view. The problem is that when a worker becomes an investor in the firm that employs him, he may be placing too many eggs in one basket, and risks losing both his job and his savings should that one firm happen to fail. Thus a more prudent form of savings would be a diversified investment portfolio, as is typical of most pension funds. Trade unionists have been voicing this objection to employee ownership for years (Patard, 1982a; Jochim, 1982:154), and Peter Drucker makes a similar point (1974:191, 1976:8).

The relative insecurity of employee ownership in comparison to a diversified investment portfolio becomes particularly apparent when it is suggested that employees should accept employee ownership in the place of a pension plan. In the 1975 worker buyout of South Bend Lathe, the possibility of using workers' pension assets to finance the purchase was briefly considered but was turned down at the workers' insistence (Blasi and Whyte, 1981:331). Converting pension plans into ESOPs has also held many attractions for the managers of conventional firms. Unlike pension plans, ESOPs allow cash that is earmarked for employees' retirement to be kept within the firm, rather than constantly flowing out of it. For firms that fear takeovers, converting pension plans into ESOPs is also a quick way to place a large block of friendly capital in managers' hands. In 1981, this tactic was used to deflect takeover threats both at Grumman Corporation and at Harper and Row. Both firms, however, were subsequently sued for this action. Grumman was sued by the Labor Department, on the grounds that its actions were not in the best interests of the beneficiaries of its pension plan (Caudell-Feagan, 1983; Sing, 1984). Harper and Row was sued by its employees, who were particularly upset by the fact that the ESOP had apparently paid almost twice the current market value for its shares (*Employee Ownership*, September, 1983, p. 8).

The risks to which workers' capital stakes in their businesses are exposed also make it possible for employee ownership to have an ultimately negative influence on morale. This is because employee ownership can cause employees to become unnecessarily distressed by the inevitable short-term fluctuations in the price of a company's stock, and extremely discouraged in the face of a long-term decline. These consequences have led eventually to the termination of a large number of employee stock bonus and stock purchase programs, particularly during the Depression, but also in the years since (Patard, 1982a; O'Toole, 1979).

All of these difficulties raised by the use of employees as a source of investment capital for their firms help to underline the importance of the tax incentives that the federal government offers to corporations to encourage them to set up these plans. As a result of these incentives, the ESOPs constitute forms of capital that employers receive in their employees' names, but not at their expense. The federal government's role in stimulating the spread of employee ownership in the contemporary United States will be considered in greater detail below.

The Government Role

It has been hard to look for very long at any of the major reasons that American employers have had for turning workers into owners without noticing a number of ways in which the federal government has been involved in these trends. The attractions of using ownership to motivate and control a labor force owe much to what the government has done to drive up the cost of the conventional employment relationship. That is, employers often use independent contractors, divest plants, and create employee stock ownership plans either to avoid federal income tax withholding and social insurance expenses or to escape the consequences of the National Labor Relations Act. Employers are encouraged to use employee ownership as a source of investment, similarly, largely by the tax deductions and tax credits associated with the various types of employee stock ownership plans. By picking up much of the tab for these plans, the federal government makes it possible to use employee ownership as a source of capital, without taking the money out of employees' own pockets, and therefore without allowing employee ownership to become a negative influence on morale.

Why is the American government so ready to encourage employee ownership in these various ways? In many cases, government efforts to promote employee ownership have not been the direct result of lobbying efforts or other organized activities by any major political groups, but have instead come at the initiative of the legislators themselves. Some of the reasons why American lawmakers have recently become so interested in employee ownership were discussed in Chapter 1. There appears to be a widespread impression in Washington that employee ownership has the potential to restore prosperity to the American economy in ways that are uniquely compatible with the nation's institutions and traditions. This is often expressed in the thought that current legislative efforts on behalf of employee ownership are serving as an "Industrial Homestead Act."

Actual government actions with regard to employee ownership have in practice not been a simple function of these legislative good intentions, but have instead been a good deal more complicated in a number of ways. First, some federal inducements for converting workers into owners have not been deliberately intended to have this result, but are instead indirect and unintended consequences of legislation that was enacted to serve entirely different ends. This is true of all the tax laws and social insurance legislation that have inadvertently driven up the cost of conventional employment relationships. Second, various arms of the federal government have occasionally worked at cross purposes in this field, with one branch or agency systematically undermining the work of another. Third, on certain specific issues a good deal of vigorous lobbying by interested parties has indeed been involved.

For legislation affecting employee stock ownership plans, the most crucial event appears to have been the establishment of a connection between Louis Kelso and Senator Russell Long in 1973. Senator Long immediately became employee ownership's most vigorous champion in the Congress, and he continues to fill that role as this book goes to press.

Senator Long's first major act on behalf of employee stock ownership was a largely defensive move. When the Employee Retirement Income Security Act of 1974 was first being discussed, there was a strong possibility that the use of employee stock ownership plans would have been drastically restricted by this bill. Since the legislation was primarily concerned with the safety of employees' retirement funds, it is not surprising that the act would have taken a tough stance against investing employees' pension funds in their employers' own stocks. As a result of Long's efforts, the final version of the ERISA bill did give legal recognition to the employee stock ownership plans.

Another consequence of ERISA was to give ESOPs the right to borrow money, a provision that gave birth to the leveraged ESOP. Since 1974, many of Long's efforts have been designed to offer additional financial inducements to corporations for setting up these plans. A rationale that is frequently offered in defense of these financial incentives is that since the ESOPs are expensive to establish and their motivational consequences remain largely unknown, corporations will not go to the trouble of setting up these plans unless the federal government can make it worth their while. As the plans mature and begin to prove their worth, the hope is that special tax credits will no longer be required.

The first tax credits for ESOPs were included in the Tax Reduction Act of 1975. This act gave corporations a tax credit equal to 10% of the value of new capital investments they made in their firms, and as a result of Long's efforts they could earn an additional 1% credit by donating an equivalent sum to an ESOP. In 1976, this potential tax credit was increased by an additional 1/2%, provided that this additional donation was matched dollar-for-dollar by voluntary contributions from employees to their ESOP accounts.

For Long, the most serious limitation of these investment-based tax credits was that they were directed largely at capital-intensive firms. For labor-intensive firms with little capital investment relative to their total payroll costs, an additional 1% on top of their investment tax credit was still not sufficient to motivate them to incur the expense of setting up an ESOP. It is for this reason that Long sought to establish a "payroll-based" tax credit for ESOPs, as such a tax credit would have a particular appeal to the labor-intensive firms that had been unmoved by the earlier investment-based credit. A payroll-based tax credit for ESOPs was finally incorporated into the Economic Recovery Tax Act of 1981. This act phased out the earlier investment-based tax credit, and left a new payroll-based tax credit in its place (see Table VIII).

In addition to these major milestones, Long has also backed a number of other pieces of legislation designed to facilitate the ESOPs' introduction and to make improvements in their structure. In 1976, he supported a bill that rebuked such federal agencies as the IRS and the Labor Department for drafting internal regulations that would have restricted the ESOPs' use in ways directly contrary to the legislators' intent (Granados, 1980:19; Frisch, 1982:195–196). Some legislative efforts to modify the internal structures of the ESOPs will be discussed later in this chapter. By one count, a total of sixteen pieces of legislation dealing with employee stock ownership plans were enacted between 1973 and 1981 (Ludwig and Curtis, 1981:211).

The federal government has not been as generous in facilitating worker buyouts of closing plants as it has been in encouraging employee stock ownership plans. For workers who have been interested in making these purchases, however, loans, loan guarantees, technical assistance, and feasibility studies have intermittently been made available through such federal agencies as the Economic Development Administration, the Department of Housing and Urban Affairs, and the Small Business Administration. Legislation to put this assistance on a more regular institutional footing has also occasionally been passed in one house or another, and in 1980, one of these bills made it into law. Called the Small Business Employee Ownership Act, this bill authorized the Small Business Administration to make loan guarantees available to a wide variety of employee-owned firms.

The history of these efforts to pass federal legislation to assist employee-owned divestitures has been recounted in a series of articles by Joseph Blasi and William F. Whyte (Whyte and Blasi, 1980; Blasi and Whyte, 1981; Blasi, Mehrling, and White, 1983). Support for this legislation came initially from a small number of Congressmen in the House who represented areas that threatened to be particularly hard-hit by the current wave of plant closures. These Representatives later linked up with groups of social scientists from Harvard and Cornell and won the support of Senator Long. Eventually, they secured working majorities in both the Senate and the House. This group's efforts have been hampered, however, by a lack of any serious support from either business or organized labor. One sign of their lack of real political muscle has been the fact that administrative agencies charged with implementing the bills they pass have been known to drag their heels for months before taking any steps to put the legislation into practice (see *Employee Ownership*, September, 1981, p. 2, and Sachs, 1983).

In attempting to account for the popularity of worker buyout legislation with the Congress, Blasi and Whyte have noted its resonance with American political tradition, but have also called attention to some more specific arguments that were eventually written into the Small Business Employee Ownership Act of 1980 (Blasi and Whyte, 1981:323–325). The bill begins by stating generally that employee ownership can save jobs and promote small business, and then turns to more specific comments about the two most prominent situations in which workers were likely to purchase their firms. In the case of firms threatened with closure, the bill argues that loan guarantees to worker buyouts will be less a drain on the federal treasury than the unemployment compensation, welfare, and job creation expenses that would otherwise result (see also Bluestone and Harrison, 1982:72–78). For more prosperous firms, the bill notes that employee ownership is a "feasible and desirable" way for retiring small businessmen to divest their firms. Whyte and Blasi have also pointed out that this latter aspect of the legislation prompted three out of the four national organizations that represent small business to give testimony in favor of the bill (Whyte and Blasi, 1980).

The Congress has also acted in recent years to preserve and expand the role of independent contractors in the U.S. economy. The initiative for this legislation actually originated with the IRS, which has sought since the late 1960s to restrict the size of this category in order to minimize the loss of revenue that results from the absence of withholding taxes for these workers. The more the IRS has pressured the industries involved, however, the more they have appealed to Congress for help. Thus this issue has now aroused more lobbying activity than any other aspect of federal ownership policy. Hearings on independent contractors conducted in the House in 1979 and in the Senate in 1982 attracted a virtual "who's who" of trade associations representing businesses that make use of these workers (U.S. Congress, House Committee on Ways and Means, 1979; U.S. Congress, Senate Committee on Finance, 1982).

In response to such lobbying efforts, Congress in 1978 forbade the IRS to impose any further restrictions on the use of independent contractors until the Congress itself had taken legislative action to define their future status. In practice, this left employers free to make greater use of independent contractors than ever before. Moreover, when Congress finally incorporated a new definition of the independent contractor category into the Tax Equity & Fiscal Responsibility Act of 1982, the explicit purpose of this legislation was to create a so-called "safe harbor" for employers that would facilitate the use of such workers.

Thus in all three arenas—worker buyouts, employee stock ownership, and independent contracting—it is now federal policy to encourage the transformation of American workers into owners. It is this federal encouragement that is most new about efforts to make workers owners in the United States today, and that also does more than anything else to lend significance to these efforts. If the existing federal encouragements for converting workers into owners are retained or continue to be enhanced, then the proportion of worker-owners and self-employed laborers in the American labor force is also quite likely to continue to grow.

From Employee Ownership to Workers' Control?

Of the mechanisms for making workers owners in the contemporary United States, the newest and potentially the most significant is clearly the ESOP. As a result both of worker buyouts and the establishment of ESOPs in conventionally owned firms, the ESOPs are rapidly spreading throughout the economy. What is the future of these funds? If they continue to grow in number and in size, what impact will they have on the internal operations of their firms? Already, employees own a majority of the stock in an estimated 1,200 American firms, and own ten percent or more of the stock in at least 30 firms that are among or near the Fortune 500 in size (Sing, 1984:7).

Some of the possibilities inherent in the spread of the ESOPs were already anticipated by Peter Drucker in 1976. In a work that was subtitled *How Pension Fund Socialism Came to America*, Drucker wrote that as a result of the capital that had accumulated in employee pension funds, the American economy was already both worker-owned and worker-controlled. Drucker even declared that

> In terms of Socialist theory, the employees of America are the only true "owners" of the means of production. Through their pension funds they are the only true "capitalists" around, owning, controlling, and directing the country's "capital fund" (Drucker, 1976:2).

Drucker appears to have based these rather extravagant claims on the following line of reasoning. First, Drucker estimated that approximately 25% of the equity in American industry was owned by pension funds of one kind or another. Because in most corporations, such stock percentages are "more than enough for control" (1976:1), Drucker leaped to the conclusion that pension funds already do in fact control the American economy.

Drucker has subsequently been disputed on both of these points. James

Henry pointed out that the portion of American stocks owned by pension funds in 1974 was probably not 25%, but 15% (Henry, 1977). By the early 1980s, this figure had reached 20-25% (Barber, 1982:32), but remained well short of the "50-if not 60%" that Drucker had predicted for 1985 (Drucker, 1976:1).

More important than the issue of the size of the pension fund holdings has been the question of their implications for control. Two aspects of the way in which pension fund investments are normally allocated make it somewhat ludicrous to describe them as instruments of workers' control. First, pension fund holdings are normally widely dispersed, and most funds are therefore merely passive minority shareholders in the companies they invest in. Second, workers typically have no say in how these funds are invested, because the funds are usually governed by management-selected boards of trustees. Drucker himself was often led by considerations of this sort to grant self-contradictorily that pension funds do not give control to workers, but make them mere "beneficial owners" (1976:69) or "investors" (1976:82).

Once Drucker's claims had been disposed of, several sources have begun to suggest that while his "pension fund socialism" was not yet a reality, it someday might be. This thinking is farthest advanced in Sweden, where union leaders have long participated in the administration of pension fund assets, and where a new type of wage earner investment fund has recently been proposed that could eventually acquire a controlling interest in most large Swedish firms (Meidner, 1978, 1981; Ohman, 1983; Albrecht, 1983). A number of authors have been quite explicit in seeing these Swedish wage earner investment funds as potential vehicles for a peaceful "transition to socialism" (Martin, 1977; Stephens, 1979; Esping-Anderson, 1981; Kesselman, 1982; Burkitt, 1983). In the United States, more modest efforts have also been initiated to see if workers cannot acquire greater control over the pension funds that are currently accumulating in their names (Rifkin and Barber, 1978; Barber, 1982; O'Cleireacain, 1981; Fager, 1982).

While American efforts to bring about workers' control through pension funds have so far born little practical fruit, worker ownership of individual firms appears in many ways to be a more promising path to workers' control. While pension fund assets are typically widely dispersed, this form of investment is concentrated right in an employee's own workplace, which may be the only work site about which employees care enough to participate on a regular basis. Moreover, while "pension fund socialism" would require national coordination to be practicable, this form of workers control can be introduced piecemeal in individual firms.

Other favorable consequences for workers' control follow from the structure of the ESOPs. It has been pointed out that when employees own stock in their companies on an individual basis, they often fail to vote their shares, or dissipate their voting power by selling off shares in response to financial need. The fact that ESOPs consolidate employee's individual share accounts into one large perpetual trust, however, encourages employee shares to be voted in a single powerful block. This is something that theorists of employee stock ownership were advocating as early as the 1920s (Patard, 1982a; 49). More recently, the capacity of ESOPs to provide a basis for workplace democracy has been given a practical demonstration in such newly established worker-owned ventures as the Rath and Hyatt Clark plants. Nationwide, the National Center for Employee Ownership estimates that employees exercise the control rights associated with their ownership in about half of the majority employee-owned firms (*Employee Ownership*, March, 1983, p. 1).

Insofar as ESOPs do serve as a basis for workplace democracy, they may also constitute a form of workers' control that is unusually resistant to the degeneration phenomenon. The laws governing ESOPs require each employee's individual holdings to be carefully accounted for, and provide for these funds to be distributed automatically to workers as they retire. These features appear closely analogous to the system of "internal debt accounting" recommended by Ellerman for preventing the degeneration of democratic firms. In addition, federal laws normally require newly hired employees to be included in their companies' ESOPs no later than a year after they have been hired. This provision will thus discourage the emergence of separate classes of owners and nonowners within democratic ESOP firms.

While ESOPs thus show a great deal of potential to create forms of worker ownship that are accompanied by meaningful and long-lasting forms of workers control, their actual use to date has fallen far short of this promise. So far, employee ownership appears to be bringing power to workers primarily in failing firms, or where retiring owners can find no other buyers for their firms. In firms like Rath and Hyatt Clark, workers' control has thus brought little more power to workers than the right to cut their own wages or to lay themselves off. In more prosperous firms, in the meantime, the ESOPs have generally not brought power to workers, but have served instead as instruments of managers' control.

ESOPs have so far served managers' interests in a number of ways. Reference has already been made to the fact that managers select the trustees who control the voting power of an ESOP's "leveraged" shares. Managers also accumulate allocated shares much more rapidly than rank-and-file employees. This is true first of all because shares in ESOPs are normally allocated not per person, but on the basis of salaries. A manager who earns ten times the salary of another employee acquires ten times as many shares. In addition, while shares in tax credit ESOPs are immediately fully vested, shares in leveraged ESOPs are vested in accordance with complex formulas, which may require employees to serve for ten or fifteen years before acquiring full ownership and control of their stock. It is also permissible for allocations to leveraged ESOPs to be weighted according to age or years of service, or to exclude whole categories of employees. It is legal for participation in an ESOP to be restricted to salaried employees, and to exclude all wage earners or unionized employees (Carlson, 1976:308; Jochim, 1982:162, 168).

ESOPs favor managers' interests not only with respect to lower ranking employees, but also with respect to outside shareholders in their firms. When ESOPs are created through issues of new shares, for examples, they dilute the existing shareholders' stock. And insofar as managers gain control over this ESOP stock, this also helps to insulate managers from outside shareholders' control, as is illustrated most dramatically by the use of ESOPs as a takeover defense. As the *Wall Street Journal* reported in February 1984, there is now a clear danger that the nation's employee stock ownership plans are being turned into "management entrenchment stock ownership plans" (Williams, 1984). With respect to the future of capitalism, the ESOPs thus show few signs of taking the United States closer to anything worthy of the name of "socialism," but they do breathe powerful new life into theories of "managerial revolution" (e.g., Burnham, 1941).

Within the federal government, both Congressmen and agencies that have been involved in the design and administration of the ESOP program have often expressed concern over these uses of the ESOPs on a number of grounds. ESOPs are both intended and legally required to be of benefit to a broad proportion of a firm's employees, rather than to managers alone. When managers use ESOPs primarily to enrich themselves and to insulate themselves from outside shareholders' control, they frustrate the purpose of the ESOP laws, and may also run afoul of many other regulations as well. These include both state and federal security and exchange laws, and laws that require employee benefit plans to be administered in the interests of their beneficiaries and not of their trustees.

Federal concerns about managers' use of ESOPs to serve their own interests have taken a number of concrete forms. The Department of Labor announced in 1983 that it would henceforth "take a much more aggressive posture in evaluating the use of any employee benefit plans as takeover defense strategies" (*Employee Ownership*, June, 1983, p. 7). In the spring of 1984, the Labor Department lived up to this pledge by threatening to sue Carter Hawley's ESOP fiduciaries if they took improper action in that company's takeover fight (Sing., 1984).

Misgivings about the one-sided uses of ESOPs and other benefit plans have also occasionally prompted the Congress to act. In 1981 and 1982, Congress imposed restrictions on so-called "top heavy" benefit plans. According to the 1982 law, "top heavy plans" are defined as plans in which 60% or more of the benefits go to "key" employees. The category of "key" employees includes all company officers, employee-owners who earn more than $150,000 per year, the ten largest employee-owners, and all employees who own 5% or more of the company's stock. The 1982 law did not prohibit these top heavy plans, but it did require them to contribute at least 3% of *all* participants' salaries to their accounts every year, unless the key employees' allocation percentage is less. The same law also imposed accelerated vesting schedules on these top heavy plans (*Employee Ownership*, December, 1982, p. 2).

Another set of steps that Congress has taken to limit managers' opportunities to use ESOPs primarily for their own benefit has consisted of various legislative provisions requiring voting rights in ESOP stocks to be "passed through" to their beneficiaries rather than being exercised at the discretion of management-selected trustees. Federal lawmakers appear to have had a number of reasons for backing such laws. One is an expectation that employee ownership will lose much of its social psychological meaning and motivational consequences if it is not accompanied by some form of control. Another common argument is that the ESOP program was set up to benefit employees, not just managers, and giving voting rights to plan beneficiaries is the best way to make sure that these plans are indeed responsive to their needs.

In public corporations, federal law currently requires complete pass through of voting rights on all allocated shares. This includes all shares in tax credit ESOPs, since they are immediately allocated, plus all shares in leveraged ESOPs on which the loans have been paid off. In closely held firms, voting rights must be passed through only for major issues such as mergers and acquisitions that require the support of more than a majority of shareholders in order to be approved. This limited pass through provision for closely held corporations was added to the ESOP regulations only in 1978.

That 1978 law appears now to have been the high water mark of Congressional support for the pass through of voting rights in ESOPs. Since that time, federal support for these provisions has noticeably declined. One major cause prompting many Congressmen to reconsider their positions on this issue was the fact that numerous firm owners vociferously objected to this change in the plans. Many firm owners who had established ESOPs prior to 1978 felt that Congress had no right to impose such a retroactive change on them, and they flocked to the newly formed ESOP Association of America in order to lobby for the repeal of this law (Granados, 1980). These objections have also contributed to an impression that the 1978 pass through provision is now seriously retarding the further spread of ESOPs to closely held firms. In 1981, a bill calling for the repeal of the limited voting rights pass through in closely held corporations passed the Senate with only three dissenting votes, but was not acted upon in the House. In the following year, similar bills were introduced in both the Senate and the House, and it appears to be only a question of time before this provision is repealed (*Employee Ownership*, September, 1982, p. 7, and December, 1983, p. 6).

The relative political weakness of employee ownership in the United States stands out even more clearly when one contrasts the American situation to the current proposal for wage earner investment funds in Sweden. Support for this reform in Sweden begins with the fact that Sweden has the most heavily unionized and possibly also the most politically powerful working class in the Western world (Stephens, 1979; Stephens and Stephens, 1982; Esping-Anderson and Friedland; 1982). The proposal for wage earner investment funds originated in Sweden's largest trade union in the early 1970s, and was adopted with some modifications by the Social Democratic Party in 1978. When the Social Democrats returned to power in 1982, the passage of this legislation was virtually assured; a bill to establish the wage earner investment funds was formally introduced in the Swedish Parliament in November 1983.

The contrasting political origins of employee ownership proposals in the United States and Sweden is clearly reflected in the form these proposals take. In the United States, ESOPs are financed through government subsidies and employers' voluntary gifts; in Sweden, the wage earner investment funds are to be financed through a tax on employers' "excess" profits. In the United States, ESOPs are commonly vehicles of managers' control; Sweden's wage earner investment funds are to be controlled by employee representatives, with their voting power to be divided equally between local and national union organizations (Sonning, 1984).

As in Sweden, employee ownership in the United States has been accompanied by workers' control primarily when unions have been involved in its design. Some reasons why American unions are generally skeptical about employee ownership have already been discussed. As a result of these misgivings, union leaders have generally approached worker ownership with great reluctance, and have bargained for it only when they have felt that they had little choice (Whyte *et al.*, 1983, Chapter 5). When unions have become involved in employee ownership, however, they have sought to make the best of what they consider to be a bad situation, and have insisted that workers' gains in ownership should be accompanied by gains in control. Thus local union involvement in the buyouts of Denver Yellow Cab and the Rath and Hyatt Clark plants helped lead to the adoption of unusually democratic structures by these firms. In companies in which employees have acquired ownership through concession bargaining, unions have also sought representation for worker-owners on company boards. As a result of these efforts, workers' representative have gained admission to the boards of such companies as Chrysler and Eastern Airlines. At the annual meeting of Pan American shareholders held in May 1984, employees' representatives also used the voting power of their stock to block a reorganization of the company. The employee representatives had feared that the company's proposed new structure would allow it to set up a new nonunion subsidiary, as several other airlines had already done (*Los Angeles Times*, May 9, 1984, p. IV-1; Northrup, 1983).

All of this suggests that not much more workers' power is likely to come out of worker ownership than goes into it at the start. Occasional acts of philanthropy aside, power is not something that is very frequently just given away. It is therefore unrealistic to expect American workers to acquire any meaningful degree of power from forms of employee ownership that they receive passively as gifts from their employer or the federal government. Worker ownership in the United States is unlikely to have significant consequences for workers' control, unless American workers summon up the will and the power to insist that it should.

This conclusion is also supported by the case studies reported in the previous four chapters of this work. In those instances, workers were able to establish their own organizations as a result of the power they derived from their ties to each other and from the nature of their work. Later entrants to these organizations who had these same resources were also incorporated into the ownership of these firms. In none of these organizations, however, was ownership or the power associated with it ever extended to categories of workers who were not in a position to insist that it should.

Conclusion

Several early readers of this manuscript complained that they found this final chapter somewhat inconsistent with the rest of the book in tone. While earlier chapters presented generally sympathetic treatments of employee ownership in a variety of forms, this chapter has been largely a catalogue of real and potential abuse.

This difference in tone had its origin in differences in the causal processes giving rise to employee ownership in these instances that clearly separate them from the cases of employee ownership discussed earlier in this work. The employee-owned firms described in the four previous chapters were all created by and for the employee-owners themselves. If there was anyone whose interests one needed to be concerned about in those cases, it was the employees who were not being allowed to become co-owners of those firms. In the forms of employee ownership examined in this chapter, in contrast, employees are becoming owners at the initiative of someone else, a fact that in itself encourages inquiry into the motives of these Greeks bearing gifts.

This initial skepticism has here been reinforced by data on the actual workings of employee ownership in many of these forms. Due to problems with stock valuations and the absence of voting rights, the General

Accounting Office concluded flatly that ESOPs in closely held firms "generally were not being operated in the best interest of participants" (U.S. General Accounting Office, 1980: 6). Examinations of worker buyouts of failing firms and of conversions of employees into independent contractors have in many cases yielded even more disturbing results.

There is a danger that by emphasizing this potential for abuse, I have done an injustice to firms like Washington's International Group Plans that have extended ownership to their employees on fair or even generous terms. Whether these cases outnumber the abusive ones is at present impossible to say. Another disquieting aspect of all of these forms of employee ownership, in fact, is how little systematic information is being collected about any of them. At this point, we cannot even say with certainty how many ESOPs or independent contractors there are. As for what the consequences of these innovations have been, at present we have little more than isolated case studies and anecdotes to rely on.

Given the potential for abuse inherent in all of these developments, they clearly deserve much closer scrutiny than they currently receive. This was the conclusion of the General Accounting Office report on ESOPs that appeared in 1980, and it applies with even greater force to independent contracting arrangements and to worker buyouts of failing firms.

In the absence of better safeguards, we should prepare now for the current wave of enthusiasm for employee ownership in the United States to subside, and for some hard questions to begin to be asked. Already, in firms like Harper and Row, employees are asking whether employee ownership is so wonderful that it was worth giving up their pension fund. As ESOPs do begin to accumulate more stock, workers may also want to know whether the stock is really worth what it was valued at and why owning a significant amount of stock has not brought them more control.

It seems inevitable that such issues will eventually force us to rethink what the goals we seek from employee ownership really are, and to ask whether there are not better ways to promote employee ownership than the ones we are using now. About the long-term future of employee ownership in this country, however, I have little doubt. Governments almost everywhere are trying to turn their nations' employees into owners, by one means or another, for good reasons or bad. In the United States, we have some particularly strong reasons for putting employee ownership on our national agenda and keeping it there. For Americans to become owners of their workplaces may or may not prove to be America's answer to socialism; it may or may not be America's answer to Japan; but before it was any of those things, it was the American Dream. American workers want to own their own businesses, and since this is a democracy, I suspect that someday most of them will.

Bibliography

Abe, Masatoshi A., and Brian C. Brush
1976 "On the Regulation of Price and Service Quality: The Taxicab Problem," *Economics and Business*, 16, No. 3 (Autumn):
105–111.

Abell, Peter, and Nicholas Mahoney
1980 *Economic and Social Potential Of Industrial Cooperatives in Developing Countries*. London: International Co-operative Alliance.

Abrahamsson, Bengt
1977 *Bureaucracy or Participation: The Logic of Organization*. Beverly Hills: Sage
Publications.

Adizes, Ichak and Elisabeth Mann Borgese, eds.
1975 *Self-Management: New Dimensions to Democracy*. Santa Barbara, Ca.: Clio
Press.

Agassi, Judith Buber
1974 "The Israeli Experience in the Democratization of Work Life," *Sociology
of Work and Occupations*, 1: 52–81.

Albrecht, Sandra
1983 "Sweden: Nationwide Debate on Worker Investment," *Workplace
Democracy*, 10, No. 2: 12–15.

Alchian, Armen, and Harold Demsetz
1972 "Production, Information Costs, and Economic Organization,"
American Economic Review, 62: 777–795.

Alrich, Howard, and Robert N. Stern
1983 "Resource Mobilization and the Creation of U.S. Producers'
Cooperatives 1835–1935," *Economic and Industrial Democracy*, 4: 371–406.

Allen, Michael Patrick
1981 "Power and Privilege in the Large Corporation: Corporate Control and
Managerial Compensation," *American Journal of Sociology*, 86: 1112–1123.

American Center for the Quality of Work Life
1978   *Industrial Democracy in Europe: A 1977 Survey*. American Center for the
            Quality of Work Life.

American Dental Association
1963   "The 1962 Survey of Dental Practice II. Income of Dentists by Loca-
            tion, Age and Other Factors," *Journal of the American Dental Association*,
            66 (1963): 554–561.

1964   "The Dental Partnership," *Journal of the American Dental Association*, 69
            (1964): 499–500.

Aristotle
1962   *The Politics*. Translated by T.A. Sinclair. Baltimore, Md.: Penguin.

Aronowitz, Stanley
1972   "Left-Wing Communism: The Reply to Lenin," in *The Unknown Dimen-
            sion: European Marxism since Lenin*. Edited by Dick Howard and Karl E.
            Klare. New York: Basic Books.

Auchincloss, Louis
1963   *Powers of Attorney*. Boston: Houghton Mifflin.
1974   *The Partners*. Boston: Houghton Mifflin.

Avineri, Shlomo
1968   *The Social and Political Thought of Karl Marx*. London: Cambridge
            University Press.

Avrich, Paul
1963   "The Bolshevik Revolution and Workers' Control in Russian
            Industry," *Slavic Review*, (March): 47–63.
1965   "What is 'Makhaevism?'" *Soviet Studies*, 17: 66–75.

Azrael, Jeremy R.
1966   *Managerial Power and Soviet Politics*. Cambridge, Ma.: Harvard Univer-
            sity Press.

Bailes, Kendall E.
1977   "Alexei Gastev and the Soviet Controversy over Taylorism, 1918–24,"
            Soviet Studies, 29: 373–394.

1978   *Technology and Society under Lenin and Stalin: Origins of the Soviet Technical
            Intelligentsia, 1917–1941*. Princeton, New Jersey: Princeton University
            Press.

Barber, Randy
1982   "Pension Funds in the United States: Issues of Investment and Con-
            trol," *Economic and Industrial Democracy*, 3: 31–73.

Barkai, Haim
1977   *Growth Patterns of the Kibbutz Economy*. Amsterdam: North-Holland
            Publishing.

Batstone, Eric
1979   "Systems of Domination, Accommodation, and Industrial
            Democracy," in *Work and Power: The Liberation of Work and the Control of*

Political Power. Edited by Tom R. Burns, Lars Erik Karlsson, and Veljko Rus. London: Sage Publications.

1983   "Organization and Orientation: A Life Cycle Model of French Cooperatives," *Economic and Industrial Democracy*, 4: 139–161.

Batstone, Eric, and P. L. Davies
1976   *Industrial Democracy: European Experience*. London: Her Majesty's Stationery Office.

Baumgartner, Tom, Tom Burns, and Dusko Sekulic
1979   "Self-Management, Market, and Political Institutions in Conflict: Yugoslav Development Patterns and Dialectics," in *Work and Power: The Liberation of Work and the Control of Political Power*. Edited by Tom R. Burns, Lars Erik Karlsson, and Veljko Rus. London: Sage Publications.

Beaglehole, Ernest
1931   *Property: A Study in Social Psychology*. London: Allen & Unwin.

Beck, Leif C.
1972a   "Why Large Law Firms Have Not Incorporated," *Law Office Economics and Management*, 12: 516–520.
1972b   "Dividing Group Practice Income: Don't Let it Divide the Group," *Pennsylvania Medicine*, 75 (November): 35–37.
1981   "New Tax Law for Partnerships of Professional Corporations," *Law Office Economics and Management*, 22: 211–219.

Beck, Leif C., and Vasilios J. Kalogredis
1977a   "Practical Considerations of Group Practice," *Delaware Medical Journal*, 49: 534–541.
1977b   "Further Considerations in Establishing a Group Practice," *Delaware Medical Journal*, 49: 589–590, 596–600.

Becker, Lawrence C.
1977   *Property Rights: Philosophic Foundations*. London: Routledge & Kegan Paul.

Beesley, M. E.
1973   "Regulation of Taxis," *Economic Journal*, 93, March: 150–172.

Bell, Daniel
1962   *The End of Ideology: On the Exhaustion of Political Ideas in the Fifties*. Revised edition. New York: The Free Press.
1973   *The Coming of Post-Industrial Society*. New York: Basic Books.

Bellas, Carl
1972   *Industrial Democracy and the Worker-Owned Firm*. New York: Praeger.

Bellis, Paul
1979   *Marxism and the U.S.S.R.: The Theory of Proletarian Dictatorship and the Marxist Analysis of Soviet Society*. London: MacMillan.

Bendix, Reinhard
1956   *Work and Authority in Industry*. New York: Harper & Row.
1962   *Max Weber: An Intellectual Portrait*. Garden City, New York: Anchor Books.

Ben-Ner, Avner
1981   "On Cooperatives and Hired Labor: Two Step Optimization and In-
            stability." Unpublished working paper. Institute for Social and Policy
            Studies, New Haven, Connecticut.
1982   "Changing Values and Preferences in Communal Organizations:
            Econometric Evidence from the Experience of the Israeli Kibbutz," in
            Participatory and Self-Managed Firms: Evaluating Economic Performance.
            Edited by Derek C. Jones and Jan Svejnar. Lexington, Massachusetts:
            Lexington Books.
1984   "On the Stability of the Cooperative Type of Organization," *Journal of
            Comparative Economics* 8, 247–260.

Ben-Ner, Avner, and Egon Neuberger
1982   "Israel: the Kibbutz," in *The Performance of Labour-Managed Firms.* Edited
            by Frank H. Stephen. London: Macmillan.

Ben-Raphael, Eliezer
1976   "The Stratification System of the Kibbutz," in *Rural Communities: Inter-
            Cooperation and Development.* Edited by Yehuda H. Landau, *et al.* New
            York: Praeger.

Berg, Ivar
1970   *Education and Jobs: The Great Training Robbery.* Baltimore, Maryland:
            Penguin Books.

Bergman, Edward M., and James I. Stein
1983   *Cooperative Forms of Organization in the Taxicab Industry.* Chapel Hill,
            North Carolina: Department of City and Regional Planning, Univer-
            sity of North Carolina.

Berle, Adolf, and Gardener Means
1968   *The Modern Corporation and Private Property.* Revised Edition. New York:
            Harcourt, Brace & World.

Berman, Katrina V.
1967   *Worker-Owned Plywood Companies: An Economic Analysis.* Pullman,
            Washington: Washington State University Press.

1982   "The Worker-Owned Plywood Cooperatives," in *Workplace Democracy
            and Social Change.* Edited by Frank Lindenfeld and Joyce Rothschild-
            Whitt. Boston: Porter Sargent.

Bernstein, Paul
1974   "Run Your Own Business: Worker-Owned Plywood Firms," *Working
            Papers for a New Society*, 2, No. 2: 24–34.

1976   "Necessary Elements for Effective Worker Participation in Manage-
            ment," *Journal of Economic Issues*, 10: 490–522.

1981   "Worker Ownership and Community Redevelopment," *The Corporate
            Examiner*, March: 3A-3D.

Bettelheim, Charles
1975   *Economic Calculation and Forms of Property: An Essay on the Transition Be-*

tween Capitalism and Socialism. Translated by John Taylor. New York: Monthly Review Press.

Blasi, Joseph Raphael
1978   *The Communal Future: The Kibbutz and the Utopian Dilemma.* Norwood, Pennsylvania: Norwood Editions.

Blasi, Joseph R., Perry Mehrling, and William F. Whyte
1983   "The Politics of Worker Ownership in The United States," in *International Yearbook of Organizational Democracy*, vol. I: *Organizational Democracy and Political Processes.* Edited by Colin Crouch and Frank A. Heller. New York: Wiley & Sons.

Blasi, Joseph R., and William Foote Whyte
1981   "Worker Ownership and Public Policy," *Policy Studies Journal*, 10: 320–337.

Blau, Judith R., and Alba, Richard D.
1982   "Empowering Nets of Participation," *Administrative Science Quarterly*, 27: 363–379.

Blau, Peter M.
1970   "A Formal Theory of Differentiation in Organizations," *American Sociological Review*, 35: 201–218.

Blauner, Robert
1964   *Alienation and Freedom.* Chicago, Illinois: University of Chicago Press.

Blaustein, Albert P., and Charles O. Porter
1954   *The American Lawyer: A Summary of the Survey of the Legal Profession.* Chicago: University of Chicago Press.

Bluestone, Barry, and Bennett Harrison
1980   "Why Corporations Close Profitable Plants," *Working Papers for a New Society*, 7, No. 3: 15–23.
1982   *The Deindustrialization of America: Plant Closings, Community Abandonment, and the Dismantling of Basic Industry.* New York: Basic Books.

Blumberg, Paul
1966   "Workers' Management in Comparative Analysis." Doctoral dissertation, University of California, Berkeley.
1968   *Industrial Democracy: The Sociology of Participation.* New York: Schocken Books.

Bodine, Larry
1979   "Owning Stock in a Law Firm," *National Law Journal*, 1, No. 38 (June 4): 1, 10–11.

Bolweg, J. F.
1976   *Job Design and Industrial Democracy: The Case of Norway.* Leiden: Martinus-Nijhoff.

Bonacich, Edna
1973   "A Theory of Middleman Minorities," *American Sociological Review*, 38: 583–594.

Bonacchi, Gabriella M.
1976–77   "The Council Communists Between the New Deal and Fascism," *Telos*, No. 30 (Winter): 43–72.

Boughner, Jackson L.
1962   "Taking in a New Partner," *Law Office Economics and Management*, 3, No. 3: 235–246.

Bourdieu, Pierre and Jean-Claude Passeron
1977   *Reproduction in Education, Society and Culture*. London: Sage Publications.

Bower, Ward
1977   "The 1972 Economic Census of Law Firms," in *The Law Office Manager's Problem Solver*. Chicago: Callaghan.

Bradley, Keith, and Alan Gelb
1981   "Motivation and Control in the Mondragon Experiment," *British Journal of Industrial Relations*, 19: 211–231.
1982a   "The Replication and Sustainability of the Mondragon Experiment," *British Journal of Industrial Relations*, 20: 20–33.
1982b   "The Mondragon Cooperatives: Guidelines for a Cooperative Economy?," in *Participatory and Self-Managed Firms*. Edited by Derek Jones and Jan Svejnar. Lexington, Massachusetts: Lexington Books.

Braverman, Harry
1974   *Labor and Monopoly Capital: The Degradation of Work in the Twentieth Century*. New York: Monthly Review Press.

Brill, Steven
1983   *The American Lawyer Guide to Leading Law Firms, 1983–1984*. 2 vols. New York: Am-Law Publishing.

Brinton, Maurice
1970   *The Bolsheviks & Workers' Control 1917 to 1921*. London: Solidarity.

Brus, Wlodzimierz
1972   *The Market in a Socialist Economy*. London: Routledge & Kegan Paul.
1975   *Socialist Ownership and Political Systems*. Translated by R.A. Clarke. Boston: Routledge & Kegan Paul.

Buber, Martin
1949   *Paths in Utopia*. Translated by R.F.C. Mull. Boston: Beacon Press.

Burawoy, Michael
1978   "Toward a Marxist Theory of the Labor Process: Braverman and Beyond," *Politics & Society*, 8: 247–312.
1979   *Manufacturing Consent: Changes in the Labor Process under Monopoly Capitalism*. Chicago: University of Chicago Press.

Burke, Edward J.
1981   "Median Partner Salary in Large Firm: $101,208," *National Law Journal*, 3, No. 40 (June 15): 2.

Burke, Thomas R., *et al.*
1978   "The Office Meeting—A Symposium," in *The Law Office Manager's Problem Solver.* Chicago: Callaghan.

Burkitt, Brian
1983   "Employee Investment Funds: A Crucial Element in the Transition to Socialism," *Economic and Industrial Democracy*, 4: 103–115.

Burnham, James
1941   *The Managerial Revolution.* New York: John Day.

Cafferata, Gail Lee
1982   "The Building of Democratic Organizations: An Embryological Metaphor," *Administrative Science Quarterly*, 27: 280–303.

Callinicos, Alex
1977   "Soviet Power," *International Socialism*, No. 103 (November): 7–18.

Campbell, Alastair, *et al.*
1977   *Worker-Owners: The Mondragon Achievement.* London: Anglo-German Foundation for the Study of Industrial Society.

Cantor, Daniel J.
1974   "Internal Compensation for Partners (or Shareholders), Associates and Staff." *Law Office Economics and Management*, 15, No. 2: 154–176.
1978   "Dividing Law Firm Income—The Smith System and Its Mutations" in *The Law Office Manager's Problem Solver.* Chicago: Callaghan.

Caplow, Theodore
1959   *The Sociology of Work.* New York: McGraw-Hill.

Carevic, Mico
1974   "Social Property in the Drafts of the Constitutions," *Socialist Thought and Practice*, 14, No. 2: 3–17.

Carlin, Jerome E.
1966   *Lawyers Ethics: A Survey of the New York City Bar.* New York: Russell Sage.

Carlson, D. Bret
1976   "ESOP and Universal Capitalism," *Tax Law Review*, 31: 289–315.

Caudell-Feagan, Michael
1983   "ESOPs . . . How to Implement Them Successfully and Utilize Them Strategically," *Management Review*, 72, No. 12 (December): 423–45.

Center for Research in Ambulatory Health Care Administration
1976   *The Organization and Development of a Medical Group Practice.* Cambridge, Massachusetts: Ballinger Publishing Company.

Cherns, Albert, ed.
1980   *Quality of Working Life and the Kibbutz Experience.* Norwood, Pennsylvania: Norwood Editions.

Chinoy, Eli
1955   *Automobile Workers and the American Dream.* Boston: Beacon Press.

Christiansen, R. O.
1980   "Impact of Employee Stock Ownership Plans on Employee Morale,"
            American Journal of Small Business, 5, No. 1 (July–September): 22–29.

Clamp, Chris
1983   "Mondragon Meets the Recession," *Workplace Democracy*, 10, No. 2
            (Spring): 10–11.

Clarke, Tom
1978   "Industrial Democracy: The Institutionalized Suppression of Industrial
            Conflict?," in *Trade Unions Under Capitalism.* Edited by Tom Clarke and
            Laurie Clements. Hassocks, Sussex: Harvester Press.

Clegg, Hugh
1960   *A New Approach to Industrial Democracy.* Oxford: Blackwell.

Coates, Ken, and Tony Topham, eds.
1970   *Workers' Control.* London: Panther Books.

Coch, Lester, and John R. P. French, Jr.
1948   "Overcoming Resistance to Change," *Human Relations*, 1: 512–532.

Coffman, Richard B.
1977   "The Economic Reasons for Price and Entry Regulation of Taxicabs:
            A Comment," *Journal of Transport Economics and Policy*, 11: 288–297.

Coker, Francis W., ed.
1949   *Democracy, Liberty, and Property: Readings in the American Political Tradition.*
            New York: Macmillan.

Collins, Randall
1979   *The Credential Society.* New York: Academic Press.

Comisso, Ellen
1979   *Workers' Control Under Plan and Market: Implications of Yugoslav Self-
            Management.* New Haven: Yale University Press.
1980   "Yugoslavia in the 1970's: Self-Management and Bargaining," *Journal
            of Comparative Economics*, 4: 192–208.
1981   "Workers' Councils and Labor Unions: Some Objective Tradeoffs,"
            Politics & Society, 10: 251–279.

Conquest, Robert
1967   *Industrial Workers in the USSR.* New York: Praeger.

Conte, Michael, and Arnold S. Tannenbaum
1978   "Employee-Owned Companies: Is the Difference Measurable?," *Monthly
            Labor Review*, July: 23–28.

Cornell Self-Management Working Group
1975   "Toward a Fully Self-Managed Industrial Sector in the United States,"
            Administration and Society, 7, No. 1: 85–106.

Covarrubias, A., and J. Vanek
1976   "Self-Management in the Peruvian Law of Social Property," in
            Organizational Democracy: Participation and Self-Management. Edited by G.
            David Garson and Michael P. Smith. Beverly Hills: Sage Publications.

Dahl, Robert A.
1970   *After the Revolution?* New Haven: Yale University Press.

Dahrendorf, Ralf
1959   *Class and Class Conflict in Industrial Society.* Stanford, California: Stanford University Press.

Davis, Louis E.
1973   "The Question of Ownership," *Working Papers for a New Society,* 1, Summer: 89–90.

Davis, Louis E., and Albert B. Cherns, eds.
1975   *Quality of Working Life.* 2 vols. New York: The Free Press.

Davis, Louis E., and James C. Taylor
1979   *Design of Jobs,* 2nd edition. Santa Monica, California: Goodyear.

Davy, S. J.
1983   "Employee Ownership: One Road to Productivity Improvement," *Journal of Business Strategy* 4, No. 1 (Summer): 12–21.

Derber, Charles
1983a   "Managing Professionals: Ideological Proletarianization and Post-Industrial Labor," *Theory and Society,* 12: 309–341.
1983b   "Sponsorship and the Control of Physicians," *Theory and Society,* 12: 561–601.

Derber, Milton
1970   *The American Idea of Industrial Democracy, 1865*–1965. Urbana, Illinois: University of Illinois Press.

Derrick, Paul
1947   *Lost Property: Proposals for the Distribution of Property in an Industrial Age.* London: G.F. Tomkin.

DiMaggio, Paul
1982   "Cultural Capital and School Success: The Impact of Status Culture Participation on the Grades of U.S. High School Students," *American Sociological Review,* 47: 189–201.

DiMaggio, Paul J., and Walter W. Powell
1983   "The Iron Cage Revisited: Institutional Isomorphism and Collective Rationality in Organizational Fields," *American Sociological Review,* 48: 147–160.

Djilas, Milovan
1957   *The New Class.* New York: Praeger.
1969   *The Unperfect Society: Beyond the New Class.* Translated by Dorian Cooke. New York: Harcourt, Brace & World.

Don, Yehuda
1977   "Dynamics of Development in the Israeli Kibbutz," in *Cooperative and Commune: Group Farming in the Economic Development of Agriculture.* Edited by Peter Dorner. Madison, Wisconsin: University of Wisconsin Press.

Drucker, Peter F.
1949   *The New Society: The Anatomy of the Industrial Order.* New York: Harper & Brothers.

1974   *Management: Tasks, Responsibilities, Practices.* New York: Harper & Row.
1976   *The Unseen Revolution: How Pension Fund Socialism Came to America.* New York: Harper & Row.

Eaton, Jack
1978   "The Relevance of Mondragon to Britain," *The Political Quarterly*, 49: 478–483.
1979   "The Basque Workers' Cooperatives," *Industrial Relations Journal*, 10: 32–40.

Eckert, Ross D.
1970   "The Los Angeles Taxi Monopoly: An Economic Inquiry," *Southern California Law Review*, 43: 407–453.
1973   "On the Incentives of Regulators: The Case of Taxicabs," *Public Choice*, 14 (Spring): 83–99.

Eden, Dov
1975   "Organizational Membership vs. Self-Employment: Another Blow to the American Dream," *Organizational Behavior and Human Performance*, 13: 79–94.

Edelman, Joseph
1977   "Soviet Jews in the United States: A Profile" *American Jewish Year Book*, 77: 157–181.

Edelstein, J. David, and Malcolm Warner
1976   *Comparative Union Democracy: Organization and Opposition in British and American Unions.* New York: Wiley.

Edwards, Richard
1979   *Contested Terrain.* New York: Basic Books.

Ellerman, David
1975a   "The 'Ownership of the Firm' is a Myth," *Administration & Society*, 7: 27–42.
1975b   "Capitalism and Workers' Self-Management," in *Self-Management: Economic Liberation of Man.* Edited by Jaroslav Vanek. Baltimore, Maryland: Penguin.
1977   "On the Legal Structure of Workers' Cooperatives," *News from the Federation for Economic Democracy*, 1, No. 2: 1–2.
1982a   *The Socialization of Entrepreneurship: The Empresarial Division of the Caja Laboral Popular.* Somerville, Massachusetts: Industrial Cooperative Association.
1982b   "On the Legal Structure of Workers' Cooperatives," in *Workplace Democracy and Social Change.* Edited by Frank Lindenfeld and Joyce Rothschild-Whitt. Boston: Porter Sargent.

Emery, Fred E., and Einar Thorsrud
1969   *Form and Content in Industrial Democracy.* London: Tavistock.

Engels, Friedrich
1939   *Herr Eugen Duehring's Revolution in Science.* Translated by Emile Burns. Edited by C.P. Dutton. New York: International Publishers.

Epstein, Cynthia Fuchs
1981   *Women in Law*. New York: Basic Books.

Esping-Anderson, Gosta
1981   "From Welfare State to Democratic Socialism: The Politics of Economic Democracy in Denmark and Sweden," in *Political Power and Social Theory*, vol. 2. Edited by Maurice Zeitlin. Greenwich, Connecticut: JAI Press.

Esping-Anderson, Gosta, and Roger Friedland
1982   "Class Coalitions in the Making of West European Economies," in *Political Power and Social Theory*, vol. 3. Edited by Maurice Zeitlin. Greenwich, Connecticut: JAI Press.

Estrin, Saul, and William Bartlett
1982   "The Effects of Enterprise Self-Management in Yugoslavia: An Empirical Survey," in *Participatory and Self-Managed Firms: Evaluating Economic Performance*. Edited by Derek C. Jones and Jan Svejnar. Lexington, Massachusetts: Lexington Books.

Etzioni, Amitai
1958   "The Functional Differentiation of Elites in the Kibbutz," *American Journal of Sociology*, 64, No. 5: 476–487.

Fager, Chuck
1982   "Can Pension Funds Save the Frostbelt?," *In These Times*, 6, No. 12: 8–9.

Fain, T. Scott
1980   "Self-Employed Americans: Their Number Has Increased," *Monthly Labor Review*, 103, No. 11: 3–8.

Fielding, G. J., and Roger Teal
1978   *Proceedings of Conference on Taxis as Public Transit*. Institute of Transportation Studies, University of California, Berkeley and Irvine.

Fine, Barry Dov (later Dov Eden)
1970   "Comparison of Organizational Membership and Self-Employment." Doctoral dissertation, University of Michigan.

Freidson, Eliot
1975   *Doctoring Together: A Study of Professional Social Control*. New York: Elsevier.
1979   "The Organization of Medical Practice," in *Handbook of Medical Sociology*. Third edition. Edited by Howard E. Freeman, Sol Levine, and Leo G. Reeder. Englewood Cliffs, New Jersey: Prentice-Hall.

Frieden, Karl
1980   *Workplace Democracy and Productivity*. Washington, D.C.: National Center for Economic Alternatives.

Frisch, Robert A.
1982   *ESOP for the '80s*. Rockville Centre, New York: Farnsworth Publishing.

Galante, Mary Ann
1983   "Meet the Permanent Associate," *National Law Journal*, 6, No. 7 (October 24): 1, 28, 30.

Galbrait, John Kenneth
1967   *The New Industrial State*. Boston: Houghton Mifflin.

Garson, G. David, ed.
1977   *Worker Self-Management in Industry: The West European Experience*. New York: Praeger.

Gelb, Pat M.
1981   *Taxi Regulatory Revision in San Diego, California: Background and Implementation*. Interim Report. Washington, D.C.: Urban Mass Transit Administration, U.S. Department of Transportation.

Gelb, Pat M., Steven B. Colman, and Robert M. Donnelly
1980   *Taxi Regulatory Revision in Portland, Oregon: Background and Implementation*. Interim Report. Washington, D.C.: Urban Mass Transit Administration, U.S. Department of Transportation.

Gelb, Pat M., Robert M. Donnelly, and Lidano A. Boccia
1980   *Taxi Regulatory Revision in Seattle, Washington: Background and Implementation*. Interim Report. Washington, D.C.: Urban Mass Transit Administration, U.S. Department of Transportation.

Gerson, Ben, and David Berreby
1981   "New Choices in Firm Structure," *National Law Journal*, 4, No. 10 (November 16): 1, 25, 27.

Gibson, Robin
1968   "Relations within the Law Firm," *Practical Lawyer*, 14, May: 35-48.

Goldberg, Ze'ev
1969   "The Kibbutz Utopia Materializing," in *Israel Towards a New Society*. Edited by Yehuda Gothelf. Tel Aviv: Israel Press.

Goldman, Paul, and Donald R. Van Houten
1980   "Uncertainty, Conflict, and Labor Relations in the Modern Firm I: Productivity and Capitalism's 'Human Face'," *Economic and Industrial Democracy*, 1: 63-98.

Goldstein, S. G.
1978   "Employee Share-Ownership and Motivation," *Journal of Industrial Relations*, 3: 311-330.

Goodey, Chris
1974   "Factory Committees and the Dictatorship of the Proletariat (1918)," *Critique*, No. 3 (Autumn): 27-47.

Gorz, Andre
1967   *Strategy for Labor: A Radical Proposal.* Translated by Martin A. Nicolaus
            and Victoria Ortiz. Boston: Beacon Press.
Goulden, Joseph C.
1972   *The Superlawyers: The Small and Powerful World of the Great Washington Law
            Firms.* New York: Weybright and Talley.

Gouldner, Alvin W.
1975-76   "Prologue to a Theory of Revolutionary Intellectuals," *Telos,* No. 26
            (Winter): 3-36.
1979   *The Future of Intellectuals and the Rise of the New Class.* New York: Oxford
            University Press.
Graham, Fred E.
1972   "Group Versus Solo Practice: Arguments and Evidence," *Inquiry,* 9,
            No. 2: 49-60.

Gramm, Warren S.
1981   "Property Rights in Work: Capitalism, Industrialism, and
            Democracy," *Journal of Economic Issues,* 15: 363-375.
Gramsci, Antonio
1977   *Antonio Gramsci: Selections from Political Writings (1910-1920).* Edited by
            Quintin Hoare. Translated by John Mathews. New York: Interna-
            tional Publishers.

Granados, Luis L.
1980   "Employee Stock Ownership Plans: An Analysis of Current Reform
            Proposals," *University of Michigan Journal of Law Reform,* 14, No. 1 (Fall):
            15-50.
Granelli, James S.
1978   "It's Time to Slice the Pie," *National Law Journal,* 1, No. 14 (December
            18): 1, 12.

Greenberg, Edward S.
1975   "The Consequences of Worker Participation: A Clarification of the
            Theoretical Literature," *Social Science Quarterly,* 56, No. 2 (September):
            191-209.

1980   "Participation in Industrial Decision Making and Work Satisfaction:
            The Case of Producer Cooperatives," *Political Science Quarterly,* 60:
            551-569.

1981   "Industrial Self-Management and Political Attitudes," *American Political
            Science Review,* 75: 29-42.
Griffin, Larry J., and Arne L. Kalleberg
1981   "Stratification and Meritocracy in the United States: Class and Oc-
            cupational Recruitment Patterns," *British Journal of Sociology,* 32: 1-38.

Gronlund, Laurence
1965   *The Cooperative Commonwealth.* Cambridge, Mass.: Harvard University Press.

Gunn, Christopher
1980a   "Plywood Co-operatives of the Pacific Northwest: Lessons for Workers' Self-Management in the United States," *Economic Analysis and Workers' Management*, 14: 393–416.
1980b   "Toward Workers' Control," *Working Papers*, 7, No. 3: 4–7.

Gutierrez-Johnson, Ana
1978   "Compensation, Equity, and Industrial Democracy in the Mondragon Cooperatives," *Economic Analysis and Workers' Management*, 12: 267–287.

Hammer, Tove Helland, and Robert N. Stern
1980   "Employee Ownership: Implications for the Organizational Distribution of Power," *Academy of Management Journal*, 23, No. 1: 78–100.

Hammer, Tove Helland, Robert N. Stern, and Michael A. Gurdon
1982   "Worker Ownership and Attitudes Toward Participation," in *Workplace Democracy and Social Change.* Edited by Frank Lindenfeld and Joyce Rothschild-Whitt. Boston: Porter Sargent.

Harper, Timothy
1982   "The Joel Hyatt—H&R Block Alliance: A 1,000 Lawyer Firm?," *National Law Journal*, 5, No. 8 (November 1): 1, 8–9.

Hartmann, Heinz
1979   "Works Councils and the Iron Law of Oligarchy," *British Journal of Industrial Relations*, 17: 70–82.

Heinz, John P., and Edward O. Laumann
1982   *Chicago Lawyers: The Social Structure of the Bar.* New York: Russell Sage Foundation.

Heller, Frank A., and Bernhard Wilpert
1981   *Competence and Power in Managerial Decision-Making.* Chichester: Wiley.

Henry, James
1977   "How Pension Fund Socialism Didn't Come to America," *Working Papers for a New Society*, 5, Winter: 78–87.

Herman, Edward S.
1981   *Corporate Control, Corporate Power: A Twentieth Century Fund Study.* Cambridge: Cambridge University Press.

Hickson, David J., D. S. Pugh, and Diana Pheysey
1969   "Operations Technology and Organizational Structure: An Empirical Reappraisal," *Administrative Science Quarterly*, 14: 378–397.

Hirschman, Albert O.
1970   *Exit, Voice, and Loyalty: Responses to Decline in Firms, Organizations, and States.* Cambridge, Massachusetts: Harvard University Press.

Hobbes, Thomas
1929   *Leviathan*. London: Oxford University Press.

Hochner, Arthur.
1978   "Worker Ownership and the Theory of Participation." Doctoral disser-
        tation, Harvard Univresity.

Hoffman, Paul
1973   *Lions in the Street: The Inside Story of the Great Wall Street Law Firms*. New
        York: Dutton.
1982   *Lions of the Eighties: The Inside Story of the Powerhouse Law Firms*. Garden
        City, New York: Doubleday & Company.

Holyoake, George Jacob
1906   *The History of Co-operation*. 2 vols. Revised ed. New York: Dutton.

Horvat, Branko.
1975   "The Labor-Managed Enterprise," in *Self-Governing Socialism*, vol. II.
        Edited by Branko Horvat, Mihailo Markovic, and Rudi Supek. White
        Plains, New York: International Arts and Sciences Press.

Horvat, Branko, Mihailo Markovic, and Rudi Supek, eds.
1975   *Self-Governing Socialism*. 2 vols. White Plains, New York: International
        Arts and Sciences Press.

Houseman, Gerald L.
1979   *G. D. H. Cole*. Boston: Twayne Publishers.

Howitt, Doran
1982   "Employee Ownership: A Capital Idea," *Inc.*, April.

Hughes, Everett C.
1971   "Social Role and the Division of Labor," in *The Sociological Eye: Selected
        Papers*. Chicago: Aldine Atherton.

Hughes, Graham
1983   "Valuing Your ESOP Shares," *Employee Ownership*, 3, no. 3
        (September): 4–5.

Hunnius, Gerry
1973   "Workers' Self-Management in Yugoslavia," in *Workers' Control: A
        Reader on Labor and Social Change*. Edited by Gerry Hunnius, G. David
        Garson and John Case. New York: Vintage Books.

Hunt, Robert C., Jr.
1970   "Formula Distribution of Net Income," *Legal Economic News*, October.
        Reprinted in *The Law Office Manager's Problem Solver* (Chicago:
        Callaghan).

Iadov, V. A.
1979   "Orientation - Creative Work," in *Soviet Work Attitudes: The Issue of Par-
        ticipation in Management*. Edited by Murray Yanowitch. White Plains,
        New York: M. E. Sharpe, Inc.

IDE (Industrial Democracy in Europe International Research Group)
1981   *Industrial Democracy in Europe.* New York: Oxford University Press.

Iezzi, John G.
1981   "Branch Office Syndrome Hits Firms Nationwide," *National Law Journal*, 6, No. 2 (April 6): 20-22, 29.

International Taxicab Association
1984   *Does Taxicab Deregulation Make Sense?* Rockville, Maryland: International Taxicab Association.

Jacobs, Dan N., and Ellen Frankel Paul, eds.
1981   *Studies of the Third Wave: Recent Migration of Soviet Jews to the United States.* Boulder, Colorado: Westview Press.

Jain, Hem C., ed.
1980   *Worker Participation: Success and Problems.* New York: Praeger.

Jenkins, David
1973   *Job Power: Blue and White Collar Democracy.* Garden City, New York: Doubleday.

Jochim, Timothy C.
1982   *Employee Stock Ownership and Related Plans: Analysis and Practice.* Westport, Connecticut: Quorum Books.

Johnson, Ana Gutierrez, and William Foote Whyte
1977   "The Mondragon System of Worker Production Cooperatives," *Industrial and Labor Relations Review*, 31: 18-30.

Jones, Derek C.
1975   "British Producer Cooperatives and the Views of the Webbs on Participation and Ability to Survive," *Annals of Public and Cooperative Economy*, 46: 23-44.
1976   "British Producer Co-operatives," in *The New Worker Co-operatives.* Edited by Ken Coates. Nottingham: Spokesman Books.
1977   "The Economics and Industrial Relations of Producer Cooperatives in the United States, 1791-1939," *Economic Analysis and Workers' Management*, 11: 295-317.
1978   "Producer Cooperatives in Industrialized Western Economies: An Overview," *Annals of Public and Cooperative Economy*, 49: 149-161.
1979   "U.S. Producer Cooperatives: The Record to Date," *Industrial Relations*, 18: 342-357.
1980   "Producer Co-operatives in Industralised Western Economies," *British Journal of Industrial Relations*, 16: 141-154.

Jones, Gareth R.
1983   "Transaction Costs, Property Rights, and Organizational Culture: An Exchange Perspective," *Administrative Science Quarterly*, 28: 454-467.

Kalleberg, Arne L., and Larry J. Griffin
1980   "Class, Occupation, and Inequality in Job Rewards," *American Journal of Sociology*, 85: 731–769.

Kanter, Rosabeth Moss
1972   *Commitment and Community: Communes and Utopias in Sociological Perspective*. Cambridge, Massachusetts: Harvard University Press.

Kapeliush, Ia. S.
1979   "Public Opinion in Electing Managers," in *Soviet Work Attitudes: The Issue of Participation in Management*. Edited by Murray Yanowitch. White Plains, New York: M. E. Sharpe.

Karabel, Jerome
1976   "Revolutionary Contradictions: Antonio Gramsci and the Problem of Intellectuals," *Politics & Society*, 6: 123–172.

Kardelj, Edvard
1975   "The Integration of Labor and Social Capital Under Workers' Control," in *Self Management: New Dimensions to Democracy*. Edited by Ichak Adizes and Elisabeth Mann Borgese. Santa Barbara, California: Clio Press.
1979   "Social Ownership and Socialist Self-Management," *Socialist Thought and Practice*, 19, No. 2: 46–57.
1981   *Contradictions of Social Property in a Socialist Society*. Belgrade: Socialist Thought and Practice.

Kaye, Harvey J.
1981   "Antonio Gramsci: An Annotated Bibliography of Studies in English," *Politics and Society*, 10: 335–353.

Kazan, Nick
1971   "Can Free Enterprise Speed Up Our Garbage Collection?," *New York*, July 12.

Kelso, Louis O., and Mortimer J. Adler
1958   *The Capitalist Manifesto*. New York: Random House.
1961   *The New Capitalists: A Proposal to Free Economic Growth From the Slavery of Savings*. New York: Random House.

Kelso, Louis O., and Patricia Hetter
1967   *How to Turn Eighty Million Workers Into Capitalists on Borrowed Money*. New York: Random House.

Kesselman, Mark
1982   "Prospects for Democratic Socialism in Advanced Capitalism: Class Struggle and Compromise in Sweden and France," *Politics & Society*, 11: 397–438.

Kimbell, Larry J., and John H. Lorant
1973   "Methods for Systematic and Efficient Classification of Medical Practices," *Health Services Research*, 8: 46–60.

King, Charles D., and Mark van de Vall
1978   *Models of Industrial Democracy: Consultation, Co-determination and Workers'*
        Management. The Hague: Mouton.

Kitch, Edmund W., Marc Isaacson, and Daniel Kasper
1971   "The Regulation of Taxicabs in Chicago," *Journal of Law and Economics*,
        14: 285–350.

Knight, Peter T.
1976   "Social Property in Peru: The Political Economy of Predominance,"
        Economic Analysis and Workers' Management, 10 (Fall).

Kohak, Erazim V.
1972   "Possessing, Owning, Belonging," *Dissent*, 19: 453–462.

Kohn, Melvin L.
1976   "Occupational Structure and Alienation," *American Journal of Sociology*,
        82: 111–130.

Kohn, Melvin, and Carmi Schooler
1969   "Class, Occupation, and Orientation," *American Sociological Review*, 34:
        659–678.

Kozlova, G. P.
1969   "Izmenenie soderzhaniia truda v sviazi s tekhnicheskim progressom"
        (Change in the Content of Work in Connection with Technical Pro-
        gress), in *Sotsial'nye problemy truda i proizvodstva* (Social Problems of Work
        and Production). Edited by G. V. Osipov and Ia. Shepanskii.
        Moscow: "Mysl'."

Krevnevich, V. V.
1977   "Avtomatizatsiia kak uslovie povysheniia soderzhatel'nosti truda i
        udovletvorennosti trudom" (Automation as a Condition of the Raising
        of the Content of Work and Satisfaction with Work), *Sotsiologicheskie*
        issledovaniia (Sociological Research), No. 1: 85–92.

Kurland, Samuel
1947   *Cooperative Palestine: The Story of Histadrut.* New York: Sharon Books.

Labour Party
1980   *Workers Cooperatives.* London: The Labour Party.

Ladinsky, Jack
1963   "Careers of Lawyers, Law Practice, and Legal Institutions," *American*
        Sociological Review, 28: 47–54.

Larner, R. J.
1970   *Management Control and the Large Corporation.* New York: Dunellen.

Larson, Daniel, Dr. Darroll Stanley, and James Warren
1981   "ESOP Valuations of Closely Held Company Stock," *Financial Planner*,
        January: 22–26.

Larson, Magali Sarfatti
1977   *The Rise of Professionalism: A Sociological Analysis.* Berkeley: University of
        California Press.

Laumann, Edward O. and John P. Heinz
1979   "The Organization of Lawyers' Work: Size, Intensity, and Co-Practice
            of the Fields of Law," *American Bar Foundation Research Journal*, No. 2:
            217–246.

Lavine, Douglas
1979   "It's Harder to Make Partner," *National Law Journal*, 2, No. 3 (October
            1): 1, 34.

Leibowitz, Arleen, and Robert Tollison
1980   "Free Riding, Shirking, and Team Production in Legal Partnerships,"
            Economic Inquiry, 18: 380–394.

Lenin, V. I.
1929   *What is to be Done?* New York: International Publishers.
1940   *Left-Wing 'Communism:' An Infantile Disorder.* New York: International
            Publishers.
1961   *The State and Revolution.* Reprinted in *The Essential Left: Four Classic Texts
            on the Principles of Socialism.* London: Allen & Unwin.

Leviatan, Uri
1980   "Hired Labor in the Kibbutz: Ideology, History and Social
            Psychological Effects," in *Work and Organization in Kibbutz Industry.*
            Edited by Uri Leviatan and Menachem Rosner. Norwood, Penn-
            sylvania: Norwood Editions.

Leviatan, Uri and Menachem Rosner
1980   *Work and Organization in Kibbutz Industry.* Norwood, Pennsylvania: Nor-
            wood Editions.

Lewellen, W. G.
1971   *The Ownership Income of Management.* New York: National Bureau of
            Economic Research.

Lieberstein, Samuel
1975   "Technology, Work, and Sociology in the USSR: The NOT Move-
            ment," *Technology and Culture*, 16: 48–66.

Light, Ivan H.
1972   *Ethnic Enterprise in America: Business and Welfare Among Chinese, Japanese
            and Blacks.* Berkeley, California: University of California Press.

Lipset, Seymour Martin, Martin A. Trow, and James J. Coleman
1956   *Union Democracy: The Internal Politics of the International Typographical
            Union.* New York: The Free Press.

Littler, Craig R., and Graeme Salaman
1982   "Bravermania and Beyond: Recent Theories of the Labour Process,"
            Sociology, 16: 251–269.

Livingston, D.T., and James B. Henry
1980   "The Effect of Employee Stock Ownership Plans on Corporate Profits,"
            The Journal of Risk and Insurance, 47: 491–505.

Lloyd, Emily, and Alex Taft
1978   *Boston Taxi Study: Final Report.* Boston: Mayor's Office of Transportation.

Locke, Edwin A., and David M. Schweiger
1979   "Participation in Decision-Making: One More Look," *Research in Organizational Behavior,* 1: 265–339.

Locke, John
1924   *Two Treatises of Civil Government.* New York: Dutton.

Long, Richard J.
1978a   "The Effects of Employee Ownership on Organizational Identification, Employee Job Attitudes, and Organizational Performance: A Tentative Framework and Empirical Findings," *Human Relations,* 31: 29–48.

1978b   "Relative Effects of Share Ownership Versus Control on Job Attitudes in an Employee-Owned Company," *Human Relations,* 31: 753–763.

1979   "Desires For and Patterns of Worker Participation in Decision Making After Conversion to Employee Ownership" *Academy of Management Journal,* 22: 611–617.

1980   "Job Attitudes and Organizational Performance under Employee Ownership," *Academy of Management Journal,* 23: 726–737.

1981   "The Effects of Formal Employee Participation in Ownership and Decision Making on Perceived and Desired Patterns of Organizational Influence: A Longitudinal Study," *Human Relations,* 34: 847–876.

1982   "Worker Ownership and Job Attitudes: A Field Study," *Industrial Relations,* 21: 196–215.

Lorant, John H., and Larry J. Kimbell
1976   "Determinants of Output in Group and Solo Medical Practice," *Health Services Research,* 11: 6–20.

Ludwig, Ronald L., and John E. Curtis, Jr.
1981   "ESOPs Made Substantially More Attractive as a Result of Economic Recovery Tax Act," *Journal of Taxation,* October: 208–211.

MacPherson, C.B.
1962   *The Political Theory of Possessive Individualism: Hobbes to Locke.* New York: Oxford University Press.

Margolick, David M.
1979   "Frayed Nerves at Hinshaw Culbertson: 8 Bolt Chicago Firm in Rift Over Divvying Up Work," *National Law Journal,* Nov. 12: 2.

Marsh, Thomas R., and Dale E. McAllister
1981   "ESOPs Tables: A Survey of Companies with Employee Stock Ownership Plans," *Journal of Corporation Law,* 6: 551–623.

Martin, Andrew
1977   "In Sweden, A Union Proposal for Socialism," *Working Papers for a New Society,* V, No. 2: 46–58.

Marx, Karl
1965   *Pre-Capitalist Economic Formations*. Translated by Jack Cohen. Edited by
            E.J. Hobsbaum. New York: International Publishers.
1967   *Capital: A Critique of Political Economy, Volume III*. New York: Interna-
            tional Publishers.
1971   *The Grundrisse*. Edited by David McLellan. New York: Harper & Row.
1972   *On America and the Civil War*. Edited and translated by Saul K. Padover.
            New York: McGraw-Hill.

Mason, Ronald M.
1982   *Participatory and Workplace Democracy: A Theoretical Development in Critique
            of Liberalism*. Carbondale, Illinois: Southern Illinois University Press.

Masson, R. T.
1971   "Executive Motivations, Earnings, and Consequent Equity Perfor-
            mance," *Journal of Political Economy*, 79: 1278–1292.

Mayer, Kurt
1953   "Business Enterprise: Traditional Symbol of Opportunity," *British Jour-
            nal of Sociology*, 4: 160–180.

Mayer, Kurt B., and Sidney Goldstein
1964   "Manual Workers as Businessmen," in Arthur B. Shostak and William
            Gomberg, eds., *Blue-Collar World: Studies of the American Worker*.
            Englewood Cliffs, N.J.: Prentice-Hall.

McClaughry, John
1972   *Expanded Ownership*. Fond due lac, Wisconsin: Sabre Foundation.

McLendon, Robert B.
1978   "Getting the Most Out of the Firm Meeting," in *The Law Office
            Manager's Problem Solver*. Chicago: Callaghan.

Mechanic, David
1978   *Medical Sociology*. Second Edition. New York: The Free Press.
1979   "Physicians," in *Handbook of Medical Sociology*. Third edition. Edited by
            Howard E. Freeman, Sol Levine, and Leo G. Reeder. Englewood
            Cliffs, New Jersey: Prentice-Hall.

Meidner, Rudolf
1978   *Employee Investment Funds: An Approach to Collective Capital Formation*. Lon-
            don: George Allen and Unwin.
1981   "Collective Asset Formation Through Wage-earner Funds," *Interna-
            tional Labour Review*, 120: 303–317.

Meister, Albert
1984   *Participation, Associations, Development and Change*. New Brunswick, New
            Jersey: Transaction Books.

Metzger, Bert L.
1974   "Profit Sharing: Capitalism's Reply to Marx," *Business and Society Review*, No. 11 (Autumn): 37–45.
1981   "On Profit Sharing in the U.S. and the Philosophy of Profit Sharing," *Economic and Industrial Democracy* 2: 97–102.

Metzger, Bert L., ed.
1979   *The Future of Profit Sharing*. Evanston, Illinois: Profit Sharing Research Foundation.

Metzger, Bert L., and Jerome A. Colleti
1971   *Does Profit Sharing Pay? A Comparative Study of the Financial Performance of Retailers with and without Profit Sharing Programs*. Evanston, Illinois: Profit Sharing Research Foundation.

Meyers, Frederic
1964   *Ownership of Jobs: A Comparative Study*. Los Angeles: Institute of Industrial Relations, University of California.

Michels, Robert
1962   *Political Parties: A Sociological Study of the Oligarchical Tendencies of Modern Democracy*. Translated by Eden and Cedar Paul. New York: The Free Press.

Milenkovitch, Deborah
1971   *Plan and Market in Yugoslav Economic Thought*. New Haven: Yale University Press.
1977   "The Case of Yugoslavia," *American Economic Review*, 67: 55–61.

Mill, John Stuart
1871   *Principles of Political Economy*, 7th Edition. London: Longmans.

Miller, Jon
1980   "Access to Interorganizational Networks as a Professional Resource," *American Sociological Review*, 45: 479–496.

Mills, D. Quinn
1983   "When Employees Make Concessions," *Harvard Business Review*, 61, No. 3 (May–June): 103–113.

Mitchell, J. B.
1982   "Gain-Sharing: An Anti-Inflation Reform," *Challenge*, 25, No. 3: 18–25.

Moberg, David
1981   "Should the Union Give Back or Buy In?," *In These Times*, December 23: 3,6.

Moldenhauer, Howard H.
1971   "Formula and Non-Formula Systems for Distributing Partnership Net Income," *Nebraska State Bar Journal*, 20, No. 1: 5–24 and No. 2: 61–78.

Montagna, Paul D.
1968   "Professionalization and Bureaucratization in Large Professional Organizations," *American Journal of Sociology*, 74: 138–145.

Moore, Wilbert E.
1943 "The Emergence of New Property Conceptions in America," *Journal of Legal and Political Sociology*, 1, No. 3-4 (April): 34-58.

Mulder, Mauk
1971 "Power Equalization through Participation?," *Administrative Science Quarterly*, 16: 31-38.

Nash, June, Jorge Dandler, and Nicholas S. Hopkins, eds.
1976 *Popular Participation in Social Change: Cooperatives, Collectives, and Nationalized Industry*. The Hague: Mouton.

Naylor, Guy
1968 *Sharing the Profits*. London: Garnstone Press.

Nelson, Robert L.
1981 "Practice and Privilege: Social Change and the Structure of Large Law Firms," *American Bar Foundation Research Journal*: 97-140.

New York Stock Exchange, Office of Economic Research
1982 *People and Productivity: A Challenge to Corporate America*.

Newhouse, Joseph P.
1973 "The Economics of Group Practice," *Journal of Human Resources*, 8, No. 1: 37-56.

Noble, David F.
1978 "Social Choice in Machine Design: The Case of Automatically Controlled Machine Tools, and a Challenge for Labor," *Politics & Society*, 8: 313-347.

Nomad, Max
1932 "White Collars and Horny Hands," *Modern Quarterly*, 6, No. 3: 68-76.
1959 *Aspects of Revolt*. New York: Bookman Associates.

Northrup, Hebert R.
1983 "The New Employee-Relations Climate in Airlines," *Industrial and Labor Relations Review*, 36: 167-181.

Oakeshott, Robert
1978 *The Case for Workers' Co-ops*. London: Routledge & Kegan Paul.

Obradovic, Josip
1975 "Workers' Participation: Who Participates?," *Industrial Relations*, 14: 32-44.

Obradovic, Josip, and William N. Dunn, eds.
1978 *Workers' Self-Management and Organizational Power in Yugoslavia*. Pittsburgh: University Center for International Studies, University of Pittsburgh.

O'Cleireacain, Carol
1981 "Getting Serious About Pension Funds," *Working Papers for a New Society*, 8, No. 4: 17-21.

Ogden, S. G.
1982 "Trade Unions, Industrial Democracy and Collective Bargaining," *Sociology*, 16: 544-565.

Ohman, Berndt
1983   "The Debate on Wage-Earner Funds in Scandinavia," in *International Yearbook of Organizational Democracy*, vol. I: *Organizational Democracy and Political Processes*. Edited by Colin Crouch and Frank A. Heller. New York: Wiley & Sons.

Orren, Harding A.
1974   "The 'Hale and Dorr System' Revisited," *Law Office Economics and Management*, 15, No. 2: 148–153.

Osborn, John Jay, Jr.
1979   *The Associates*. Boston: Houghton Mifflin.

O'Toole, James
1979   "The Uneven Record of Employee Ownership," *Harvard Business Review*, November–December: 185–197.

Ouchi, William G.
1980   "Markets, Bureaucracies, and Clans," *Administration Science Quarterly*, 25:129–141.

Panitch, Leo
1981   "Trade Unions and the Corporatist State," *New Left Review*, No. 125 (January–February): 21–43.

Pannekoek, Anton
1975   "Workers' Councils," in *Root & Branch: The Rise of the Workers' Movements*. Edited by Root & Branch. Greenwich, Conn.: Fawcett.

Paratransit Services
1983   *The Experiences of U.S. Cities with Taxicab Open Entry*. Rockville, Maryland: International Taxicab Association.

Patard, Richard
1982a   "ESOP Deja Vu: The Employee Stock Ownership Movement of the 1920's." Unpublished manuscript distributed by the National Center for Employee Ownership, Arlington, Virginia.
1982b   "Employee Stock Ownership in the 1920's," *Employee Ownership*, 2, No. 3 (September): 4–5.

Pateman, Carole
1970   *Participation and Democratic Theory*. New York: Cambridge University Press.

Pejovich, Svetozar, ed.
1978   *The Codetermination Movement in the West: Labor Participation in the Management of Business Firms*. Lexington, Massachusetts: Lexington Books.

Perry, Stewart E.
1978   *San Francisco Scavengers: Dirty Work and the Pride of Ownership*. Berkeley, California: University of California Press.

Proudhon, P.J.
1966   *What is Property?* Translated by Benjamin R. Tucker. New York: Howard Fertig.

Pugh, D. S., *et al.*
1969   "The Context of Organization Structures," *Administrative Science Quarterly*,
            14: 91–114.

Rachleff, Peter
1974   "Soviets and Factory Committees in the Russian Revolution," *Radical
            America*, 8, No. 6: 79–114.

Ramsey, Harvie
1977   "Cycles of Participation: Worker Participation in Sociological and
            Historical Perspective," *Sociology*, 11: 481–506.

Ransom, William L.
1925   "Property Ownership as a Social Force," in *Popular Ownership of Property:
            Its Newer Forms and Social Consequences. Proceedings of the Academy of Political
            Science*, 11, No. 3. Edited by William L. Ransom and Parker Thomas
            Moon. New York: Columbia University.

Rayman, Paula
1981   *The Kibbutz Community and Nation Building.* Princeton, New Jersey:
            Princeton University Press.

Reed, Richard C.
1983   "Business Development: Providing the Incentive," *National Law Journal*,
            5, No. 47 (August 1): 22, 53.

Reich, Michael
1972   "The Evolution of the United States Labor Force," in *The Capitalist
            System: A Radical Analysis of American Society*. Edited by Richard C. Ed-
            wards, Michael Reich, and Thomas E. Weisskopf. Englewood Cliffs,
            N.J.: Prentice-Hall.

Reisner, Edward J.
1978   "Trapping and Training the Legal Associate," in *The Law Office
            Manager's Problem Solver*. Chicago: Callaghan.

Rhodes, Lucien
1984   "That Daring Young Man and his Flying Machines," *Inc.*, 6, No. 1
            (January): 42–52.

Rhodes, Susan R., and Richard M. Steers
1981   "Conventional *vs* Worker-Owned Organizations,' *Human Relations*, 34:
            1013–1035.

Rifkin, Jeremy
1977   *Own Your Own Job.* New York: Bantam.

Rifkin, Jeremy, and Randy Barber
1978   *The North Will Rise Again: Pensions, Politics, and Power in the 1980s.*
            Boston: Beacon Press.

Rosen, Corey
1981   *Employee Ownership: Issues, Resources and Legislation. A Handbook for
            Employees and Public Officials.* Arlington, Virginia: National Center for
            Employee Ownership.
1983   "An Emerging Political Issue," *Workplace Democracy*, 10, No. 1 (Winter):
            8–10.

Rosen, Corey, and Katherine Klein
1983   "Job-creating Performance of Employee-Owner Firms,' *Monthly Labor Review*, 106, No. 8 (August): 15–19.

Rosen, Corey, and William F. Whyte
1982   "Employee Ownership: Saving Businesses, Saving Jobs," *Commentary*, Spring: 16–19.

Rosenstein, Eliezar
1970   "Histadrut's Search for a Participation Program," *Industrial Relations*, 9, No. 2 (February): 170–186.

1977   "Worker Participation in Israel: Experience and Lessons," *Annals of the American Academy of Political and Social Science*, 431: 113–122.

Rosner, Menachem
n.d.   *The Kibbutz as a Way of Life in Modern Society*. Givat Haviva, Israel: The Center for Social Research on the Kibbutz.

Rosner, Menachem, and Nanni Cohen
1983   "Is Direct Democracy Feasible in Modern Society? The Lessons of the Kibbutz Experience," in *Democracy, Equality, and Change: The Kibbutz and Social Theory*. Edited by Menachem Rosner. Darby, Pennsylvania: Norwood Editions.

Ross, Irwin
1980   "What Happens When the Employees Buy the Company," *Fortune*, June 2: 108–111.

Rothschild-Whitt, Joyce
1979a   "Conditions for Democracy: Making Participatory Organizations Work," in *Co-ops, Communes & Collectives: Experiments in Social Change in the 1960s and 1970s*. Edited by John Case and Rosemary C.R. Taylor. New York: Pantheon.

1979b   "The Collectivist Organization: An Alternative to Rational-Bureaucratic Models," *American Sociological Review*, 44: 509–527.

1983   "Worker Ownership in Relation to Control: A Typology of Work Reform," in *International Yearbook of Organizational Democracy*, vol. I: *Organizational Democracy and Political Processes*. Edited by Colin Crouch and Frank A. Heller. New York: Wiley.

Rucker, R. D.
1979   "Workers' Control of Production in the October Revolution and Civil War," *Science and Society*, 43: 158–185.

Rumberger, Russell W.
1981   "The Changing Skill Requirements of Jobs in the U.S. Economy," *Industrial and Labor Relations Review*, 34: 578–590.

Rus, Veljko
1970   "Influence Structure in Yugoslav Enterprise," *Industrial Relations*, 9: 148–160.

Russell, Raymond
1979   "Sharing Ownership in the Workplace." Doctoral dissertation, Harvard University.
1982   "The Rewards of Participation in the Worker-Owned Firm," in *Workplace Democracy and Social Change.* Edited by Frank Lindenfeld and Joyce Rothschild-Whitt. Boston: Porter-Sargent.
1983   "Class Formation in the Workplace: The Role of Sources of Income," *Work and Occupations*, 10: 349-372.

Russell, Raymond, Art Hochner, and Stewart E. Perry
1979   "Participation, Influence, and Worker Ownership," *Industrial Relations*, 18: 330-341.

Sachs, Stephen
1983   "Political Obstacles to Workplace Democracy," *Workplace Deocracy*, 10, No. 1 (Winter): 6-7.

Sacks, Stephen R.
1983   *Self-Management and Efficiency: Large Corporations in Yugoslavia.* London: Allen & Unwin.

Saive, Marie-Anne
1980   "Mondragon: An Experiment with Co-operative Development in the Industrial Sector," *Annals of Public and Co-operative Economy* 51: 223-255.

Sammons, Donna
1984   "Accounting for Growth," *Inc.*, 6, No. 1 (January): 75-82.

Satow, Roberta Lynn
1975   "Value-Rational Authority and Professional Organizations: Weber's Missing Type," *Administrative Science Quarterly*, 20: 526-531.

Sawyer, Thomas E.
1979   *The Jewish Minority in the Soviet Union.* Boulder, Colorado: Westview Press.

Scaff, Lawrence A.
1981   "Max Weber and Robert Michels," *American Journal of Sociology*, 86: 1269-1286.

Schlatter, Richard
1951   *Private Property: The History of an Idea.* New York: Russell & Russell.

Schmedel, Scott R.
1983   "Professionals Are Urged to Stay Incorporated Despite Loss of Some Benefits Under 1982 Law," *Wall Street Journal*, November 14: 54.

Schreiber, Chanoch
1975   "The Economic Reasons for Price and Entry Regulation of Taxicabs," *Journal of Transport Economics and Policy*, 9: 268-279.

Schumpeter, Joseph A.
1950   *Capitalism, Socialism and Democracy.* Third edition. Harper Torchbooks. New York: Harper & Row.

Segal, Geraldine R.
1983   *Blacks in the Law: Philadelphia and the Nation.* Philadelphia: University of Pennsylvania Press.

Shatz, Marshall
1967   "Jan Waclaw Machajski: The Conspiracy of the Intellectuals," *Survey*, No. 62 (January): 44–57.

Shelhav, Moshe, and Naphtali Golomb
1980   "The Sociotechnical Projects in Kibbutz Industries: Three Years of Planned Change Effort, Evaluation, Strategy and Prospect," in *Quality of Working Life and the Kibbutz Experience.* Edited by Albert Cherns. Norwood, Pennsylvania: Norwood Editions.

Shirom, Arie
1972   "The Industrial Relations Systems of Industrial Cooperatives in the United States, 1880–1935," *Labor History,* 13: 533–551.

Silard, Andrei
1981   "On the History of Workers' Councils," *Telos*, No. 48 (Summer): 49–64.

Simmel, Georg
1950   *The Sociology of Georg Simmel.* Translated by Kurt H. Wolff. New York: The Free Press.

Sing, Bill
1984   "Employee Stock Plans Focus of Controversy in Corporate Takeovers," *Los Angeles Times*, May 14, IV-1, 7.

Singer, Rube
1982   "Auto Design Changes Doom the Clark Plant," *In These Times*, 6, No. 13: 12.

Sirc, Ljubo
1979   *The Yugoslav Economy Under Self-Management.* New York: St. Martin's Press.

Sirianni, Carmen
1980   "Workers' Control in the Era of World War I: A Comparative Analysis of the European Experience," *Theory and Society*, 9: 29–88.
1982   *Workers Control & Socialist Democracy: The Soviet Experience.* London: Verso Editions.
1983   "Council and Parliaments: The Problems of Dual Power and Democracy in Comparative Perspective," *Politics & Society*, 12: 83–123.

Sloan, Allan
1981   "An Idea Whose Time Has Come?," *Forbes*, 128, No. 2 (July 20): 75–78.

Smart, D. A., ed.
1978   *Pannekoek and Gorter's Marxism.* London: Pluto Press.

Smigel, Erwin O.
1969   *The Wall Street Lawyer: Professional Organization Man?* Second edition.
            Bloomington, Indiana: Indiana University Press.
Smith, Reginald Herber
1940   *Law Office Organization.* Chicago: American Bar Association Journal.
Sonning, Staffan
1984   "The Employee Fund Issue Moves Toward a Decision," *Political Life in
            Sweden*, No. 17 (January). New York: Swedish Information Survey.
Speiser, Stuart M.
1977   *A Piece of the Action: The Quest for Universal Capitalism.* New York: Van
            Nostrand Reinhold.

Spenner, Kenneth
1979   "Temporal Changes in Work Content," *American Sociological Review*, 44:
            968–975.
1983   "Deciphering Prometheus: Temporal Change in the Skill Level of
            Work," *American Sociological Review*, 48: 824–837.
Stanic, S.
1980   "Ownership," in *A Handbook of Yugoslav Socialist Self-Management.* Edited
            by Bogdan Trifunovic. Belgrade: Socialist Thought and Practice.
Starr, Paul
1982   *The Social Transformation of American Medicine.* New York: Basic Books.
Stein, Barry
1976   "Collective Ownership, Property Rights, and Control of the Corpora-
            tion," *Journal of Economic Issues*, 10: 298–312.

Stephens, Evelyne Huber
1980   *The Politics of Workers' Participation: The Peruvian Approach in Comparative
            Perspective.* New York: Academic Press.
Stephens, Evelyne Huber, and John D. Stephens
1982   "The Labor Movement, Political Power, and Workers' Participation in
            Western Europe," in *Political Power and Social Theory*, vol. 3. Edited by
            Maurice Zeitlin. Greenwich, Connecticut: JAI Press.
Stephens, John D.
1979   *The Transition from Capitalism to Socialism.* London: MacMillan.

Stern, Robert, et al.
1980   *Employee Ownership in Plant Shutdowns: Prospects for Employment Stability.*
            Kalamazoo, Michigan: W.E. Upjohn Institute for Employment
            Research.
Stevens, Mark
1981   *The Big Eight.* New York: Macmillan.
Stewart, James B.
1983   *The Partners: Inside America's Most Powerful Law Firms.* New York: Simon
            and Schuster.

Stojanovic, Svetozar
1975   "Between Ideals and Reality," in *Self-Governing Socialism*, Vol. I. Edited
        by Branko Horvat, Mihailo Markovic, and Rudi Supek. White Plains,
        New York: International Arts and Sciences Press.

Strauss, George
1982   "Workers Participation in Management: An International
        Perspective," *Research in Organizational Behavior*, 4: 173–265.

Street, John
1983   "Socialist Arguments for Industrial Democracy," *Economic and Industrial
        Democracy*, 4: 519–539.

Swaine, Robert T.
1948   *The Cravath Firm and Its Predecessors, 1819–1948*. 3 vols. New York: Ad
        Press Ltd.

Tabb, J. Yanai, and Goldfarb, Amira
1966   *Workers' Participation in Management*. New York: Pergamon Press.

Talmon, Yonina
1972   *Family and Community in the Kibbutz*. Cambridge, Mass.: Harvard.

Tannenbaum, Arnold A.
1968   *Control in Organizations*. New York: McGraw-Hill.

Tannenbaum, Arnold S., *et al.*
1974   *Hierarchy in Organizations: An International Comparison*. San Francisco:
        Jossey-Bass.

Tawney, R.H.
1920   *The Acquisitive Society*. New York: Harcourt, Brace & World.

Teague, Elizabeth
1983   "Workers' Control or Workers Controlled," *Workers Under Communism*,
        No. 4 (Fall): 22–24.

Thimm, Alfred L.
1980   *The False Promise of Codetermination: The Changing Nature of European
        Workers' Participation*. Lexington, Massachusetts: Lexington Books.

Thomas, Henk
1980   "The Distribution of Earnings and Capital in the Mondragon Co-
        operatives," *Economic Analysis and Workers' Management*, 14: 364–392.

Thomas, Henk and Chris Logan
1982   *Mondragon: An Economic Analysis*. London: George Allen and Unwin.

Thornley, Jenny
1981   *Workers' Co-operatives: Jobs and Dreams*. London: Heinemann.

Tocqueville, Alexis de
1945   *Democracy in America*. 2 vols. Edited by Phillips Bradley. New York:
        Vintage Books.

Toscano, David J.
1983   "Toward a Typology of Employee Ownership," *Human Relations*, 36:
        581–602.

Travostino, Joan M.
1980   "Regulating Multistate Law Firms," *Stanford Law Review*, 32: 121–1233.

Trist, E. L., *et al.*
1963   *Organizational Choice: Capabilities of Groups at the Coal Face Under Changing Conditions*. London: Tavistock.

Tucker, Robert C., ed.
1972   *The Marx-Engels Reader*. New York: Norton.

Useem, Michael
1980   "Corporations and the Corporate Elite," *Annual Review of Sociology*, 6: 41–77.

U.S. Congress, House Committee on Ways and Means
1979   *Independent Contractors: Hearings Before the Subcommittee on Select Revenue Measures on H.R. 3245, June 20, July 16 and 17, 1979*. Washington, D.C.: U.S. Government Printing Office.

U.S. Congress, Joint Economic Committee
1976   *Employee Stock Ownership Plans (ESOPs): Hearing Before the Joint Economic Committee, Congress of the United States, Parts 1 and 2, December 11 and 12, 1975*. Washington, D.C.: U.S. Government Printing Office.

U.S. Congress, Senate
1981a   Senator Long speaking on "Expanded Ownership—Its Importance to the Free Enterprise System," an address initially delivered on March 16, 1981, to the Government Affairs Committee of the ESOP Association of America, 97th, Cong., 1st Sess., 27 March, *Congressional Record*, 127, No. 50.

U.S. Congress, Senate
1981b   Senator Long speaking for the Expanded Ownership Act of 1981, S. Res. 1162, 97th Cong., 1st Sess., 12 May, *Congressional Record*, 127, No. 72.

U.S. Congress, Senate Committee on Finance
1982   *Independent Contractor Tax Proposals: Hearing Before the Sub-Committee on Oversight of the Internal Revenue Service on S. 2369, April 26, 1982*. Washington, D.C.: U.S. Government Printing Office.

U.S. Department of Commerce, Bureau of Industrial Economics
1984   *Franchising in the Economy 1982–1984*. Washington, D.C.: U.S. Government Printing Office.

U.S. General Accounting Office, Office of the Comptroller General
1980   *Employee Stock Ownership Plans: Who Benefits Most in Closely Held Companies?* Washington, D.C.: U.S. Government Printing Office.

Ussenin, V. I., *et al.*
1979   "Soviet Workers and Automation of the Production Process," in *Automation and Industrial Workers: A Fifteen Nation Study*, Vol. 1, Part 1. Edited by Jan Forslin, Adam Sarapata, and Arthur M. Whitehill. Oxford: Pergamon Press.

252   BIBLIOGRAPHY

Vanek, Jaroslav
1970   *The General Theory of Labor-Managed Market Economies.* Ithaca, New York:
            Cornell University Press.
1971   *The Participatory Economy: An Evolutionary Hypothesis and a Strategy for
            Development.* Ithaca, New York: Cornell University Press.
1975   *Self-Management: Economic Liberation of Man.* Baltimore, Md.: Penguin.

Vanek, Jaroslav, ed.
1977   *The Labor-Managed Economy.* New York Cornell University Press.

Verba, Sidney, and Goldie Shabad
1978   "Workers' Council and Political Stratification: The Yugoslav Ex-
            perience," *American Political Science Review,* 72: 80–95.

Vidich, Charles
1976   *The New York Cab Driver & His Fare.* Cambridge, Massachusetts:
            Schenkman.

Viteles, Harry
1966–1968   *A History of the Co-operative Movement in Israel.* 7 vols. London: Vallen-
            tine, Mitchell.

Vogel, Ezra F.
1979   *Japan as Number 1: Lessons for America.* Cambridge, Massachusetts: Har-
            vard University Press.

Wachtel, Howard M.
1973   *Workers' Management and Workers' Wages in Yugoslavia: The Theory and Prac-
            tice of Participatory Socialism.* Ithaca, New York: Cornell University
            Press.

Wallace, Michael, and Arne L. Kalleberg
1982   "Industrial Transformation and the Decline of Craft: The Decomposi-
            tion of Skill in the Printing Industry, 1931–1978," *American Sociological
            Review,* 47: 307–324.

Walters, Francis W.
1968   "The Peasant and the Village Commune," in *The Peasant in Nineteenth-
            Century Russia.* Edited by Wayne J. Vucinich. Stanford, California:
            Stanford University Press.

Webb, Sidney and Beatrice
1897   *Industrial Democracy.* London: Longmans.

Webb, Sidney and Beatrice
1920   *A Consultation for the Socialist Commonwealth of Great Britain.* London:
            Longhmans, pp. 154–167. Reprinted in Ken Coates and Tony
            Topham, eds., *Workers Control.* Revised edition. London: Panther
            Books, pp. 66–72.

Weber, Max
1946   *From Max Weber: Essays in Sociology.* Translated and edited by H. H.
            Gerth and C. Wright Mills. New York: Oxford University Press.
1947   *The Theory of Social and Economic Organization.* Edited by Talcott Parsons.
            Translated by A. M. Henderson and Talcott Parsons. New York: The
            Free Press.

1968   *Economy and Society*. 2 vols. Edited by Guenther Roth and Claus Wittich. Berkeley, California: University of California Press.

Weil, Robert I., and Paul D. Roy
1981   "Statistics About and for Lawyers," *Law Office Economics and Management*, 22, No. 2: 220–235.

Weyher, Harry F., and Hiram Knott
1982   *The Employee Stock Ownership Plan*. Chicago: Commerce Clearing House.

Whyte, William Foote, and Joseph R. Blasi
1980   "From Research to Legislation on Employee Ownership," *Economic and Industrial Democracy*, 1: 395–415.

Whyte, William Foote et al.
1983   *Worker Participation and Ownership: Cooperative Strategies for Strengthening Local Economies*. Ithaca, New York: ILR Press.

Wiles, Peter John de Je Fosse
1977   *Economic Institutions Compared*. Oxford: B. Blackwell.

Williams, David J.
1980   "The Economic Reasons for Price and Entry Regulation of Taxicabs: A Comment," *Journal of Transport Economics and Policy* 14:105–112.

Williams, John D.
1984   "Buyouts Made With ESOPs Are Critizized," *Wall Street Journal*, February 21, pp. 35, 53.

Williamson, Oliver E.
1964   *The Economics of Discretionary Behavior: Managerial Objectives in a Theory of the Firm*. Englewood Cliffs, N.J.: Prentice-hall.
1980   "The Organization of Work: A Comparative Institutional Assessment," *Journal of Economic Behavior and Organization*, 1: 5–38.
1981   "The Economics of Organization: The Transaction Cost Approach," *American Journal of Sociology*, 87: 548–577.

Windmuller, John P., ed.
1977   *Industrial Democracy in International Perspective*. Annals of the American Academy of Political and Social Science, 431.

Woodward, Joan
1965   *Industrial Organization: Theory and Practice*. New York: Oxford University Press.

Woodworth, Warner
1981   "Forms of Employee Ownership and Workers' Control," *Sociology of Work and Occupations*, 8: 195–200.

Yanowitch, Murray
1978   "Pressures for More 'Participatory' Forms of Economic Organization in the Soviet Union," *Economic Analysis and Workers' Management*, 12: 403–417.

Yassour, Avraham, ed.
1977   *Kibbutz Members Analyze the Kibbutz*. Cambridge, Mass.: Institute for Cooperative Communities.

Yudin, Yehuda
1975   "Industrial Democracy as a Component in Social Change: The Israeli
            Approach and Experience," in *Self-Management: New Dimensions to
            Democracy*. Edited by Ichak Adizes and Elisabeth Mann Borgese. Santa
            Barbara, California: Clio Press.

Yunker, James A.
1977   "The Social Dividend Under Market Socialism," *Annals of Public &
            Cooperative Economy*, 48, No. 1 (January–March).

Zdravomyslov, A.G., Rozhin, V.P., and Iadov, V.A., eds.
1970   *Man and His Work*. Translated and edited by Stephen P. Dunn. White
            Plains, N.J.: International Arts and Sciences Press. Originally
            published in Moscow by "Mysl" Publishing House, 1967.

Zeitlin, Maurice
1974   "Corporate Ownership and Control: The Large Corporation and the
            Capitalist Class," *American Journal of Sociology*, 79: 1073–1115.

Zimbalist, Andrew
1975   "The Limits of Work Humanization," *Review of Radical Political
            Economics*, 7, No. 2: 50–59.

Zimbalist, Andrew, ed.
1979   *Case Studies on the Labor Process*. New York: Monthly Review Press.

Zirkle, Thomas E.
1970   "Group Practice—Part III: Interpersonal Dynamics," *Journal of the
            American Osteopathic Association*, 69: 1053–1056.
1972   "Dividing Income in Group Practice," *Journal of the American Osteopathic
            Association*, 71: 808–811.

Zukin, Sharon
1977–78   "The Paris Conference on Self-Management," *Telos*, No. 34 (Winter):
            148–157.
1981   "The Representation of Working-Class Interests in Socialist Society:
            Yugoslav Labor Unions," *Politics & Society*, 10: 281–316.

Zupanov, Josip
1975   "Participation and Influence," in *Self-Governing Socialism*, Vol. II. Edited
            by Branko Horvat, Mihailo Markovic, and Rudi Supek. White Plains,
            New York: International Arts and Sciences Press.

Zwerdling, Daniel
1977   "At IGP, It's Not Business as Usual," *Working Papers for a New Society*, 5,
            No. 1 (Spring): 68–81.
1979   "Employee Ownership: How Well Is It Working?" *Working Papers for a
            New Society*, 6, No. 1: 15–27.

Subject Index

Index of Proper Names